THE EDWARD DOUGLASS WHITE
LECTURES ON CITIZENSHIP

OTHER PUBLISHED LECTURES IN THIS SERIES:

Individual Freedom
and
Governmental Restraints

By WALTER GELLHORN

LOUISIANA STATE UNIVERSITY PRESS

Baton Rouge

Second Printing, 1958

COPYRIGHT 1956 by WALTER GELLHORN

Library of Congress Catalog Card Number: 56–13001

Manufactured in the United States of America

Acknowledgments

DURING the autumn of 1955 Richard McKeon, Distinguished Service Professor of Greek and Philosophy at the University of Chicago, Robert K. Merton, Professor of Sociology at Columbia University, and I were commissioned by the National Book Committee to study the freedom to read, in all its aspects. The results of our work appeared in a report entitled "The Freedom to Read: Perspective and Program," submitted by us in 1956 to the National Book Committee, which plans to publish it. My indebtedness to Messrs. McKeon and Merton is very large. Discussions with them extended over a period of four months. No one could long listen to the conversation of two such erudite and broadly cultivated gentlemen without appropriating some of their information and insights. I drew upon them in writing Chapter II of this book. Neither Mr. McKeon nor Mr. Merton has, however, seen the chapter, and so neither of them shares responsibility for the views it states.

David J. Bardin and Sheldon Turtletaub, Harlan Fiske Stone Scholars and members of the Class of 1956 at Columbia Law School, were kind enough to give me valuable aid when I needed it. I gladly acknowledge their help, with warm thanks.

I am grateful to Louisiana State University for its invitation to deliver the Edward Douglass White Lectures in 1956. This book is based upon those lectures. No lecturer could hope for more cordial consideration and hospitality than the University community—administration, faculty, and students—so generously extended to me in Baton Rouge. I am especially appreciative of the kind exertions of Paul M. Hebert, dean of the Law School, to assure the success of the lectures.

WALTER GELLHORN

May 1956

Table of Contents

INDIVIDUAL FREEDOM AND
GOVERNMENTAL RESTRAINTS

1

Changing Attitudes Toward the Administrative Process

VESTIGES of the savage remain in all of us. Everyone experiences occasional nostalgia for the good old primitive days, free from government. We groan in concert about the price we have to pay for civilization—though, in the end, only the anarchists at the one extreme and, at the other, the advocates of repealing the Sixteenth Amendment really appear convinced that taxes are unbearable. We also groan, though as a rule not in concert, about other aspects of government, whose inescapable function it is at times to prevent and at times to compel conduct far from the wishes of governed individuals. Our necks fit into yokes less readily than do the oxen's, and we bellow more loudly when the yokes are felt. That is why, so long as vocal chords have not been paralyzed by terror, cries of concern or outrage usually provide the unharmonious accompaniment of new governmental measures.

If the American administrative process, which has had its most noteworthy growth during the past quarter century, had developed without a background of determined grumbling by vigorous viewers with alarm, the future historian would have been perplexed by the abnormality of silence. But no one need be worried in behalf of the distant scholar who seeks to interpret our age. A full quota of attacks on governmental theory and practice will satisfy him that American adrenal glands were functioning at capacity during these significant years.

While our contemporary period differs from no other in respect of expressed distaste for governmental exertions, this moment in history nevertheless does have a feature that distinguishes it from the rest. Within this brief span of years the defenders and detractors of the administrative process have all but exchanged roles, and have done so with almost unbelievable abruptness. The chorus of concern about the administrative process peals forth today with no abatement of yesteryear's volume; but the choristers are different, and those who formerly joined most lustily in the singing now seek to still it. As a matter of fact, they sometimes even urge Congress to investigate daring critics of procedures they themselves so recently denounced.

The transfer of adjudicatory responsibilities from the traditional courts to the as yet untraditionalized administrative agencies aroused anxious debate from the first, and the debate continues today. The methods of the new adjudicators have been praised and blamed—praised for being functional without unfairness, blamed for being incautiously careless of litigants' rights in ways that fairminded judges would have avoided. I should like to speculate about why the praisers and blamers have recently switched sides.

Conceivably, of course, there is nothing more to the problem than discovering whether one likes or dislikes the results reached by the administrators. In this view all the pother about administration is a delusion—of oneself or of others. All that counts is whether one approves the end product. There is undoubtedly a great deal to be said for this explanation. Some of those who formerly inveighed against administrative proceedings were at bottom concerned with the governmental policies committed to the administrators rather than with the administrators themselves—though, like a bull infuriated by banderillas, they may have only partly identified the source of their irritation. On the other hand many who in the mid-thirties were cheering the newly created agencies of the New Deal were making essentially the same error as their opponents. They imagined that the administrative agency had a sort of built-in point of view. They, like those who were perturbed on the other side, believed that some inner current ineluctably made the administrative agency an instrument of social and economic progressivism —with which they vaguely sympathized. Of course neither the supporters nor the attackers of administrative agencies were accurate in their perceptions. Both groups learned as the years passed that the administrative process is not a stream running always in the same direction, but, rather, a mechanism capable of being steered.

The Early Battle Lines

To recognize the maneuverability of the administrative process is not to detract from the positive achievements of the administrators of the mid-thirties. A shattering depression had damaged the nation's morale as well as its business. Resentments ran deep in a population rightly or wrongly convinced that their economic lives were effectively in the power of too few and too unenlightened hands. Elsewhere in the world men were exhibiting an alarmingly ready willingness to exchange political liberty for promises of material welfare. Even in this country the corrosives of discontent had begun to lodge in the crannies of our political structure. Cracks might have widened into fissures if the acids of that difficult period had not soon been somewhat diluted by the legislation of the early Roosevelt years. The administrative agencies of that time, said James M. Landis, a former Harvard Law School dean who had himself become a government official, reflected " an effort to grant protection to the common man in the realization of new liberties born of a new economic order. The continuity of the common man's radio programs, the security of his bank deposits, his protection against unfair discrimination in employment, his right to have light and power at reasonable rates, his protection against fraud and chicanery in our securities markets, his right to cheap railroad travel—to mention only a few of the necessities of modern life—these are some of the new liberties which make up the right of today's common man to the pursuit of happiness, and these liberties for their protection today seek the administrative and not the judicial process." [1]

These economic " liberties " were indeed more actively recognized than in the years immediately before. Recognition was reinforced by administrators many of whom, at least in the beginning, were convinced that they were shaping a new and better society. In fact, new shapes did emerge. None can deny, for example, that the vast strengthening of labor organizations was facilitated if not made possible by legal safeguards of collective bargaining; and, while there may yet be disagreement about the desirability of the result, there can be no disagreement that American society has been profoundly altered.

Nor can one ignore the changes in American financial mores that the mid-thirties wrought. We have but recently seen their fruit. What had threatened for a moment to be The Depression of 1954 turned out to be a mere squiggle on the economic graphs; a Republican administration and a financial community that had once been bitterly hostile to " governmental interference " joined in assuring the public that the Securities and Exchange Commission, the Federal Deposit Insurance Corporation, and the unemployment insurance authorities would see to it that nobody was seriously hurt when the business boom began to show signs of deflating. And, in truth, few people were. Bank depositors remained tranquil; there were no bank closings. The stock market trembled; but it was not shoved toward disaster by the ruthless manipulative practices that were common until so recently. The ranks of the jobless increased; but unemployment insurance payments cushioned the shock of reduced purchasing power, so that credit withdrawals led to no chain reaction of insolvency.

Events thus gave substantial support to Kenneth Davis' view that the developments of "positive government"—that is, of governmental action taken affirmatively to fend off the pitilessness of life—have confounded the Marxists. "Marx failed to foresee that government could protect against the abuses of free enterprise, that government could intervene to prevent extreme maldistribution. Marx failed to foresee the potentialities of taxing and spending to provide for the general welfare. *Marx failed to foresee the modern regulatory agency.*" [2]

But if the Marxists failed accurately to estimate the dynamics of the democratic system functioning through appointed officials, so too did some of the enthusiasts over official accomplishments fail accurately to estimate their limitations. Many believed that administrators, selflessly devoted to the general welfare and scientifically equipped to make the pertinent decisions, would ultimately assume the role of economic planners for the public good. This belief was widely shared, though with quite different emotions, by friends and enemies of the administrative process alike. Time has shown that "both the thrill and the chill failed to take into account basic factors limiting the managing and ' planning' potentialities of the administrative process." [3] Indeed, there is much evidence that even in the avowedly "planned economies" of the totalitarian countries there has been a quiet abandonment of any notion that industrial production can desirably be planned centrally.[4]

In any event, whether or not the thrill and the chill were entirely justified, the line between "liberals" and "reactionaries " could be charted not long ago with adequate precision in terms of their professed attitudes toward administrative bodies. By and large the liberals believed that administrators could be relied upon for wise and just decisions, and that, as a corollary, they should as far as possible be free from judicial supervision that might rigidify administrative procedures or supplant the informed administrative conclusions. Of course, friends of the administrative process did not believe that administrators were always at their best or that their procedures left no room for improvement. Quite to the contrary, substantial exertions were undertaken toward the end, as Robert Jackson put it, of " adapting the administrative process to the magnitude of its task." [5] But the liberals did at least have general faith that the process was perfectible. Meanwhile, they confidently believed that no serious harm was being done to offset the good wrought by dispassionate specialists.

Those who disliked the policies the administrators enforced did not share this confidence. Nor were all convinced that de-emphasis of judicial power was wise. The judges, after all, had valiantly stricken down a number of statutes and had shown little enthusiasm about the efforts of " reformers " to tinker with the American way of life. Few of them as yet owed their appointments to the Roosevelt administration. They represented the ideals and values that had proved their worth in the past, and they, more than a newly created corps of administrators—composed of zealots, politicians, and, worst of all, wild-eyed professors—could be counted on to preserve the citizen's rights. From the first days of the New Deal the organized bar declaimed against " the evils notoriously prevalent " in administrative tribunals, and warned that " the judicial branch of the federal government is being rapidly and seriously undermined "—a warning to which was added the gloomy prediction that unless existing tendencies were somehow checked, the courts were "in danger of meeting a measure of the fate of the Merovingian kings."[6] While perhaps only a few lawyers were erudite enough to know exactly what that fate had been, they were confident that it was a sorry one. The "right wing" drew together to save the courts and to stem the encroaching tide of administration. Their early efforts to "improve" the administrative process took the form of legislation that would have virtually disemboweled it.[7]

Support for these efforts came from somewhat unexpected quarters. The greatly respected Roscoe Pound, shedding the scholarly methods that had brought him fame, declared without first investigating the matter very closely that ten unfortunate tendencies could be discerned in administrative action. These included "a tendency to decide without a hearing, or without hearing one of the parties," "a tendency to decide on the basis of . . . evidence not produced," and "a tendency to make decisions on the basis of preformed opinions and prejudices."[8] Ignoring other scholars' detailed studies of actualities in the regulatory areas, Professor Pound repeatedly emphasized his unflattering characterization of public administration;[9] and though his views were subjected to severe criticism, because they reflected the very tendencies he ascribed to others, they undoubtedly helped color the legal profession's attitude toward the newer agencies of government.

As late as 1944, when cannonading was ominously heavy on a somewhat more urgent front, the firing continued against the administrative process. "Justice cannot stand half free and half enslaved," declared a prominent Ohio lawyer. "We cannot have, in this country, two systems of dispensing justice—one . . . safeguarded by restrictions and limitations and privileges which have been found to be wise and necessary through centuries of experience, and another system administered largely in disregard of our principles of jurisprudence, largely in disregard of the limitations, restrictions and privileges which our courts have found it wise and necessary to observe." [10] And as soon as World War II was at an end dominant elements of the Congress, under the special leadership of Senator Pat McCarran and Representatives Hatton W. Sumners and Francis E. Walter, moved quickly to limit administrative authority while expanding judicial review. Their efforts led to enactment of the Federal Administrative Procedure Act of 1946.[11]

The Turning Tide

Almost at the moment when the administrative process was supposedly being put in its place once and for all, attitudes toward it began to change. Consider one example. The National Labor Relations Board, long an object of execration, had complained in 1947 that while its work load had increased by some 60 per cent, its appropriation had been decreased by 25 per cent, so that it was being strangulated by unmasticated business. Soon afterward the elements of Congress that had expressed the greatest fears about such agencies as the NLRB greatly expanded the Board's jurisdiction by giving it power to proceed against unions as well as employers. Thereupon its operating funds mounted quickly. By 1953 it was receiving from Congress an appropriation three times larger than it had been given a decade earlier.

Other adminstrative agencies had similar experiences. Having been damned roundly the night before, they awoke the next morning to find themselves apparently once more in favor. As time went on the few senators who could remember the palmy days made speeches about the " subversion of the administrative process." [12] They complained particularly that personnel and policy changes had transformed the agencies into old lions, perhaps noble in appearance but in fact toothless, tired, and impotent—or, if still potent, using their potency to wrong purposes. Among the previously administration-minded professors a certain disenchantment became manifest. Within the academic groves could be heard mutterings that perhaps the courts were abdicating their responsibilities, and should stand readier than in the past to review adminisrative acts, while diminishing their deference to the supposed administrative expertness.[13]

The reversal of attitudes toward administrative proceedings is strikingly reflected in Congressional reaction to *Wong Yang Sung* v. *McGrath*, decided by the Supreme Court in 1950.[14] Wong, a Chinese seaman, had been ordered deported after a hearing that concededly fell below the standards of the Administrative Procedure Act of 1946. The single question before the Supreme Court was whether administrative hearings in deportation cases must conform to that statute's requirements.

One of the most earnestly declared purposes of the Administrative Procedure Act had been to curtail what its sponsors believed was a widespread practice of embodying in one person the inconsistent duties of prosecutor and judge. The then supporters of the administrative process regarded this as a vastly overblown issue, but rarely did the backers of the proposed legislation fail to inveigh against the " combination of functions " that they thought was usual. As a matter of fact, this practice was never as general as the critics of the administrative agencies supposed; five years before the 1946 statute was enacted a search of the whole field of federal administration had brought to light only four minor examples of commingling of functions.[15] Until a short while previously, it is true, the Immigration and Naturalization Service had been one of the offenders, for it had indulged the objectionable practice of merging the duties of judge and prosecutor in the single person of the officer assigned to conduct a deportation hearing. But even that agency had mended its ways after a critical investigation by a special committee appointed by the Secretary of Labor,

within whose jurisdiction the Service was then lodged.[16]   In
June of 1940, however, the Service was transferred from
the Department of Labor to the Department of Justice, and
thus came under the direction of the Attorney General.
Then, growing tougher, it had reverted to its former methods.
In the hearing of Seaman Wong the Supreme Court discovered " a perfect exemplification " of the very practices
that had been so vigorously condemned in earlier years.

The duality of functions found to have occurred in Wong's
case, the Court said in an opinion by Mr. Justice Jackson, " if
objectionable anywhere, would seem to be particularly so in
the deportation proceeding, where we frequently meet with
a voteless class of litigants who not only lack the influence
of citizens, but who are strangers to the laws and customs
in which they find themselves involved and who often do
not even understand the tongue in which they are accused.
Nothing in the nature of the parties or proceedings suggests
that we should strain to exempt deportation proceedings
from reforms in administrative procedure applicable generally to federal agencies." And so the Court held that the
public authorities had used illegal methods in finding poor
Wong deportable.

The decision was noted with interested satisfaction in the
professional periodicals. The *Notre Dame Lawyer* thought
that the Supreme Court had acquired some of Senator Mc-
Carran's spirit; the *Ohio State Law Journal* was confident
that the " intent of the framers " had been followed by the
judges; and other law review editors joined in the congratu-
latory refrain.[17]   But those who had ostensibly been intent
on safeguarding individuals from the dangers of administrative abuse did not greet Wong's triumph over " bureaucratic despotism " with the rejoicing one might have expected. The Supreme Court spoke on February 20, 1950.
The Congress spoke back on September 27, 1950. It enacted
a rider to an Appropriation Act that in terms exempted

" exclusion or expulsion of aliens " from the provisions of
the Administrative Procedure Act. Then, in the Immigration and Nationality Act of 1952, popularly known as the
McCarran-Walter Act after its chief sponsors (who were
also, it will be recalled, chief sponsors of the Administrative
Procedure Act), the exemption was copper-riveted by providing that exclusion and deportation hearings could from
now on be held by any immigration officer the Attorney
General might care to designate, who could also simultaneously discharge whatever other duties the Attorney General
might prescribe. Thus was *Wong Yang Sung* v. *McGrath*
overruled.[18]

The legislative aftermath of that case lays a shadow of
doubt upon the genuineness of some noisily expressed fears
of administrative injustice. The shadow would perhaps not
be heavy if this episode stood alone. After all, a substantial
segment of the Congress has traditionally shown symptoms
of xenophobia, reflected in a stiffly unsympathetic attitude
toward the problems of aliens.[19] Despite the Supreme Court's
repeated comments in the 1920's that administrative proceedings involving the foreign born were lacking in the security
associated with judicial proceedings,[20] and despite the notorious insensitivity with which the Immigration and Naturalization Service at times discharged its duties, the would-be
revisionists of the administrative process never focussed their
attention on this running sore. They preferred instead to
concentrate on administrators whose conduct was positively
Chesterfieldian compared with that of the alien-hunters. So
if the erstwhile anti-administrators had done no more than
express anew their confidence in immigration officers, they
would merely have been consistently inconsistent.

In recent years, however, the old time foes of " the bu-
reaucracy " have gone much farther. They have cheerfully
thrust into administrative hands a vastly enlarged respon-

sibility for decisions of utmost delicacy. Even a partial catalog is impressive:

1. Censorial powers have been exercised with scanty adverse reaction from those who once fulminated against the dangers of administrative despotism;

2. The withholding of governmental information from the public affected by it has come to be taken virtually for granted, confidence being reposed in the administrators who will decide what it is safe for the public to know; [21]

3. The individual's "loyalty" and his possible riskiness to the nation's security have been adjudged by administrators with slight attention to the procedural norms thought essential in other sorts of adjudications;

4. Detention of political deviants in times of crisis has been authorized, not on the basis of proof that they have committed an offense but on the basis of an administrator's *ex parte* decision that perhaps they might do so in future;

5. The Attorney General has been empowered to prescribe regulations for the registration of printing presses and mimeograph machines of Communist organizations—a measure that prompted a leading newspaper executive to exclaim, " This is the nearest thing to press licensing that has existed on this continent since colonial times. Not only is it a departure from principles established for three centuries in the English speaking world; it is, inferentially, a tribute to the efficacy of Communist propaganda that no American ought to make " ; [22]

6. A board has been created to determine the Communist orientation of organizations whose activities are in no way challenged as unlawful, with the consequence that administrators may supervise the labeling not only of drugs and foodstuffs (as in the past) but also of labor unions, old age pension groups, and lawyers guilds;

7. The Department of State, controlling the issuance of passports to those who have desired to leave and of visas to those who have desired to enter the United States, has decisively affected human lives; and, despite its habitual disregard of the allegedly essential procedural safeguards, the Department of State has yet to incur the wrath of the former anti-administrationists on this score;

8. The Department of Justice has had power to affect human lives even more decisively, indeed one might be tempted to say definitively, through exercising or failing to exercise its power to withhold deportation of an individual who might be killed or imprisoned in the country of his origin; but " the bureaucrats " have been little censured for choosing to decide these life-and-death issues on the basis of informal procedures and undisclosed evidence;

9. Illegal wiretapping, notorious though little rebuked, has jeopardized the citizen's privacy; and those who formerly foresaw possible abuses of administrative discretion now join in supporting persistent legislative efforts to authorize discreet wiretapping;

10. The Post Office Department has cooly decided whether or not to deliver foreign periodicals and other printed materials to addressees in this country, acting upon its own judgment of the reader's " legitimate needs " for the publications in question; and it has done so without criticism from those who used to declaim against " bureaucratic despots " and " administrative absolutists."

During the period in which these and other new powers have been granted or old ones fortified, the former friends and the former detractors of the administrative process have been circumnavigating the globe of government, traveling in opposite directions. The friends, starting from a point on the globe that might be labeled extreme support, have now traveled all the way to the station of extreme fear. The detractors, starting from extreme fear, have seemingly reached the point from which the friends had so recently departed.

The New " Radicals "

This exchange of attitudes may facilely be explained in terms of concern over national security. The needs of security are indeed acutely sensed by many persons of good will and sober judgment. Those needs render palatable many measures that might otherwise offend. Alexander Hamilton observed that external threats are the most powerful molders of national conduct, bending after a time " even the ardent love of liberty." Continual danger, he said, " will compel nations the most attached to liberty to resort for repose and security to institutions which have a tendency to destroy their civil and political rights. To be more safe, they, at length, become willing to run the risk of being less free." [23] As in Hamilton's day, so also in ours; the tremors foreseen in 1788 are felt realities now. Many endorse with great sincerity steps that may conceivably strengthen national safety, even when those steps may entail some loss of freedom or occasional injustice to individuals. We face today not a sharply drawn choice between an absolute good and an absolute evil, but between one good and another—what " the Greeks thousands of years ago recognized as a tragic issue, namely, the clash of rights, not the clash of wrongs " ; [24] and we have perfected no calculus for resolving that clash.

But the facile explanation does not fit all the facts. In the first place, many who deplore entrusting the administrator with the powers catalogued above, do so precisely because they fear that the nation's security has thus been jeopardized rather than buttressed. In the second place, some who have willingly enlarged administrative authority in new realms while deploring its existence in old, may have been moved chiefly by impulses wholly unrelated to their doubtlessly

genuine concern about national security. Some supporters
of the more recent forms of official repressivism may be the
very persons who in earlier years, when national security
was no issue at all, were utterly unmoved by abusiveness in
the immigration service or by obtuseness among the postal
censors. They may, in short, be repression-minded as a
matter of taste rather than need.

The fact is, of course, that a persuasive reason for repressivism can always be found, and, indeed, always has been
found, by those who seek it. Well before Soviet imperialism
threatened this country there were men who, in the name of
defending traditional American values and institutions, were
ready (consciously or not) to abolish them. Know-Noth-
ingism and Ku-Kluxism in earlier times were mass manifesta-
tions of this curious coalescing of defense and surrender, of
purported preservation and actual destruction; every generation has produced similar phenomena.[25] I do not for an
instant mean to impugn the true patriotism of the many
devoted Americans who think that today's new administrative look is a badly needed response to unprecedented perils.
Among those who are seemingly fired by patriotic passion,
however, are some to whom the term " pseudo-conservative "
has been usefully applied—persons who talk " conserva-
tively " but act otherwise; persons who talk, for example,
about the desperate dangers of " Big Government " while
simultaneously urging that governmental power be extended
farther and farther into zones previously deemed inap-
propriate.[26]

It is the pseudo-conservative rather than the genuinely conservative element that remains blind to the possibility of
" allegiance through principled recalcitrance," [27] and is carefree about the risk that measures aimed at " subversion "
may conceivably suppress mere dissidence. " All discussion,
all debate, all dissidence," Judge Learned Hand has said,
" tends to question, and in consequence to upset, existing

convictions "—which, he adds, is precisely its purpose and its justification.[28] But to an authoritarian-minded person, the upsetting of existing convictions is far from a " justification " of discussion; it is, rather, a reason for its suppression. Though very few people outspokenly condemn variety of opinion or originality of thought, many believe inwardly that society is better off without it. Today, as in Mill's day, " originality is the one thing which unoriginal minds cannot feel the use of." [29]

This is by no means a peculiarly American quality. To intimate that it is would be harsh and unfair. Walter Bagehot remarked sardonically in 1874 that persecution of those who were different might almost be said to exist as a fundamental rule of life: " It is so congenial to human nature, that it has arisen everywhere in past times, as history shows; that the cessation of it is a matter of recent times in England; that even now, taking the world as a whole, the practice and theory of it are in a triumphant majority. Most men have always much preferred persecution, and do so still; and it is therefore only natural that it should continually reappear in discussion and argument." [30] Strands of suspicion and hostility and resentment have run through the fabrics of all countries in all ages, though of course the strands are always given color and emphasis by local factors. In our own time and in our own country the atmosphere of international tension has tinted the strands—but, I suggest, some of the strands were there beforehand.

The New " Reactionaries "

It is not the purpose of this essay, however, to critcize or to characterize those who now find elements of safety in governmental methods they formerly condemned. Its purpose, rather, is to sketch why some of the former upholders of the administrative process (I was undoubtedly among them) now feel that what were mainly imaginary dangers have become real—and frightening.

Unfitness Coupled With Unreviewability. During the years of major contention about the administrative process, the great bulk of administrative decisions involved either the ascertainment of past occurrences or the enunciation of informed judgments about future economic or technological developments. The " facts " were to be found in the light of objective evidence about specific non-repetitive events— as, for example, when determining whether an allegedly injured employee had in fact been injured in the course of his employment; or whether an employer had discriminatorily discharged employees who sought to organize for collective bargaining; or whether farmers had been victimized by a commission agent at a distant stockyard to which they had shipped cattle for sale.

Still under the guise of finding facts, the administrative agencies were also sometimes called upon to make " guesstimates " about the future—as, for example, when they decided whether or not integration of public utility companies would be functionally useful in rendering service; or whether the issuance of a radio broadcasting station license to one rather than another applicant would assure better service for the public; or whether a schedule of rates would be adequate to compensate a railroad without unduly burdening the shipper in times to come; or whether a certificate of public convenience and necessity should be granted to an air carrier. In these matters, the agencies of necessity dealt in forecasts or opinions about future events, and they exercised a judgment quite different from that involved in evaluating evidence bearing upon a past or present occurrence. Nevertheless, as Judge Barrett Prettyman insisted, these estimates of the future could not be " fashioned from pure fantasy, speculation devoid of factual premise." Mere subjectivism

did not suffice as a basis of action. The administrative judgments were required to have " a hard core of factual possibility, which can be ascertained and evaluated only upon the
basis of present and past events and conditions," so that the
rationality of the agencies' guesstimates could be demonstrated even though others might conceivably have reached
different conclusions.[31]

Finally, many agencies had the power to make rules and
regulations—" sub-legislation," as it has sometimes been
called—that had the same effect as statutes. But those rules
were not immune from later challenge. They were subject
to precisely the same examination in court as though enacted
by the legislature itself; and, moreover, they were valid only
when within the scope of the power the legislature had
delegated.

These various powers were indeed vastly important. Note,
however, that they had two common characteristics. First,
they dealt for the most part with essentially economic issues.
Second, they almost invariably involved factual judgments
that could be made with presumably greater skill by specialists than by persons who had less continuous contact with
the sorts of issues to be decided. The same cannot be said
about the matters that now stir the concern of the " liberals "
who formerly viewed administrative proceedings with com-
placency or active approval.

Sheer specialization of work does not inevitably make for
expertness. Some specialization is nothing more than a convenience, as when minor adjudicatory functions are assigned
to administrators rather than judges, lest the regular business
of the courts be overborne by petty affairs—as would happen,
for example, if federal judges instead of employees of the
Bureau of Old Age and Survivors Insurance had to pass on
the nearly two million pension claims that are adjudicated
annually. The administrators who perform that work become specialists without being able to claim any particular

expertness. Similarly, administrators who make decisions concerning such abstractions as " obscenity," " security," and " loyalty," which bulk so large in the newer realms of administration, are not experts though they may sometimes be specialists. No well defined educational process or routinized training has equipped them, as distinct from judges and jurors, to determine the delicate issues of philosophy, aesthetics, psychology, or political theory that arise in contemporary administration. It is precisely here that administrative judgment is most subject to miscalculations, distortions, and delusions.

With the benefit of hindsight all of us console ourselves with thoughts of our intellectual superiority over those who made mistakes in earlier days. Unlike them, we do not believe in witches; we do not think that religious differences merit burning at the stake, either for the benefit of the burned or the burners; we marvel that two generations ago President Noah Porter of Yale demanded that William Graham Sumner discontinue using as a textbook the supposedly too radical *Study of Sociology* by Herbert Spencer, whom we now think of as a doctrinaire apostle of self-reliance and laissez faire; and we find ourselves amused that in 1940 Bertrand Russell was barred from teaching mathematics and logic in the College of the City of New York lest he demoralize its sheltered student body, after his writings had been attacked by a taxpayer as " lecherous, salacious, libidinous, hurtful, venerous, erotomaniac, aphrodisiac, atheistic, irreverent, narrow-minded, untruthful, and bereft of moral fibre."

If we feel superior to those who went before, we are probably deluded by our own self confidence. The men who made the decisions of yesterday at which we scoff today were for the most part as well intentioned and as intelligent as are we ourselves, or our administrative officials, and, with allowances for differences in time and space, just about as learned.

" Orthodox Christians who are tempted to think that those who stoned to death the first martyrs must have been worse men than they themselves are, ought to remember that one of those persecutors was Saint Paul." [32]

The point need not be further belabored. Human understanding is a chancy thing. That is why entrusting to any person the power, through censorship in any form, to shut off communication at its source is to run a great risk. Nowadays that risk is being taken with gay abandon by persons who used to be fearful of administrative errors. The censors they support are unlikely to have an expertise warranting special deference toward their findings. Yet, as will be shown more fully in a later chapter, their determinations are often dispositive of what can be read. Especially in matters of taste, where so little can be established objectively, real danger exists that an entirely fictitious expertness may limit the review of administrative rulings in a way that to all intents and purposes gives sanction to administrative fiat. Here, much more than in the areas of economic and social adjustment, there may be true need for judicial supercession of administrative commands.*

* Professor Louis Schwartz of Pennsylvania has made a strong plea that judges rather than administrators should shape the large outlines of national *economic* policy where Congress has not itself marked them but has left policy development to others. He maintains, in this connection, that there is a sense "in which judges have more ' expertise' than commissioners. If the latter are expert in their special fields, the former are experts in synthesis. Daily confronted with the entire range of social conflict, the judges acquire perspective, become aware, as no commissioner can, of all the conflicting goals towards which a society struggles." Louis B. Schwartz, Legal Restrictions of Competition in the Regulated Industries, 67 Harv. L. Rev. 436, at 473–474 (1954). In my estimation, the asserted superiority of a judge's perspective is even more clearly present where the permissible limits of expression are in issue.

Consider in this context, also, the position stated by William J. Butler, The Rising Tide of Expertise, 15 Fordham L. Rev. 19, at 34–35 (1946): ". . . the expert, if he expects to have any special consideration accorded to his judgments, must be one who deals in a field which involves genuine knowledge and some approximation of certainty. Another qualification which the judgment of the expert must have is that it be addressed to a problem

Consider another power of tremendous consequence, executed with finality by persons of no special qualifications: the power given the Attorney General to save an alien from deportation " to any country in which in his opinion the alien would be subject to physical persecution." [33] This power to preserve a human being from a violent fate at the hands of his fellow-countrymen has been regarded by the courts as virtually beyond their control.

The immigration officials to whom the Attorney General has delegated his authority may and do make their life-and-death decisions upon the basis of information not communicated to the affected individual.[34] They may, and they apparently do, conclude that a former Communist need fear no persecution from the Rhee government, having been assured by the Korean consul in San Francisco that the " Korean Government always welcomes home with open arms all those Prodigal Sons who truly repented and return home for mercy and guidance." [35] They may, and they apparently do, conclude that a turncoat Titoist has nothing to fear in Yugoslavia—and this in the face of uncontradicted testimony to the contrary by a former chief of the Foreign Press Department in the Tito government, now a professor of Modern European History in this country, and by the Dean of the Serbian Cathedral of St. Sava in New York City.[36] They may, and they apparently do, conclude on the basis of information never revealed to the affected alien or to the reviewing courts that the mainland of China will not be insalubrious for a non-sympathizer with the Communist regime there.[37]

This is not to say that the power to withhold deportation is never exercised. During the year which ended June 30, 1954, fifty-three out of 258 applications filed during that year were acted upon favorably. But a recent task force report to

which is solvable within his own field. Thus, the physician is no expert when he advocates euthanasia."

the House Committee on the Judiciary stated some harsh conclusions about the administration of this branch of the law. Applications were denied, it was feared, " in many cases where threat of physical persecution in the country to which the deportee is destined may have been claimed with a reasonable degree of probability." The deciding officers " do not appear to be properly educated and trained to judge the difficult and involved elements entering into the cases before them." Many of them " simply do not possess the necessary intellectual background which would permit them to evaluate the imponderable factors related to the alien's social and political past, his activities, his family ties, and his other connections which may be the direct or indirect cause of persecution in the countries placed in the Soviet orbit." Moreover, few of those who make these vital discretionary determinations have " sufficient knowledge of the past, recent, and current history of the many countries of Europe and Asia where physical persecution for political reasons is a matter of everyday practice. Not many of them know how Soviet terrorism operates behind the Iron Curtain and whom and why it singles out for destruction. . . . [A]pparently well justified claims of fear of persecution in at least three countries now dominated by international communism have been flatly rejected without the presentation of anything even remotely resembling a factual rebuttal of the claims made by the deportee." [38]

Obviously, a matter of this sort cannot be handled by application of rigid rules. Discretion must exist if findings are to be shaped by the fluctuating circumstances of individuals and the political organisms that affect their lives. But, in bestowing that necessary discretion upon the administrators of immigration laws, we should not fool ourselves into thinking that we have assigned the work to " experts." Nor should we be content to accept their say-so as the absolutely final judgment when a fellow human's existence is at stake.

Seemly adherence to American belief in the importance of the individual demands more than that. At the very least, the administrative decision should be reviewable to the extent of establishing its rationality.

Before passing to another topic, let us consider one more example of inexpertness combined with unreviewability in law administration. Under the law as it stands today, each consul of the United States has sole and uncontrolled power to deny visas to foreigners within his consular area who desire to enter the United States as immigrants or visitors.[39]

American consuls are undoubtedly devoted public servants of blameless character. But their traditional functions are to promote commerce, report economic developments, and protect American lives and property. None of these activities provide on-the-job training in visa administration. Once upon a time, according to A. A. Berle, Jr., a former assistant secretary of state and ambassador of the United States, the denial of a visa had been governed by " pretty mechanical tests," and so the task could be " put in the. hands of a ministerial officer without great difficulty." But the untroubled quietude of the past is no more; the work today raises delicate and difficult questions because statutes have greatly elaborated the conditions of eligibility. Still, decisions remain as of yore entirely within the discretion of the consuls, whom Mr. Berle characterizes as " boys that are just coming into the service." The result, he adds, is that " you would have these little difficult questions, with absolute power, frequently the power of life or death, vested in a youngster, usually of good intentions, and frequently of very little experience, and with not only no control over him, but in the outlying districts, nobody with whom he could even consult." [40]

No functional justification exists for endowing an official with such unqualified authority to be negative. The only outspoken effort to suggest a justification came from Senator

McCarran's committee, which in 1950 viewed the consular veto power over visas as " an additional barrier to the entry of inadmissible aliens." [41] Perhaps it is. But if an additional barrier is needed for that purpose, we could greatly improve the present design. The existing system seems to keep out the fit along with the unfit, and as a rule nobody need become aware of the mistakes. It does happen, of course, that unwise decisions are sometimes made in cases involving persons prominent in the social, business, or academic life of other countries, and that this causes a certain diminution of good will toward the United States.[42] It is a fact that a number of international scientific congresses that would otherwise have met in this country (to the great advantage of American scientists) have gone elsewhere, to avoid the embarrassments of denied or unduly delayed visas.[43] It is true that some of our consuls " display a considerable degree of shyness " in deciding to recommend the temporary admission, as nonimmigrants, of certain aliens who desire to come to the United States and whose entry could not be deemed prejudicial to this country's interests—and it is true that their " shyness " has lowered the nation's prestige.[44] Nonetheless, the consul's word is law, so long as the word is " No! "

Consuls cannot be blamed for overly rigid policies framed by Congress. Nor can they be blamed for not having special qualifications for the performance of work only tangentially related to their main interests. The fault in the present situation lies, as in the instances previously given, in the American public's willingness to entrust these important tasks to inexpert persons whose judgment is altogether beyond external review. The American Bar Association's Section of Administrative Law has recommended creating a Board of Visa Appeals, as an administrative mechanism to control the now uncontrolled discretion of the individual consul. This is a badly needed first step toward bringing visa

administration within the reach of law. "It is difficult to
find any other situation in our whole administration" the
lawyers have asserted, "in which so crucial a power is lodged
in the initial operating officer beyond any possibility of
review. This . . . encourages the arbitrary and irresponsible
exercise of power. It has also been pointed out that in a
case of doubt the consul is taking the least risk in denying
the visa and thus important interests may be denied legitimate protection"—interests, it may be added, that include
those of relatives already in this country who may by unreviewable and uninformed official action be precluded from
reuniting a scattered family.[45]

The Decisiveness of Decisions. A deeply significant difference between much of the older administration and the
newer brand lies in their relative capacity for truly determina-
tive consequences.

Despite occasional howls that have suggested a great deal
more bloodshed than actually ever occurred, the somewhat
older regulatory agencies of government have rarely been
brutal in their treatment of the established interests they
regulated. The agencies have in the main been like gar-
deners concerned with topiary art, as it were, rather than
with uprooting. They have snipped here and there; sometimes they may even have snipped with a carelessness that
left raggedness in the overall effect. But their decisions have
not been likely to have a killing effect despite the irritations
they might cause.

Consider, for example, the nature of the decisions made by
the agency the anti-administrationists seemingly hated the
most, the National Labor Relations Board. If, after a full
hearing, the Board found that an employer had engaged in
an unfair labor practice, it ordered him to cease and desist
from continuing in the future what had been wrongfully
done in the past. In cases where employees had been wrong-

fully discharged, the Board might order the employer to pay them their lost wages. These money damages rarely amounted to large sums. Their assessment was remedial rather than punitive. In no case did punishment of an erring employer lie at the end of the long and openly contested proceedings; rather, the employer faced nothing more horrid than an injunction to go and sin no more. Wounding though this may have been to the employer's pride, and galling though it may have been to a company unused to collective bargaining, no order of the NLRB ever ended a going business.

Similarly, the Federal Trade Commission could direct a business concern to refrain in the future from using an unfair method of competition to which it had resorted in the past; but the Commission imposed no punishment for earlier misdeeds, nor did it prevent the business from continuing an honorable existence despite its earlier errors.

True, the Federal Communications Commission and the Civil Aeronautics Board, through their licensing powers, were given vast authority over broadcasting and air transport. But industries regulated from their infancy could be shaped from the start, without being radically altered. The administrators' authority of revocation acted, perhaps, as a Damoclean sword; yet the sword was very sparingly used (and then not to kill), and the administrators could never cause it to fall without justification demonstrable to the satisfaction of a reviewing court.

The Securities and Exchange Commission also possessed powers that in the early days seemed substantial. It was authorized to consider whether stock promoters were candid in describing the companies whose securities were about to be sold to the public. The Commission's refusal to approve a registration statement might cause the abandonment of a financial project upon which considerable toil and ingenuity might have been expended. Even so, the adverse administrative action was rarely dispositive of the fate of either financiers or of the enterprises they were seeking to finance. A particular transaction might have to be shelved, a particular practice of securities dealers might have to be modified, a particular disappointment or annoyance might be experienced. But grass was not sown in Wall Street. Its life continued in full vigor.

These powers (which are typical of those that caused concern two decades ago) are surely not inconsiderable. But they are markedly different in their consequences from the ones that now arouse alarm in formerly complacent quarters. The new radicalism has given approval to powers that tunnel into the bedrock of individual security far more deeply than has been customary.

Deportation orders, for instance, do much more than irritate those to whom they are addressed. They may result, as Mr. Justice Brandeis well said, " in loss of both property and life; or of all that makes life worth living." [46] They may destroy homes, separate families, wreck business endeavors of long standing. Nevertheless, the administrative power to issue such orders—orders that are " at times the equivalent of banishment or exile " [47]—is constantly being reinforced. Recently the Supreme Court has upheld the ouster of an alien who, having entered the United States at the age of seven, had resided here for thirty-six years during which he had acquired an American wife and four American-born children. There was, according to Mr. Justice Black, " strong evidence that he was a good, law-abiding man, a steady worker and a devoted husband and father loyal to this country and its form of government." But there was also evidence that he had made the grave mistake of having been a member of the Communist Party for a brief period in the past—a membership that had terminated well before his deportation was sought, a membership that was legal at the time it existed, a membership that was not shown to involve either knowledge of evil purposes or involvement in improper activities. Nonetheless, by legislation enacted after the alien had already ended an association that he had no reason to suppose would expose him to penalty, Congress empowered the Attorney General to deport. And deport he did, with the result that the alien lost " his job, his friends, his home, and maybe even his children, who must choose between their father and their native country." The Supreme Court felt itself powerless to interfere, saying that Congress could deal with aliens as it saw fit.[48]

The point here is not that a hapless deportee occasionally deserves our pity even more than our resentment. The point is that the administrative power, upheld despite the presence of almost all the elements of an old-fashioned tear jerker, was dispositive and not merely admonitory or remonstrative. The Court itself has recognized that " the expulsion power has been exercised with increasing severity, manifest in multiplication of grounds for deportation, in expanding the subject classes from illegal residents to legal residents, and in greatly lengthening the period of residence " during which deportation remains possible.[49] Still the judges refuse to call a halt, saying, in effect, that anything (and anybody) goes so long as the rudimentary procedural forms are observed.

One consequence is that an ever greater number of residents in the United States, foreign born but still human, live somewhat less securely than formerly. During the whole decade before World War II, for example, only 210,416 aliens were sent out of the country by deportation or by what is euphemistically called voluntary departure under official pressure. During the single year 1950, by contrast, 579,105 aliens were ushered from our midst, most of them leaving " voluntarily " in preference to being deported. In the year which ended June 30, 1952, the figure rose still further to 744,140. In 1954 the totals climbed to 1,101,228.[50] The gross figures are less revealing than they appear on the

surface, for somewhat more than 60 per cent of those deported are Mexican nationals who entered this country
illegally, and a still larger percentage of the " voluntary
departures " may be attributed to this group. Even after
they have been subtracted, however, the remainder is large.
If we exclude from our calculation all the deportees or de-
parters who were never lawfully admitted to begin with,
or who violated the conditions upon which they were temporarily admitted, and who may therefore not have very
compelling claims to consideration, we may safely estimate
that at least 2,000 permanent residents are being annually
banished from their home country. Their banishment is in
essence a punishment for things they did after their lawful
entry into the United States.

Let it not be supposed that only the Reds and the ex-Reds
are affected by the newer style of deportation for past events.
During the ten years from 1945 to 1954, for example, there
were 160,598 deportations; but of these only 163 fell into
the " subversive or anarchistic " category.[51] The official reach
goes far beyond the politically blameworthy. Thus, for instance, a man who had violated the Marihuana Tax Act
fourteen full years before Congress thought to make its
violation a ground of deportation, was seized and ousted
without any finding that his continued residence would be
undesirable; and the Supreme Court felt powerless to intervene.[52] Violations of law used to be regarded as relevant
only to a weighing of present fitness. Now the officials need
not consider present fitness at all. The bare fact of past
violation prvoides a peg on which an administrator can hang
a deportation order, thus adding " a new punishment for a
past offense." The principle established in the case of the
former Communist may, apparently, be extended as far as
logic will take it.

A business man could prosper, not only economically but
socially, despite an order of the National Labor Relations

Board or the Federal Trade Commission. Not so an ousted alien. Even less so a man adjudged to be a security risk. Such a man loses more than his present job. He also loses access to others in government or in private industry, and perhaps even beyond this country's borders.[53] Recall that often the man regarded as a security risk is in no sense a malefactor, even in the eyes of those who felt compelled to brand him. He may, for example, be an unfortunate who suffers from guilt by family relationship, or he may merely be one whose past associations raise a question about the drift of his sympathies. Yet, unlike the respondent in a Labor Board proceeding, he will henceforth obtain a passport only with great difficulty, if at all; if in the armed services, he may be assigned undesirable service under surveillance and, at least until recently and perhaps still today, he may be discharged otherwise than honorably; he cannot obtain a Federal Communications Commission license as operator or station owner; grants for research work may be withheld from him; and if the President declares the existence of an "internal security emergency," he may be interned.

One might suppose that this new-type administrative order, with its far reaching and relatively dire consequences, would be entered somewhat more cautiously than, say, the milk-and-water cease and desist orders of the Federal Trade Commission. The opposite is true. Conventional administrative orders must be preceded by notice and opportunity to be heard; the evidence upon which decision rests must be made known to the person it affects, so that he may subject it to effective counterattack; the decisional process must be deliberate, opportunity being given to analyze and to argue concerning the proposed conclusions. These procedural protections against error or injustice are absent in the area now being discussed. Nor is this change experienced exclusively in personnel security cases, though the word "security" does run like a leitmotif through many of the instances in which procedural regularity has been discarded.

The administrative bail cases, arising in deportation matters, are suggestive of the change. Substantial periods of time may elapse between the seizure of an allegedly deportable alien and the judgment as to whether or not he should be deported.[54] What shall be done with the alien during this time? To detain everyone pending final decision would be a needless cruelty quite inconsistent with our traditions. To allow every accused person to go at large, on the other hand, might expose the United States to possible injury while the proceedings were dragging on toward their close. Congress sought to solve the problem by enacting that " pending final determination of the deportability of any alien taken into custody under warrant of the Attorney General, such alien may, *in the discretion of the Attorney General* (1) be continued in custody; or (2) be released under bond . . . ; or (3) be released on conditional parole . . ." .

The practical workings of this rather sweeping exercise of " discretion " are exemplified by the case of one Zydok, who was described by the Supreme Court as follows:

> Appellant was seventeen years of age when he arrived in this country from Poland in 1913. Since then he has lived continuously in the State of Michigan. He has been a waiter in an English speaking restaurant in Hamtranck, Mich., for seventeen years and for a great part of that time he was head waiter. He owns his own home in Detroit and has a family consisting of his wife, two sons, a daughter, and five grandchildren. Both sons served in the armed forces of the United States in World War II. His grandchildren were born in this country and his daughter married here. . . . The record fails to disclose that he has violated any law or that he is engaged, or is likely to engage, in any subversive activities.

Nevertheless five of the nine Justices deemed this man, as to whom there was no disclosed evidence of subversive activities, subject to detention of indefinitely prolonged duration because a very subordinate official of the Immigration and Naturalization Service (not the Attorney General himself) said that Zydok's dossier showed involvement with the Communists; and Communists were so great a menace to the nation's welfare and safety that a person accused of being one should not be admitted to bail while the truth or falsity of the accusation was being determined.[55]

We tend, not wholly unnaturally, to accept without very critical examination any disabilities that may be imposed on Communists, and especially alien Communists. But let us look for just a moment at the implications of a case like Zydok's. If persons merely alleged (on the basis of as yet secret evidence) to be Communists are so dangerous that they must be cut off from their homes and families, why confine the Attorney General's subordinates to the seizure and indefinite detention of aliens? No one suggested that Zydok's detention was necessary to assure his obedience to a deportation order if one were ever issued after hearing. He was kept in jail, as one of the judges said, "solely because a bureau agent thinks that is where Communists should be." In effect, the Congress, with the Supreme Court's narrow approval, has empowered administrative officials to hold without bail people they deem "dangerous," before their dangerous quality has been established and without the possibility of effective supervision. Does this not give one pause? History is replete with instances in other lands of abusive police administration involving lengthy detention, without bail, of individuals against whom charges were never substantiated. The whole concept of admitting persons to bail is that individuals should not be kept in prison before trial, so long as their presence can be assured at trial and afterward. Constitutional protections are precious. They are much too precious to be risked by countenancing administrative immobilization of persons, even when those persons are alleged to be Communists.

The problem of the Zydok case does not have to be solved by allowing every accused individual to roam at large while his case is sub judice. The nation will be safer rather than weaker, however, if bailability is determined by a judicial exercise of sober discretion upon disclosed facts.

Another disturbing instance of allowing " security " to out-weigh the older notions of fair procedure is found in the case of Mrs. Ellen Knauff, the German-born wife of an American citizen.[56] The Attorney General excluded her from the United States because, he said, her admission would be prejudicial to this country's interests. But he declined to reveal the basis of this finding, nor was he willing that Mrs. Knauff should have a hearing; the Attorney General had acted on " information of a confidential nature " which he desired not to expose. The Court, by a four-to-three vote, said that Mrs. Knauff " had to stand the test of security. This she failed to meet. We find no legal defect in the manner of petitioner's exclusion."

Mr. Justice Jackson, strongly dissenting, wrote: " Security is like liberty in that many are the crimes committed in its name. The menace to the security of this country, be it great as it may, from this girl's admission is as nothing compared to the menace to free institutions inherent in procedures of this pattern. In the name of security the police state justifies its arbitrary oppressions on evidence that is secret, because security might be prejudiced if it were brought to light in hearings. The plea that evidence of guilt must be secret is abhorrent to free men, because it provides a cloak for the malevolent, the misinformed, the meddlesome, and the corrupt to play the role of informer undetected and uncorrected. . . . Congress will have to use more explicit language than any yet cited before I will agree that it has authorized an administrative officer to break up the family of an American citizen or force him to keep his wife by becoming an exile. Likewise, it will have to be much more explicit before I can agree that it authorized a finding of serious misconduct against the wife of an American citizen without notice of charges, evidence of guilt and a chance to meet it."

Members of Congress (including Representative Walter, be it said to his credit) seemingly shared Mr. Justice Jackson's sentiments, for they pressed the Attorney General to indicate what was wrong with Mrs. Knauff. About a year later the Attorney General decided that a hearing could be had. His confidential information could then be disclosed, he thought, without disaster. When the information was exposed to the light of day, it shrank to insignificance. The Board of Immigration Appeals ultimately decided that there was no substantial evidence that Mrs. Knauff had engaged in or was likely to engage in activities detrimental to the United States. More than three years after she had first been detained at Ellis Island, the Attorney General approved his board's finding, and Mrs. Knauff was at last admitted into this country.[57] Thus, in the end, she was found to be all right. But a contrary administrative fiat had been upheld. It could have determined the future existence of a young couple, whose whole marriage was at the mercy of administrators unchecked by fair procedures.

Ignatz Mezei, a cabinetmaker born in Hungary but long a resident of Buffalo, provided another example of the truly dispositive character of the new administration. Mezei left this country, having first obtained a re-entry permit, in order (he said) to visit his ailing mother. When he returned, he was denied entry and, like Mrs. Knauff, was given no hearing or information as to the cause of his difficulties. He applied to 25 other countries for admission, but was invariably rejected; the Communist countries did not want him and the rest were afraid of him, supposing that whatever it was in Mezei that menaced this powerful nation would be equally bad for them. Consequently, Mezei seemed condemned (though without having had a trial) to life imprisonment on Ellis Island.

Once again, this time by a five-to-four vote, the Supreme Court held that the detained person had no rights.[58] Once again Mr. Justice Jackson protested. " This man, who seems to have led a life of unrelieved insignificance, must have been astonished to find himself suddenly putting the Government of the United States in such fear that it was afraid to tell him why it was afraid of him. . . . Let it not be overlooked that due process of law is not for the sole benefit of an accused. It is the best insurance for the Government itself against those blunders which leave lasting stains on a system of justice but which are bound to occur on *ex parte* consideration. . . . [W]hen indefinite confinement becomes the means of enforcing exclusion, it seems to me that due process requires that the alien be informed of its grounds and have a fair chance to overcome them. This is the more due him when he is entrapped into leaving the other shore by reliance on a visa which the Attorney General refuses to honor."

Mezei's case like Mrs. Knauff's had a reasonably happy ending. After some three years of detention, he was finally accorded a hearing before a special board composed of distinguished New York attorneys. They found, upon the basis of evidence that seems to have been available without uncovering any " undercover sources," that Mezei was in fact excludible as a sometime Communist. But they then volunteered the unanimous recommendation that he be allowed to remain at liberty in this country on parole, as a harmless though perhaps not exemplary character. For several years Mezei has been among us, without, so far as is known, dire consequences. But his freedom is a matter of administrative grace. As a matter of law, he could have been kept under lock and key for the rest of his life without ever being told why.

Enough has been said to suggest some of the qualitative differences between the older and the newer fashions in administrative justice. Wise men have counselled against creating official powers that would be frightening if in the hands of our enemies. Powers like those just discussed seem to me to be of that stamp.

From Public Service to Public Suspicion

Today, to a degree not remotely approached in the past, American citizens are the objects of the suspicion of administrators rather than the objects of their services. A crusty old English gentleman, when writing to public officers in Whitehall, is said to close each of his letters with the inverted sentence: " You are, Sir, my obedient servant." Certain American officials might not see the joke. Given some of the jobs we expect them to perform, administrators can scarcely be blamed for beginning to think of citizens not as masters to be served but as potential dangers to the nation, to be scrutinized with a wary eye. Cold war with a major foreign power has understandably stimulated fears. Those fears have sometimes distorted vision. We have lost confidence in one another. We have too often generalized from the particular, so that doubts and hostilities have occasionally overflown the banks of reason. We have in too many instances qualified the belief, on which our governmental structure rests, that freedom—freedom from surveillance, freedom from governmental channeling of opinion or political activity, freedom for the maverick and the minority—will sustain our national security, while the restrictions spawned by overcautious concern will shake it.

Of course one must recognize that life is a risk from first to last. A prudent watchfulness against possible harm has never been thought antithetical to democratic conviction, and there is no reason to begin now to think that it is. In the past, however, we have for the most part kept a sane balance between recognition of the risks of evil and, on the other hand, insistence upon the citizen's " right to be let alone." When balances have had to be struck, we have taken a dim view of the dragnet, the identity card, the secret police, and the enforced orthodoxies that have characterized less free societies.

Now there is a certain instability of conviction on that score. There are those who think that perhaps " civil liberties and all that stuff " were all right in normal times, but that one must be more realistic in periods of war or other crisis involving the nation's well-being or survival. The times being what they are and seem likely to continue to be, this exception would swallow up the rule. We live in an age when crisis is the normality and peaceful quiet the anomaly. If one is to be realistic at all, one must be realistic enough to recognize that a change in our attitude toward individuals and their rights is more likely to be permanent than temporary.

In every society, in every age, and certainly in our own there are multitudes who, in Archibald MacLeish's phrase, " fear freedom or are frightened of the loneliness it implies." [59] For the most part, however, inroads on freedom are not initiated by those who prefer that others assume responsibility for directing their lives; these flabby folk become the hordes that sustain dictatorships, but they themselves are too inert to bring it to pass. We need not worry, in my estimation, that freedom will be brought low upon their initiative. Nor do I think that evilly motivated men will successfully trick us into surrendering one after another bastion in a heedless quest for an unattainably perfect security. The real danger lies among those of us who genuinely desire to protect freedom, and who think that this can best be done by limiting it.* They propose to give a little here to protect a lot there. The motive is admirable, but the judgment is unsound. The very amplitude of our American brand of freedom sometimes seduces us into believing that a good deal of it can be spent without anyone's really noticing the difference—that we can afford, as Carl Becker put it, " to take liberties with our liberty." [60] But the trouble is that small restrictions accumulate into large restrictions and, in the process, may become as habitual as, before, freedom was. Restrictions justified as necessary safeguards of freedom may in fact safeguard freedom out of existence altogether.

Nobody supposes that this sorry state has in fact been reached in the United States. A vigorously healthy libertarianism can withstand many assaults, as the British have amply proved by their resilient recovery from the restraints of exceptionally stern and alarmingly summary governmental powers in crisis years.[61] It is not too early, however, to ponder whether a danger point is at hand.

Consider, for example, the much discussed personnel security programs. Their assigned purpose is clearly justifiable. They are defended as means of guarding against infiltration into the public service and important private employments by

---

* As bearing on the motives of those who would protect freedom by limiting it, consider the remark of Harlan Fiske Stone: " History teaches us that there have been few infringements of personal liberty by the state which have not been justified . . . in the name of righteousness and public good. . . . The framers were not unaware that under the system which they created most governmental curtailments of personal liberty would have the support of a legislative judgment that the public interest would be better served by its curtailment than by its constitutional protection." These words were spoken in Justice Stone's famous dissenting opinion in Minersville School District v. Gobitis, 310 U. S. 586, at 604 (1940), the " flag salute case." That dissent, it will be recalled, was destined to become the majority view only three years later in West Virginia Board of Education v. Barnette, 319 U. S. 624 (1943) ; in the latter case Justice Jackson said, among other things: " Struggles to coerce uniformity of sentiment in support of some end thought essential to their time and country have been waged by many good as well as by evil men." (p. 640.)

individuals who might use their positions to jeopardize the nation's well-being. On the face of it this is unexceptionable. The trouble with the programs is that they are such awkward means to the defensible end.

Professor Ralph Brown of Yale, one of the most scrupulous of those who have been examining into the matter, tells us that some 12,600,000 persons employed in the United States are at any given moment subject to one or another kind of federal, state, or local security test.[62] Chief Justice Earl Warren has counted eight million Americans who require security clearances by federal officials alone; and former Senator Harry Cain, a member of the Subversive Activities Control Board, no doubt having in mind the fact that the immediate family of an employed individual may also undergo a "loyalty investigation" in the course of his obtaining a clearance, has raised the total to 20,000,000.[63] Probably both figures are subject to upward revision if one takes into account persons who, having been cleared, move on to some other employment, to be replaced in their former jobs by new recruits who must then in turn be cleared; the normal personnel turnover means that many more are cleared than there are jobs for which clearance is necessary. At any rate, within a very brief period probably at least a fifth of all persons employed in the United States (plus many of their families) have been subjected to inquiry concerning their associations, politics, and beliefs in order to weed out a tiny group about whom some suspicion might arise.*

* The numerical analysis in the text may be affected by Cole v. Young, 76 S. Ct. 861, decided June 11, 1956. The case held that existing statutes did not authorize the summary removal, on "loyalty" grounds, of federal employees who do not occupy positions affecting national security. The effects of the decision could not yet be gauged when these pages went to press. The Administration had not determined what changes, if any, to make in the existing personnel loyalty–security programs; and Congress was still considering the possibility of nullifying Cole v. Young by broadening the statutory reach. The chances seemed good, however, that there would be some reduction in the staggeringly high totals mentioned in the above text.

The consequences of this nervous peering at one another remain difficult to calculate. We know with some assurance that the campaigns to eliminate the untrustworthy have not exposed active malefactors. Not a single instance of espionage, sabotage, or similar subversiveness has come to light through a "loyalty investigation." What we know about espionage we know because of the excellent counter-espionage work of the agencies assigned to that duty, and not because of the personnel security programs. If we feel more secure because of the operations of those programs, we feel so because they have ended the employment of an indeterminate number of hypothetically potential rather than proved wrongdoers.* But this sensation of security has entailed high social costs, made higher by the needless extension of security searches into areas that had no security significance in the first place. This has happened, for instance, through investigations of personnel engaged in open, basic research where there was no question of access to secret materials, and where the integrity of the scientists involved was already well established. In such cases, as the National Science Foundation recently declared in an official report, " loyalty or security-type investigations are clearly undesirable and unlikely to serve any useful purpose." [64] Others have put the matter

---

* From the administrative point of view, there is an absolute enchantment about getting rid of "hypothetically potential rather than proved wrongdoers." The virtue of the system is that the adverse decision can never be shown to have been mistaken. The simple beauties of such a situation were anticipated in some remarks in the House of Commons on the British Alien Bill of 1793 by Mr. Grey, an opposition member: "Perhaps, indeed, some time hence, ministers, if asked to show what they had done for the service of the state, would assure the House, that but for their interference much mischief might have ensued; they might say they had sent such a person out of the country; perhaps somebody might say, 'I knew that gentleman very well, he had no views of sedition, he was a worthy and quiet man.'— 'Oh, I beg your pardon,' the minister would say, 'you do not know him so well as I do; I sent him out of the kingdom to prevent mischief; I grant you, he did nothing against the state, but that is owing to me, for I took care to prevent him.'" 30 Parliamentary History of England (Hansard, 1817), 211.

even more strongly, for it is known that "security" has sometimes meant the end of medical research focused on such wholly non-military problems as multiple sclerosis, the nervous system, and the treatment of high blood pressure.[65] Sometimes it has meant impeding badly needed military research, as when Dr. Fritz Zwicky, professor of astrophysics at California Institute of Technology, was suspended from guided missile work with not even a hint of doubt about his reliability, but seemingly because he chose to retain his Swiss citizenship; thus the United States purported to make itself more secure—by rejecting the services of one who might significantly advance the armed forces' work in rocket propulsion.[66]

Perhaps more significant in the end than costs like these, have been the more subtle erosions of previously accepted values. High officials of the Department of Justice have sharply attacked critics of procedural crudities in the personnel security programs, going so far, indeed, as to suggest that the critics are either fools or knaves. One quails before the intemperate attack of such powerful public employees. But one recalls the Supreme Court's reminder that " the history of liberty has largely been the history of observance of procedural safeguards " ; [67] and thus emboldened despite bureaucratic disapproval, one may question whether the sacrifice of fair procedures is a very effective means of preserving the American way of life.

The loyalty-security programs have certainly not achieved the ultimate of procedural refinement. One of their chief dangers lies in the fact that imperfections originally recognized as abnormalities tend to become accepted, after a time, as commonplace.* And yet the truth of the matter is that crude procedures have been producing alarmingly crude results.

* Dean Acheson, taking a retrospective glance at the federal employees loyalty program that he had joined in endorsing as a member of the Cabinet,

In about eight percent of the federal cases, it is estimated by one who has studied the matter intensively, informants upon whom reliance had been placed have later been found untrustworthy or, if trustworthy, have been incorrectly reported.[68] This is indeed a high percentage. Its significance is enlarged by the fact that the affected individual very frequently remains ignorant of his accusers and sometimes, indeed, of the nature of their accusations, so that he has little opportunity to show that the charges against him are insubstantial. Mistaken decisions are little to be wondered at in such circumstances. This is not because the adjudicators are ill-willed, but because they are precluded from learning all the facts.

The difficulties encountered by their predecessors, at home and abroad, should instruct us in what may be expected. The important British case of *Greene* v. *Secretary of State for Home Affairs* is illuminating.[69] In 1940 Greene was seized and placed in custody by the Home Secretary, acting under the applicable Defence Regulations. Despite his protests and protestations of innocence, Greene was kept in custody because confidential information gave the Government reason to think that he " was a person of hostile associations and that by reason thereof it was necessary to exercise control over him." The courts refused to intervene in his behalf. Nearly two years later he was released with a letter of regret, advising him that the charges against him were to be " re-

made this comment: ". . . it was not realized at first how dangerous was the practice of secret evidence and secret informers, how alien to all our conceptions of justice and the rights of the citizen. . . . Experience proved again how soon good men become callous in the use of bad practices. Familiarity breeds more than contempt, it breeds indifference. What was, at first, designed for cases which it was thought would be serious, sensitive and rare, became commonplace and routine. Now in cases involving no secret agent or sensitive position, a person may be branded as of doubtful loyalty and dismissed on evidence by persons whose identity not even his judges know and whose words, summarized for them, are withheld from the defendant." Dean Acheson, *A Democrat Looks At His Party* (Harper & Bros., 1955), 128–29.

garded as withdrawn." They had been made, it turned out,
by an informant who later admitted that they were false.

Lest one suppose that this reflects a foreign ineptitude un-
paralleled by efficient Americans, I regretfully add that
equally grim cases have been domestically produced.* They
stem from precisely the same procedural deficiency that
caused Greene's difficulties.[70] The Conservative barristers
of Britain were recently moved to say: " It has been disturbing to realise that, almost absent-mindedly as it were, a
system has been evolved in which the individual can suffer
substantial loss of rights through the unfettered discretion
of Ministers. What is far worse, such a decision can sometimes be arrived at without hearing the citizen's own point
of view, and occasionally on a misapprehension of the true
facts." [71] A similar comment by an American, directed at
untested reliance upon " faceless informers," might expose
him to the wrathful remark by public officers that he must
be in league with the Communists. Nonetheless, one need
not be in league with the Communists to know that abuse
has arisen in country after country when informers' secret
reports have been relied on as evidence, rather than merely
as leads to obtain evidence.

* One such case came to light just the other day. William Henry Taylor,
a former federal official now employed by the International Monetary Fund,
had in 1955 received this staggering judgment by a loyalty board: " This
board is convinced that the employee has engaged in espionage and subversive activities . . . and that he was and possibly still is an adherent to
the Communist ideology." Taylor doggedly fought for vindication. The first
necessary step was to discover what the accusations against him were. Finally
he obtained a further hearing, which lasted for two days. Eighteen months
after the original judgment was rendered, the board vacated its earlier
decision and notified Taylor that " on all the evidence there is not a
reasonable doubt as to your loyalty to the Government of the United States."
The chairman of the board explained: " Mr. Taylor and his counsel produced many live witnesses and numerous affidavits and letters which were all
favorable to him and which tended to negative much of the alleged deroga-
tory information in the file. If many of those factors had been known to us
earlier, we might not have rendered our first decision." *New York Times*,
January 7, 1956, p. 1, col. 3.

The use of reports as leads is normal police practice. Our modern administrators are taking the matter a very long step farther by using them directly as the basis of the dispositive decisions discussed in earlier pages. Not long ago the Chinese Communists announced the beginning of a new campaign against " counter-revolutionaries." One of the first byproducts of the campaign was the creation of a new state award, that of " Security Hero." [72] Three weeks after the drive had begun, a 21-year-old artisan had become " Security Hero, Class A " as a reward for having reported 281 suspects to the police. Americans shudder, and rightly so, at this unsavoury development in a country whose traditions and legal processes are so different from our own. Yet similar evils could conceivably arise here, too (as by all accounts they have arisen wherever the role of the political police has become magnified), if Americans were to discard their deep-rooted conviction that shortcuts paved with good intentions lead not to justice but to another destination.

The Individual Abides

Individuals comprise the state. The state has no existence as an abstract entity, capable of demanding homage in its own right. It exists only as an amalgam of human beings, who are its blood, bones, and sinew. The subordination of the individual and the exaltation of the state have always impressed Americans as obnoxious; and the fact that individuals are subordinated and the state is exalted in the Soviet Union has reinforced our conviction that the free way of life proceeds in a different direction. Today, however, too many administrators seek, and too often are given, powers that unduly obscure traditional protections against expedient invasions of individual rights. Harshly imposed limitations upon personal movement or upon access to employment are illustrative. The persistent campaign of the Department of Justice to legitimatize wiretapping is suggestive. The arguments against things like these are by no means one-sided. I do not propose to say that every person who is persuaded of their virtues is a traducer of America's democratic faith. I say merely that in the aggregate they reflect a shifting emphasis in governmental activity, a shift away from regulation for the public and toward policing of the public.

The results can not be weighed on scales that produce standardized measurements upon which everybody agrees. For myself, I think that the administrative huffing and puffing have produced very dubious effects. They have not, in my opinion, produced tranquillity, but have themselves engendered suspicions and nervousness that then seem to call for yet more energetic exertions.

It would be unfair, of course, to charge up against the administrators all the unpleasantnesses of our times. To some extent, however, the emphases and enthusiasms of government officials set the tone of much unofficial thinking, activity, and emotion. Perhaps encouraged by current administrative preoccupations, many Americans in their private capacity today eschew any examination of the merits of ideas or works of art or television performances or labor union demands or utterances by clergymen; instead, they examine the real or supposed " associations " of their authors. This avoidance of substantial thought means that a great deal of public debate never rises much above the level of petty gossip and hence fails to reach issues about which discussion might be useful. Our gaze too often remains fixed upon a shadowy curtain that obscures reality.

Man, it is true, has probably always sought in one way or another to escape the burden of exercising his brain. According to Socrates, once upon a time " men would accept the truth even if it were uttered by a stick or a stone, but now they ask who you are, and what are your motives." Socrates did not state at just what happy time in its history the human race was prepared to look truth in the face without becoming more interested in the face than in the truth. My own guess is that men in every age have been concerned with " who you are, and what are your motives "—though the styles do change, so that what was alarming or unpalatable in one generation may be readily accepted in the next. At any rate, heterodoxy has never been widely cherished. Even in the years of our nation's youth Alexis de Tocqueville had discovered no other land " in which there is so little independence of mind and real freedom of discussion as in America." [73] In those days, however, such fetters on discussion as may have existed were entirely self-imposed. No bureaucrat was needed to exclude foreign newspapers and periodicals, or to erect a " paper curtain " to prevent international travel, or to label organizations, or to sift the " loyal " from the " unloyal." What is truly extraordinary just now is the apparent conviction, reflected in energetic governmental activity, that Americans cannot quite be trusted —and, especially, must be most vigilantly guarded against seduction by an ideology they have long rejected with almost unanimous emphasis.

2

Restraints on Book Reading

Books are not big business in the United States. The gross annual receipts of all American publishers from the sales of all manner of books—including the *Bible, First-Grade Arithmetic, Aunt Emma's Cookbook,* and *How to Build Your Own Spaceship*—aggregated in 1955 only a bit more than half the net profits, after taxes, of the General Motors Corporation. If the term "bookstore" be given an extremely loose definition, there are perhaps 1,500 bookstores in the United States—as against 18,000 blacksmith shops. To be sure, there are other means of book distribution, including "book clubs" and public libraries. But Americans are not assiduous bookworms. Sweden, in relation to population, enjoys ten times as many public libraries as does the United States; Denmark has seven bookstores to our one; a recent series of interviews showed that while only one out of every five Americans shyly admitted that he was reading a book (or, at least, reading at a book) during the survey period, more than half the people questioned in Britain were so engaged at that time.

If quantitative measurements like these were to be given overriding significance, restraints on book reading might perhaps be unruffling. Books, however, have a special importance for the nation's health. Paradoxically, their significance derives in part from the economically "small time" character of the publishing business. The book trade is old-fashioned. It still resembles the nineteenth century more than it does the twentieth. Many small, personally operated firms compete actively with one another. Publishers of books unlike publishers of newspapers need not be press owners; so entry into business does not require a vast initial capital expenditure. The resulting entrepreneurial variety encourages the publication of books that might never appear if choice were entirely in the hands of a few industrial giants. Moreover, while best sellers are undoubtedly welcomed by even the most altruistic publisher, a small edition of a hardcover book is economically feasible; an unsuccessful book is not a major catastrophe. In this respect book publishers are released from the pressure apparently felt by those who cater exclusively to a mass market that, they fear, might vanish if any part of it were antagonized or offended.[1] Hence new ideas, which almost always antagonize or offend, are not so severely limited in books as elsewhere in our increasingly integrated society. And, apart from introducing ideas that may require extensive textual development, books remain the chief hope that diversity, and even elevation, of taste may survive the standardizing, leveling down influences of mass communications.

These considerations warrant particular attention to censorship of books, though all forms of censorship have certain common features and rest on similar hypotheses.

The Philosophic Foundations of Censorship

Censorship is a loosely used word. Strictly, it means prohibiting expression or communication. When legally enforcible, this connotes official action to prevent the writing or, if too late to prevent the writing, to prevent the publication or other circulation of what the censors deem objectionable. Today the term has been extended to wholly unofficial action as well. It embraces group activity aimed at eliminating particular works or kinds of works, or limiting their

availability, after their publication. Official censorship, based
on law or administrative regulation, usually observes the
forms of legal procedures, though its permissible content has
sometimes been defined so vaguely that the attendant procedures have given little real protection. Unofficial censorship derives its force not from legal mechanisms, but, at its
best, from persuasion and, at its worst, from implacable
economic or political pressure abetted by misuse of police
authority.

Both kinds of censorship have long been applied to books.
They generate problems that can be considered only in rela
tion to the supposed needs that arouse demands for prohib
tory controls and in the light of the dangers that the contro:s
create.

Among the wise and good men of the world there have
almost always been some who have felt that censorship ad-
vances rather than limits man's freedom. Plato, Augustine,
and Spinoza among many others asserted that no man is free
who acts erroneously because influenced by passion or mistaken ideas. When what is true and good is known, anything
that would subvert it should be controlled—not to narrow
man's freedom, but to save him from the unfreedom of
immorality or harmful doctrine that might damage him or
the community.[2] In this view censorship rests in one or
another degree upon the belief that those who are qualified
to identify evil and mistake should be empowered to prevent
their dissemination.

There is another appraisal, however, that leads to a different conclusion. Aristotle—and, in more recent times and
in our own country, Dewey and Holmes among others—
maintained that a man is free only so long as he may make
his own choices. If choice is foreclosed by another's judgment about what is virtuous or wise, freedom is lost. More
importantly, in this philosophic approach, the chances of discovering what really is virtuous or wise diminish when ex-

perimentalism and disagreement are impossible. Holmes' insistence that " the best test of truth is the power of the thought to get itself accepted in the competition of the market " is a reflection of Aristotle's democratic faith in the value of the individual's own search for virtue and his free action in association with others to secure the common good.

Censorship, in one view, aims at preserving freedom through reinforcing what its proponents regard as the true values and beliefs. Opposition to censorship, in the other view, does not derive from hostility to the virtues the pro-censors prize, but reflects, rather, a conviction that in the end the values of a free society will be attained through freedom rather than repression. The advocates of censorship, in other words, regard it as a means by which to prevent debasement of the individual virtues, the cultural standards, and the common security of democracy. Its opponents regard it, by contrast, as a danger to the freedom which fosters those virtues and standards, and without which democracy cannot survive. These two quite different conceptions must be kept in mind, because their adherents sometimes too readily believe that the other side is unconcerned with values or is uninterested in freedom. In fact, both seek the same general ends.[3] The question remains whether censorship will advance or retard their attainment.

The Revival of Book Censorship

The " omnicompetent and irrepressible " Lord Brougham strongly believed in popular education at sixpenny prices. In pursuit of that belief he organized a Society for the Diffusion of Useful Knowledge that brought forth works on, among other things, " Chemistry, Heat (with the theory of the thermometer and the steam engine), Hydraulics, Hydrostatics, Optics and Pneumatics and a Farmer's Series with something for every agricultural worker to read in the winter evenings."[4] His enthusiasm was strong enough to carry across the Atlantic. In 1829 The Boston Society for the Diffusion of Knowledge began a low-priced venture similar to Brougham's, and two years later The American Library of Useful Knowledge began operations with the declared purpose of issuing " in a cheap form a series of works, partly original and partly selected, in all the most important branches of learning."

If the publishers of paperbound books had confined themselves to this laudable and unexciting purpose, their work would no doubt have passed unnoticed. In time, however, their operations became more ambitious. Approximately 1,500 out of a total of somewhat more than 4,500 titles published in this country in 1885 were paperbound. Many, perhaps most, of these were of foreign, and notably British, origin. Whether their charm lay in their intrinsic worth or in certain deficiencies in the copyright laws of that time is unclear. At any rate, the paperbound business did not survive strengthening of international copyright protection. Not until 1939 and the early 1940's did the paperbound books once more begin to make their presence sharply felt. During that period new high-speed printing and binding methods came to the fore, enabling the cheap production of softcover books at a time when the costs of hard-cover book production were markedly rising. By 1953 close to a thousand titles were being issued in paperbound editions annually, a tenth of all the titles published in America.[5]

Mass production connotes mass distribution. In the case of the paperbound books this occurred through more than 100,-000 outlets, where in most instances the books competed for sales with magazines whose flamboyant covers sought to catch customers' eyes. Soon the paperbound books were competing not only for customers but also for flamboyancy, both external and internal. In 1955 more than 200,000,000 copies were sold.[6]

It would be manifestly unfair to the publishers of paperbound books to suggest that their products are typically unworthy. As a matter of fact, many (and their number is increasing) reflect the finest in western literary tradition. Even the " trash " is probably several cuts above the level of the pulp magazines, which have seemingly been deserted by millions of readers since the advent of cheap books. Much is said about the vulgarization of literary taste in modern times. But before becoming too despairing, let us recall that not long ago only one or two per cent of the population were among the elite who read any books at all.[7] The ready availability of paperbound books has not debauched tastes that would otherwise have been refined by the steady reading of " good books." On the contrary, the paperbounds seem to have attracted many previous total abstainers who, having discovered that reading can be fun, may have gone ever upwards and onwards with the arts.

At any rate, whatever the merits of the matter, the appearance of paperbound volumes in the mass market drew the eyes of censors as well as customers. The zeal that had once fired the Watch and Ward Society, the Society for the Suppression of Vice, and other self-anointed guardians of the public soul had all but evaporated by 1940. A succession of judicial decisions had emancipated books from the rigorous test of obscenity laid down in 1868 by Lord Chief Justice Cockburn, who believed that words, phrases, or passages could be lifted out of context and then considered as abstractions to determine whether their tendency is to " deprave and corrupt those whose minds are open to such immoral influences "[8]—a test, as one indignant litterateur exclaimed, that allows four letters to count for more than four hundred pages. The unwillingness of judges to condemn a literary work as a whole because some of its parts might offend the most sensitive reader was matched by an apparently mounting belief that anyone who could afford to spend money on books was probably past salvation, anyway. As a result, literary expression was increasingly free—and perhaps increasingly earthy.

Toleration reached the snapping point, however, when books fell within the reach of youthful and impecunious buyers. Then, in the words of Reverend James Pickett Wesberry, Chairman of the Georgia Literature Committee, " a few public-spirited citizens at last became alarmed " at the " display of salacious material freely accessible to the young and impressionable *at prices easily accommodated by young allowances*, and began to act." [9] In this context, action meant censorial efforts.

The Identification of Obscenity

Those who urge increased repression of allegedly obscene books are of course convinced that " obscenity " can be identified. In reality, however, the word does not refer to a thing so much as to a mood. It is a variable. Its dimensions are fixed in part by the eye of the individual beholder * and in part by a generalized opinion that shifts with time † and place.‡

* The National Organization for Decent Literature, the leading national lister of allegedly obscene books, has promulgated a list of some hundreds of titles containing, in addition to many volumes of no observable merit, books of serious purpose by such well-known writers as Hemingway, Faulkner, and Dos Passos. The NODL also denounces such widely read and sometimes admired books as Thomas Heggen's *Mr. Roberts*, James Jones' *From Here to Eternity*, Evan Hunter's *The Blackboard Jungle*, and Leon Uris' *Battle Cry*.

† Anne L. Haight, *Banned Books* (2nd ed.; Bowker, 1955), informs us, for example, that Jonathan Swift's *Gulliver's Travels* was " denounced on all sides as wicked and obscene " when it was published in 1726 (p. 36); in 1841 Shelley's publisher was convicted for publishing a collection of his works including such pieces as " *Queen Mab* " and " *Prometheus Unbound* " (p. 52); Walt Whitman's *Leaves of Grass* was denounced upon its publication and continued to encounter legal difficulties for years afterward (pp. 61–62); Tolstoi's *The Kreutzer Sonata* was banned by the Post Office Department in 1890, and Theodore Roosevelt denounced the author as a " sexual and moral pervert " (p. 65); Thomas Hardy's *Tess of the D'Urbervilles* and *Jude the Obscure* had rough sledding in England (p. 67).

‡ Huntington Cairns, writing in 1938 in Freedom of Expression in

Partly, too, the concept of obscenity is itself a product of censorship and concealment. Our grandfathers, we moderns hear incredulously, strained hotly for a peek of a prettily turned ankle; their voyeurism was stimulated by clothing styles reflecting a moral conviction that the existence of female legs should be kept a secret. The Japanese, conditioned by their training to regard kissing as an entirely private exercise, are said to find American movies filled with obscenity because they unabashedly portray heterosexual osculation; and as a consequence films that do not bring a blush to the most demure Americans must be drastically edited before they are deemed appropriate for general exhibition in Japan. A hundred years ago Nathaniel Hawthorne's *Scarlet Letter* was thought unfit for modest maidens, a fact that probably led to its being read so eagerly and widely as

Literature, 200 Annals of the American Academy of Political and Social Science, at 82–83, lists a number of books that had been cleared of obscenity charges in New York largely through " the unceasing efforts of two or three lawyers who, with a deep attachment to the principles of liberty, have contested every invasion of what they have regarded as the province of literature and art." Then he adds: " That the vigilance of less than a handful of the New York bar is directly responsible for the comparative freedom enjoyed by the New York book trade is apparent if we contrast the New York situation with that of Boston, where the bar is indifferent to censorship matters. In the latter city, *Antic Hay, All Quiet on the Western Front, Strange Interlude, A Farewell to Arms, The Sun Also Rises, Elmer Gantry, The World of William Clissold, Manhattan Transfer,* and scores of similar works are prohibited."

Lillian Smith's *Strange Fruit* was adjudged obscene in Massachusetts in 1945, though it did not make a similar impression in other jurisdictions. Ernest Hemingway's *To Have and Have Not* was removed from public sale and public library circulation in Detroit in 1938, but continued to sell at a brisk pace elsewhere. Erskine Caldwell's *God's Little Acre* was successfully defended in New York in 1933 against charges initiated by the Society for the Prevention of Vice; but thirteen years later it was found to be obscene in Denver, and in 1950 was accorded that same distinction in Massachusetts. As recently as 1905 the Brooklyn Public Library excluded from the Children's Room those notorious novels, *The Adventures of Tom Sawyer* and *The Adventures of Huckleberry Finn* (the latter of which had been banned from the public library of Concord, Massachusetts, as " trash and suitable only for the slums "). In 1954 the Illinois State Library system directed that Hans Christian Andersen's *Wonder Stories* should be stamped " For adult readers only."

to assure its becoming an American classic, now very grudg-
ingly studied in high school courses from coast to coast. Nobody today cringes at mention of venereal disease, but not
long ago it was one of the " dirty little secrets " that D. H.
Lawrence insisted became dirty (and slyly cherished) only
because of futile attempts to suppress mention of them [10]—
just as, in linguistics, words derive their deliciously vile con-
notations from restraints rather than from use. The late
Harry Reichenbach, press agent extraordinary, put Lawrence's
theory to practical commercial uses. He managed, by calling
attention to a row of strategically placed asterisks, to persuade the Post Office Department to deny the mails to Elinor
Glyn's *Three Weeks*. When the ban was lifted, as of course
it eventually was, the demand for the shoddy novel moved it
triumphantly to the best seller lists. According to one account, he made a " masterpiece " of an inferior painting
called " September Morn," an innocuous representation of
a nude woman standing up to her knees in sea water. Her
arms were carefully intertwined to provide a reasonably
chaste covering of her front, but only goose pimples covered
her exposed flanks. Reichenbach bribed some boys to stand
in front of a Brooklyn art dealer's window display, pointing
and grimacing at this not very exciting spectacle. An anonymous telephone call brought the " vice crusader " Anthony
Comstock storming to the scene, and, after him, the police.
All this led to vast popularity for a picture that might otherwise have hung inconspicuously in the home of some Brooklyn burgher. Seven million copies were ultimately distributed, bringing the picture within the vision of almost every
American male who patronized a barber shop; the original
was sold for some $10,000.[11]

But let us put aside for the moment the possibility that
repression creates rather than stifles the evil of obscenity.
The difficulty of definition remains. The Reverend Dr. James
Wesberry says that " determining what is or is not obscene

would not be difficult for me to do personally "—but he then
quickly acknowledges with some puzzlement that what is
obnoxious to him " would probably not get a guilty verdict
in the courts." [12] His perplexity is not unique. An international conference at Geneva on Suppression of the Circulation and Traffic in Obscene Publications accomplished
much less than had been hoped, because the delegates could
not agree upon what obscenity is.[13] One prominent censor
reportedly said a year or two ago: " I don't discriminate
between nude women, whether or not they are art. It's all
lustful to me." The remark shows, as Eric Larrabee has
observed, that one man's sex may be another's psycho-
neurosis; it casts much more light on the censor than it does
on obscenity.[14]

It is easy to make fun of the untutored; but even the
highly cultivated and literate person runs into real trouble
when he seeks to define the undefinable. A very able and
highly respected priest, for example, falls back upon " custom " and " common estimation " rather than upon precise
definition to help in applying the principle that " if this
object rouses to genital commotion, it is obscene " ; but,
recognizing that " it is not a matter of absolute certainty
that this particular object will so arouse even the normal
man," he urges acceptance of the idea that " even if it is
not certain that such and such an object will arouse to sexual
passion, nevertheless, if the probability swings in that direction, then the object is, for practical purposes, obscene." [15]
No doubt these words were not intended to be read literally,
for a net cast so widely would bring in an unsuspected catch.
Many persons profess, for example, to see a phallic symbol
in the radiator ornamentation of motor cars; shall the ornamentation, which may thus arouse a " genital commotion "
in one sensitive to symbols, be banned? In a carefully conducted survey 85 per cent of a group of boys between the
ages of 12 and 16 (the tender years of adolescence about

which censorial groups are particularly concerned) reported
" genital commotions " resulting from such varied and seemingly non-erotic stimuli as carnival rides, playing a musical
solo, fast car-driving, and seeing a column of marching
soldiers. Perhaps we could tolerate doing away with such
" obscenities " ; but what would we do about the similarly
" obscene " stimuli of taking school tests, receiving grade
cards, and listening to the national anthem? [16] Questioning
of a large number of American college women disclosed that
dancing, music, and, to some extent, reading had been among
the sources of their sexual stimulation; but far and away
the largest number very simply and directly stated that the
chief stimulus was MAN—an obscene object susceptible of
only a limited censorship.[17] In truth, if the suggested test
of obscenity were to be taken very seriously, it would lead to
a fruitless effort to fetter life itself—and would certainly
necessitate the censoring of brassiere advertisements, rock
and roll music, and " sacrosanct institutions like the pin-up
picture or the drive-in theater, which have done more to
keep sex going in America than Steinbeck has." [18] Unless
the human race is to vanish entirely, we can scarcely afford
to regard the arousing of normal sexual desires as a social
danger to be curbed at all costs.[19]

Federal Judge Ernest Tolin, faced with the perplexing
question of what constitutes obscenity, decided to consult
the settled authority of judicial utterances. His researches
were more baffling than enlightening, for in 1954 he discovered fourteen different judicial definitions of the term.[20]
" No one seems to know what obscenity is. Many writers
have discussed the obscene, but few can agree upon even
its essential nature," complained Professors Lockhart and
McClure after completing one of the most exhaustive studies
yet made in this field.[21]

Often coupled with obscenity as an object of censorial
concern is the fictional portrayal of violence and " horror."

These are somewhat more readily identified than obscenity, though, even as has been the case with obscenity, styles change from generation to generation. What was deemed outrageous yesterday may be taken for granted today. Thus, for example, an Illinois court only thirty years ago upheld a censorial refusal to permit the showing of " The Deadwood Coach," because " where gun-play, or the shooting of human beings . . . is for personal spite or revenge, and involves taking the law into one's own hands, and thus becomes a murder, the picture may be said to be immoral; it inculcates murder " [22]—a belief that has seemingly had small effect on Hollywood producers or on movie-goers. The " czar " of the comic books industry now seeks to interdict " scenes of horror, excessive bloodshed, depravity, lust, sadism, or masochism," as well as scenes dealing with " ' walking dead,' torture, vampires, ghouls and cannibalism." [23] He has at least a fighting chance of identifying them, though what constitutes " *excessive* bloodshed " may be difficult to ascertain in a nation deeply addicted to detective stories, Western movies, highway fatalities, and the development of awesome devices for producing mass death.

In any event, the main theory of censorship in this respect is the same as in instances of alleged obscenity: suppression of the written word is necessary to forestall thoughts that the unsuppressed word might stimulate—and the theory back of this is that the stimulated thoughts are steps to socially undesirable actions.[24]

The Impact of Reading on Conduct

The view that reading is readily translated into behavior is shared by many reputable persons. Mr. J. Edgar Hoover, as an example, has been quoted as contending that " the increase in the number of sex crimes is due precisely to sex literature madly presented in certain magazines. Filthy literature is the great moral wrecker. It is creating criminals

faster than jails can be built." [25] And Dr. Fredric Wertham,
a psychiatrist of high standing, has waged a virtual crusade
against comic books because his clinical observation has
convinced him that the comics have sexually stimulated and
emotionally brutalized many children.[26]

With all respect to those who accept these assertions as
self-evident truths, I doubt that the available evidence supports them. I think that they overstate the significance of
words and pictures and understate the other elements of life
that shape human behavior.

Admittedly, the premises underlying censorship have not
as yet been fully tested by empirical research. Hence one
cannot demonstrate unequivocally that books do not promote
juvenile delinquency, sexual perversion, sadism, and the
other evils the censors fear will flow from reading.* Such
objective evidence as does exist, does not sustain the fear.

We start with the proposition that an interest in pornography is seemingly not the molder of a man's personality but
the reflection of it. Indeed, certain psychological experi-

---

* Some day, I hope, a trained social historian will try seriously to discover
whether children and adults are in fact worse today than they used to be.
When I was a boy, the old folk were sure that young people were being
driven to perdition by the dime novel (*Nick Carter, Detective*; tales of the
wild, wooly west full of cowboys and Indians), by the nickelodeon, and by
burlesque shows. The British equivalent of the dime novel in those days
was the penny dreadful. Compare the remarks of Younger, J., in *Glyn* v.
Weston Feature Film Co., (1916) 1 Ch. 261, at 269–70: " We are constantly hearing of the injurious influence exercised upon the adventurous
spirit of our youth by the penny dreadful which presents the burglar in the
guise of a hero and so excites the imagination of the juvenile reader that,
adopting in the spirit of true adventure the life of his idol, he presently
finds himself in the dock branded by an unfeeling world as a common thief."
Though violence today is very violent indeed, it seems to me as a matter of
fact to be somewhat less widespread now than it was earlier in the century—
fewer black eyes and bloody noses, fewer stabbings, fewer rapes. Lizzie
Borden and her bloody hatchet antedated comic books; little children were
taught the fearful dangers of accepting candy from strangers long before
paperbound books were allegedly putting perverted ideas in people's heads;
Jack the Ripper was not stimulated by penny dreadfuls; Peeping Toms existed
before " girlie magazines."

ments suggest that one who finds pornographic elements in allegedly obscene books is very likely to discover them also in apparently innocuous books, through a process of self-selection and emphasis that the reader himself brings to the words. This same process of self-selection—this tendency to read and see what accords with pre-existing interests—probably controls the effects of reading as well as the determination of what will be read. The fact that "sex maniacs" may read pornography does not mean that they became what they are because of their reading, but that their reading became what it is because of them. Their personality, according to modern scientific findings that confirm a proposition stated long ago by the Jesuit fathers, was probably basically formed before they ever learned to read.

So far as disclosed by the most exhaustive study of juvenile delinquency yet made in America, reading seems to be of small moment in shaping antisocial tendencies. Sheldon and Eleanor Glueck searchingly inquired into numerous cases to identify the influences that produced delinquency. Reading (if it was influential at all) was of such slight significance that it was altogether omitted from their statement of "factors with probable causal significance." [27] Judge George W. Smyth, just retired after being for many years acclaimed as one of the nation's outstanding children's court judges, has described to the New York State Temporary Commission on Youth and Delinquency the causes that had seemingly contributed to delinquency in cases recently adjudged by him. Reading *difficulty* was mentioned as among the 878 causative factors that had had effect upon the troubled children before him; *reading*, no matter of what, found not a single place in his list.[28]

Judge Smyth's observation is confirmed by other workers in the field of undesirable juvenile behavior. The Bureau of Mental Health Services of the Domestic Relations Court of New York has found a marked reading retardation among the children whose conduct has brought them before the court. Far from discovering that delinquency grew out of reading, the clinicians have discovered that among New Yorkers it is more likely to grow out of inability to read.[29] This is no transitory condition, but, as a succession of studies has shown, has been true for decades. The importance of the "common sense" or "hunch" or "experience" that seeks to ascribe delinquent behavior to undesirable reading, should not be minimized. But heavily laying the finger of blame upon reading matter, even upon the despised comic books with all their crudities and offensiveness, is likely to divert attention from much more serious problems.[30] Censorship is a nostrum rather than a remedy. Reliance on it will simply delay therapeutic and preventive steps that must be taken if youthful antisocial conduct is to be lessened.

Dr. Marie Jahoda and the staff of New York University's Research Center for Human Relations recently surveyed the available studies bearing on the impact of reading on human conduct, good and bad. Every indication points to a primary conclusion: "Direct experiences have a much greater directive power on human behavior than do vicarious experiences."[31]

To say that one's personality is formed before he acquires reading habits is, of course, not the equivalent of saying that reading cannot conceivably affect behavior. Reading, like other environmental factors, may modify an individual's personality predispositions, though unlikely in itself to make a "bad" man out of a previously "good" one. The question remains, however, whether fiction will frequently provide what Dr. Wertham calls the "added impetus" to antisocial impulses, serving as a trigger mechanism to set off an explosion that otherwise might not have occurred.[32]

Nobody is in a position, on the basis of what is now known about human beings, to deny this possibility. But there is at least one other possibility to be offset against it and, more importantly, a probability that diminishes its significance as an argument in support of censorship. The offsetting *possibility* derives from the Aristotelian concept of emotional catharsis,[33] shared now by many psychiatrists who believe that aggressions and frustrations that might otherwise flare into overt conduct are not fanned to flame but, instead, are more often dissipated, or at least made temporarily quiescent, by reading.[34] The *probability* is that fictional reading (even comic book reading) about sexual conduct or about violence and brutality has small behavioral consequence as compared with the more realistic impressions derived from reading newspapers *—or even from seeing motion pictures or television that purport to mirror reality.[35] Years ago, in commenting upon some of the classics that might be deemed obscene, Lord Macaulay said: " We find it difficult to believe that in a world so full of temptations as this, any gentleman whose life would have been virtuous if he had not read Aristophanes and Juvenal will be made vicious by reading them." [36] Change Macaulay's illustrations and his point holds good today.

Unless all children are to be wrapped in cotton batting and utterly removed from the world, we cannot hope to im-

---

* On January 8, 1956, during what police and sociologists agree is the " slack season " for crime and sex, the newspaper with the largest circulation in the United States contained the following headlines, among others: " War Hero Cop Is Held in $450 Shop Holdup "; " Juliette in Negligee, Rival Romeo Elope On Bridal Eve "; " Flying To Face Kidnap Charge "; " Nudity on Deck, Sabrina's Mad "; " Wounded Cop In Life Fight—Madman Held "; " Find 3G Heroin In A Cadillac "; " Nurse Held In Drug Theft "; " Slew Man, 60, Over A Barmaid, He Says "; " Nab Four Youths in Car Arsenal." The same newspaper on January 12, 1956, contained stories under the following headings: " Lover Held, Quiz 2 More In Girl's ' Murder ' "; " Two Hold Family For 12 Desperate Hours "; " Beauty Queen, 18, Kidnaped, Raped "; " Held In Beating of Bar Pickup "; " 4 Teen-Agers Nabbed In Tinsel Car Thefts "; " Mate Pleads For Wife's Return "; " Had Two Vice Flats, Says Cop's Accuser." The dates have no special significance; they were selected only because this note happened to be written on January 8 and was looked at a second time on January 12. One may fairly assume that any other two days would have produced approximately the same sort of headlines.

munize every one of them against contact with something that might conceivably energize his savage side. G. K. Chesterton once noted a complaint that a child had been induced to kill his father with a carving knife, through having seen a similar episode in a motion picture. " This may possibly have occurred," Chesterton conceded, " though if it did, anybody of common sense would prefer to have details about that particular child, rather than about that particular picture. But what is supposed to be the practical moral of it, in any case? It is that the young should never see a story with a knife in it? . . . It would be more practical that a child should never see a real carving-knife, and still more practical that he should never see a real father. . . . It is perfectly true that a child will have the horrors after seeing some particular detail. It is quite equally true that nobody can possibly predict what that particular detail will be . . . If the kinema exhibited nothing but views of country vicarages or vegetarian restaurants, the ugly fancy is as likely to be stimulated by these things as by anything else." [37] Experts in abnormal psychology agree with Chesterton.

It is well, perhaps, to stress that in this branch of the discussion we are indeed talking about abnormal rather than normal psychology. Even if it be true that reading matter may activate the impulses of some twisted individual, can this possibility justify repressive policies that affect all alike? Should a nation's reading be tailored to fit the extremely uncertain contours of an hypothetical person with a supposedly lower threshold of resistance than is usual? A program of censorship aimed at that end must prove to be all but limitless. There is virtually no repression of expression that could not be justified as a necessary protection of isolated individuals with abnormal predispositions. Where the harmfulness of speech or writing is provable and certain, limitations in the form of penalties have always been upheld—as, for example, in the false labeling of foods, the uttering of defamations, and the inciting of riots.[38] There is a world of difference, however, between speech (or writing) as a form of demonstrably dangerous action and, on the other hand, speech (or writing) that may conceivably though improbably have some unascertainable impact upon some unidentifiable and anomalous person. The stable and well adjusted members of the community must make many sacrifices because there are unstable and disturbed members as well. But freedom of communicaton and freedom to read ought not to be among the sacrifices when the gain is so dubious and the deprivation so plain.

Let this not be read as a plea for the preservation of " bad " books. It is a plea, rather, for the proposition that the accessibility of books should not be determined censorially but selectively; * that the possibility of reader's choice should not be foreclosed, because the wisdom to make

---

* The difference between a librarian's book *selection* and book *censorship* has been acutely stated in the following terms by Dean Lester E. Asheim of the Graduate Library School, University of Chicago: ". . . the selector's approach is positive, while that of the censor is negative. . . . For the selector the important thing is to find reasons to keep the book. Given such a guiding principle, the selector looks for values, for strengths, for virtues, which will overshadow minor objections. For the censor, on the other hand, the important thing is to find reasons to reject the book. His guiding principle leads him to seek out the objectionable features, the weaknesses, the possibilities for misinterpretation. . . . The selector says, if there is anything good in this book let us try to keep it; the censor says, if there is anything bad in this book, let us reject it. And since there is seldom a flawless work in any form, the censor's approach can destroy much that is worth saving." Dean Asheim adds a fact that has not often been adequately stressed. Censors sometimes use " external criteria." When that happens, " The book is not judged on its merit as a book at all. It is used as a stick to beat its author for personal deviations, whether they are reflected in the book at all." The selector, by contrast, weighs the book rather than the author or the publisher, and " does not succumb to irrelevancy, introduced either by the prejudices of his own background or the pressures of his library's patrons." Lester E. Asheim, Not Censorship, But Selection, Proceedings of the Second Conference on Intellectual Freedom, 1953 (American Library Association, 1954) 90, at 95–97.

Attacks upon a book because of its authorship, without reference to its content, is like refusing to exhibit a picture by Picasso because one dislikes his politics.

good choices may grow even out of bad choices; and that, above all, the public not be beguiled into hoping to curb delinquent behavior by curbing reading. Our better chance, so far as the problem of delinquency is concerned, is to discover how to persuade potential delinquents to commence reading good books, rather than to waste our energies in seeking to keep reading matter out of their hands.

The Suppression of Bad Ideas

In another aspect of the matter, concern about obscenity merges into a more generalized concern about supposedly dangerous thinking. A Congressional committee, for example, has denounced a book that apparently made a serious argument in favor of polygamy, and entered another into its records because the " author is obviously trying to cash in on the Scottsboro pro-Negro agitation which was Communist-inspired." [39] Elsewhere obscenity has been detected not so much in the wording as in the content of challenges to commonly accepted convictions about the desirability of chastity or monogamy.[40] In such instances books are censorially threatened because they are the repositories of ideas deemed injurious to society, or, to put it in the more common speech of the day, because they are subversive. Opinions thought to be potentially subversive of governing authority and those thought to be subversive of the established social and moral order evoke an essentially similar reaction: They are too dangerous to be allowed to circulate! Thus the censorship of " obscenity " and the censorship of " sedition " or " propaganda " are seen to have a common core.

The Communist view, as expounded by Lenin, admits no argument about the desirability of suppressing unsettling thoughts. " Why should freedom of speech and freedom of the press be allowed? " Lenin asked. " Why should a government which is doing what it believes to be right allow itself to be criticized? It would not allow opposition by lethal weapons. Ideas are much more fatal things than guns. Why should any man be allowed to buy a printing press and disseminate pernicious opinions calculated to embarrass the government? " [41]

I fear that there are non-Communist Americans who may share this particular bit of the hated ideology.

In my estimation the proscription of writings because of their feared effects on accepted beliefs is not only unconstitutional but, on the most pragmatic basis, unwise. Since 1791 the First Amendment has stood as a safeguard of the freedom of expression. The doctrine of political freedom it is intended to implement is not a bit of eighteenth-century muddleheadedness. It reflects, rather, the lesson learned from history that truth cannot be established by proclamation and that belief cannot be created by extirpating non-believers.[42] It embodies the faith that whatever may be the short-run gains or losses along the way, in the end the national safety is endangered far less by political freedom than it is by political suppression.

Day-to-day decisions, however, are not shaped by constitutional absolutes. Nor do sons live always in the shadow of their fathers' faith. Excessive worry about disagreement, novelty, and heresy cannot be dispelled by the Spirit of 1776, but (if at all) by a cool appraisal of the contemporary scene.

What does that appraisal show? It shows, among other things, a perfectly amazing exaggeration of the extent to which dissent is abroad in the land. In the United States the main channels of communication are all but exclusively occupied by upholders of the established order. There are 1,860 daily newspapers—of which only one, with a circulation of 6,000, is Communist; [43] *Life* magazine, which on the whole does not challenge the nation's fixed attitudes, sells more than 30,000,000 more copies than all the paperbound books put together and probably has an even larger influence than these numbers suggest upon the social attitudes of the day; [44]

Time magazine, which interlards the news with its own not
very heretical views, has a circulation of 1,860,976 compared
with the petty 33,006 of the *Nation* and the even paltrier
28,589 of the *New Republic*, two journals of critical though
far from revolutionary opinion so unsettling to the good
people of Bartlesville, Oklahoma, that they have discharged
a public librarian after thirty years of service because she
insisted the magazines had a legitimate place in the library.[45]

Ah, yes, say some of our perturbed fellow citizens. That
is all very well. But it fails to take into account the
propaganda.

Differentiating propaganda from discussion or education
is not simple. As David Riesman has noted, the distinction
between the two may be as essentially subjective as the distinction between liberty and license; there is in general a
tendency to regard as propaganda the dissemination of information or the statement of opinions we dislike.[46] In any
case, we Americans tend to overestimate the effectiveness
of what we do identify as propaganda. A British professor
teasingly explained to his own countrymen that " they
[Americans] believe in machinery more passionately than
we [British] do; and modern propaganda is a scientific
machine; so it seems to them obvious that a mere reasoning
man can't stand up to it. All this produces a curiously girlish
attitude toward anyone who might be doing propaganda.
' Don't let that man come near me. Don't let him tempt me,
because if he does I'm sure to fall.' " [47]

Some of the observations made in earlier pages about the
process of self-selection in reading matter has obvious pertinence here. Extensive researches have been made into
the effectiveness of propaganda, political and other, dissemi-
nated by the mass media. Students of communication conclude that, as a rule, it is extremely difficult to impress a
communication upon persons who do not already share the
views it reflects.[48] Republicans rarely listen to Democratic

campaign speeches, and Democrats return the compliment; anti-Semites do not tune in on radio preachments about brotherly love; and Communist spokesmen do not attract large audiences of persons with emptily absorbent minds, ready to accept whatever they may hear. Propaganda seems to have its largest success as a reinforcer rather than as a disturber of existing convictions.

Moreover, a man's attitudes and courses of action are infinitely more significantly influenced by his face-to-face contacts than by what he reads or hears; this is the lesson consistently drawn from extensive analysis of voting behavior and racial prejudices.[49] Ideas do not stick like burrs. Even when they are insistently pounded home by radio or television they still can be and, it seems, for the most part are " avoided by withdrawal, deflected by resistance and transformed by assimilation." [50] The mass media have proved to be most effective when they operate in a situation of " psychological monopoly " (a situation in which books never find themselves) ; or when they seek to channel an already existent attitude (that is, for example, people who already brush their teeth might be persuaded to buy a particular toothpaste, but the idea of toothbrushing would not probably be adopted by those who had previously survived without it) ; or when they are conjoined with direct personal contacts. Surely there is even less reason to become exercised about the corrupting power of books, pallid things that are rarely taken up in the first place and that can always be put down and forgotten, than about the mass media.

In light of what we do know about these matters, suppressive efforts seem a misdirected expenditure of energy. I cannot understand, for example, why the Post Office Department is so vigilant to prevent Americans from receiving Russian publications to which, for one reason or another, they wish to refer. As former Ambassador George Kennan tartly remarked, there is probably " nothing sillier than the

fear that American library users are going to be inclined
toward communism by stumbling on communist publications
in libraries. . . . I would know of no better cure for anyone
who had illusions about communism or the Soviet Union
than to be forced to read *Pravda* or *Izvestiya* over a certain
length of time." [51] Even if Communist writers were livelier
and more persuasive than they have ever yet managed to be,
enforced ignorance would not be the best way to offset their
influence. The Advisory Committee on Prisoners of War,
named by Secretary of Defense Charles E. Wilson on May
18, 1955, to analyze the problem of "brainwashing," concluded that the uninformed soldier, the man who had never
had occasion or opportunity to know anything of communist
conceptions and achievements, was the most likely prospect
for enemy proselytizing. "The way to combat such a subject as Communism," the committee reported, "is not to hide
it or hide from it. The way to combat it is to explode it.
Americans have the means at hand—the Bill of Rights. Or
call it Democracy or Republican Government, or the American Way. 'Armed with a knowledge of American principles—and a knowledge of the enemy's—the American fighting man possesses a sword and shield which cannot be
wrested from him in combat or captivity.'" [52]

That is a sound judgment. Nations do not lose their
vitality because questions are asked, but because they remain
unanswered. "I do not recollect that any civilization ever
perished from an attack of doubt," commented José Ortega y
Gasset. "Civilizations usually die through the ossification
of their traditional faith, through an arteriosclerosis of their
beliefs." [53] Learned Hand reminds us that James Harvey
Robinson, the American historian of ideas, advanced somewhat the same thought, but in the affirmative. Robinson used
to say that we had risen from the ape because, like him, we
had insisted on "monkeying around," always meddling with
things as we found them. Judge Hand endorses the thesis,

adding his own strong conviction that " any organization of society which depresses free and spontaneous meddling is on the decline, however showy its immediate spoils." [54]

American democracy is not an inflexible thing of fixed components. It is, rather, a structure within which many persons of strongly opposed philosophies and aspirations can reach, for quite different reasons, commonly acceptable conclusions about the plans and actions required for organized living together. If ever the democratic system of the United States is overthrown, it will not be by words. It will be by acts of force and violence, made more forceful and more violent by the artificial stifling of the criticism, the controversy, and the compromise that invigorate our political institutions and make possible a peaceful coexistence of all the elements in our country. President Eisenhower well said in 1953: " As it is an ancient truth that freedom cannot be legislated into existence, so it is no less obvious that freedom cannot be censored into existence. And any who act as if freedom's defenses are to be found in suppression and suspicion and fear confess a doctrine that is alien to America." [55]

The Mechanics of Restraint

Some years ago Boston theater owners risked revocation of their licenses if a majority of a board composed of the mayor, the police commissioner, and a member of the city art commission objected to a play on grounds of " public morality or decency." To avoid the economic gamble, the theater owners subjected themselves to the judgment of a censor appointed by the mayor. The system was efficient and simple. The only trouble with it, as it turned out, was that the officials who operated the system seemed to be altogether too simple. " I do not get the impression," Professor Chafee remarked mildly, " that the holder of this office [of censor] is usually a man of extensive literary training with an established reputation as a dramatic critic. Familiarity with the

' Oedipus Rex ' of Sophocles or the ' Hippolytus ' of Euripides might lessen his fears that a total collapse of family life will be caused by the presentation of incest on the stage in O'Neill's ' Desire Under the Elms.' " [56] Nor were the mayor or the police commissioner or the art commissioner any better equipped. They were not chosen because they read widely and were accustomed to make literary evaluations. However admirable these officials might be in other respects and however honorably they might discharge their other duties, they remained (when it came to censoring plays) merely three untrained individuals in a position to transmute their tastes into edicts.

The Boston personnel problem is not unique in the annals of censorship. Probably very few official censors are warped and twisted beings of the Anthony Comstock type, neurotically preoccupied with the uncertain state of other people's morals.[57] Still, all things considered, the post of censor is not likely to attract individuals of outstanding cultural attainments.[58] The nature of their work, moreover, perforce bends their energies into finding what they are seeking.[59]

Nor do matters improve when the work of identifying objectionable writings is passed into the hands of volunteer aides. No assurance can be given that the volunteers will be especially well equipped for their labors. In a Minnesota city where more than three hundred books were censored in a move quickly emulated in other communities, the " most responsible " person has been described by an admirer as " a white-haired grandmother, who manages a small grocery store. She looks on the task of censorship as a ' matter of salvation of souls.' " [60] The National Organization for Decent Literature, which circulates lists compiled locally in some dioceses as well as a national list promulgated by the Archdiocese Council of Catholic Women of Chicago, depends upon volunteer readers to judge popular publications according to the organization's established criteria.[61]

The same is true of other citizens' groups that undertake to control the community's reading, usually with the help of local law enforcement officials who accept the unofficial lists as authoritative. In Detroit, where the Police Department's Censor Bureau seeks, as it says, to " skim off the filth " without reliance on volunteers, the police refer questionable items to the sole judgment of an assistant district attorney who determines whether they are " objectionable," only " partially objectionable," or fit for consumption. In Georgia a State Literature Commission whose original members were a Baptist clergyman and " two of the noblest and finest laymen God ever made " has been empowered to investigate " all sales of literature which they have reason to suspect is detrimental to the morals of the citizens of this State." The Commission is to hold hearings, to make findings, to " prohibit the distribution of any literature they find to be obscene," and to recommend prosecution if, notwithstanding their prohibitory order, sales continue. The members of the Commission need have no qualifications other than that they be Georgians " of the highest moral character." They must work rapidly, for they are limited to meeting for not more than thirty days in any one year; and they must be genuinely interested in their duties rather than in the rewards of office, for they receive a per diem fee of only ten dollars.[62]

The essentially amateur status of the censors lends special significance to the practical observation that their judgments are rarely reviewable. A survey of the chief mechanisms of censorship shows this to be so.

Police Action and " Private " Censorship. Most state laws and municipal ordinances aimed at suppression of allegedly objectionable literature contemplate conventional criminal proceedings in which the issue of guilt or innocence may be tested. In point of fact, not very many prosecutions occur—partly, perhaps, because prosecutors fear that they may only succeed in advertising rather than suppressing the books they dislike.

In any event, convictions have become somewhat too difficult when guilt must be established through fair trials. The courts have evinced too liberal an insistence that a book be evaluated as a whole, instead of by examining isolated passages. Of course there are still occasional convictions of sellers of " under-the-counter pornography " and, even less frequently, of books with some pretensions to seriousness. But there is no present likelihood that scientific works on psychoanalysis or sexual behavior will provide the foundations of successful prosecutions, or that the books of modern writers like James T. Farrell, William Faulkner, and John O'Hara will be adjudged violative of the law.

Writings of these sorts, however, continue to be included among the books deemed objectionable by censorial elements who may not know much about art, but who know what they don't like.

This would be tolerable if the matter stopped there—if, that is, the objectors did no more than express their opinions concerning the merits of available reading matter. There is no reason why one must depend for advice upon the *Saturday Review of Literature* or the *New York Times Book Review* if, instead, one would prefer to receive his literary guidance from a religious source, from a circle of housewives, or from a veterans' organization.

Trouble arises only when the advisers insist that their advice be accepted. Precisely that trouble does arise today with considerable frequency, in the form of pressures upon distributors and sellers of books.

Application of pressure is especially easy in the case of paperbound books. In few cities are they distributed by more than two wholesalers, whose trucks also deliver magazines and comic books to news dealers and other retailers. The police need not attack upon a broad front, but can entirely control the situation by squeezing this narrow bottleneck. Truck operators are usually heavily dependent on police tolerance of brief violations of parking regulations, during unloading operations; wholesalers' warehouses are subject to being especially closely examined by building, fire, and health inspectors. Moreover, the retailers may be municipal licensees.[63] Both wholesalers and retailers (who often combine ignorance of their rights with a disinclination to defend those of which they are aware) are therefore readily influenced by police " suggestions " that particular books be suppressed

In mid-1955 the Detroit police department, upon request, was proudly distributing its list of banned books to at least a hundred other cities, where presumably the catalog of 275 " objectionable " and 60 " partially objectionable " paperbound titles is put to some sort of semi-official use. Similarly, private groups press vigorously for dealers' observance of their censorial judgments. Often this is done by awarding seals of approval to stores that remove listed publications from sale, the award to some shopowners being coupled with threatened or actual boycotting of others. Sometimes reliance is placed upon the police to " persuade " the recalcitrants. Mayors, police commissioners, and trade association executives have frequently called for " voluntary co-operation " with the " decent citizens of the community." [64] This last phrase, being translated, means citizens who agitate for censorship. Those who do so are not always evenly motivated; they may include concerned parents, bigots of one brand or another, self-seeking officeholders who are looking for an " issue," and, often, newspapers that crusade against allegedly obscene books while simultaneously devoting their own columns to scandalism and crudities.[65]

Even when formal legal processes have been prescribed as a prelude to repressive action, " voluntary co-operation " without the legal preliminaries may bulk larger in significance. Thus, for example, during the first year of its life the

Georgia Literature Commission, presumably after complying with the statutory procedures, "suggested the withdrawal from sale of five pocket books, three so-called ' flapper ' pamphlets, and one picture pamphlet, and one art magazine " ; but during the same period the distributors were led by "voluntary co-operation " to eliminate some thirty-odd additional publications.[66] In Detroit, the police and the prosecutor read paperbound books that are voluntarily submitted for approval in advance of distribution—though one of the distributors "volunteered " only after the police notified retailers that they were handling books not yet cleared by the Censor Bureau, and might thus unwittingly expose themselves to the risk of prosecution under the obscenity laws. The result of all this co-operation is that Detroiters, young and old alike, are barred from obtaining cheap editions of many books of merit (as well as many whose authorship and titles cast doubt upon their value).

The test of what may be read in soft covers in Detroit is very simple. "If I feel that I wouldn't want my 13-year-old daughter reading it," the assistant prosecutor recently told a reporter, " I decide it's illegal." Then he added, " Mind you, I don't say that it is illegal in fact. I merely say that in my opinion it would be a violation of the law to distribute it. The distributors usually co-operate by withholding the book." [67] Since the censorial rulings are not publicly announced, Detroiters do not, as it were, know what they are missing. The distributors seem content with a system that releases them from harassment by private censorial groups, and the retailers are little concerned since they are unaware of any loss. Interviews in Detroit lead one to conclude that dissatisfaction is largely confined to a few libertarian professors (who were especially aroused when students could not procure a paperbound edition of a book assigned for reading in an American literature course; the volume was readily available in hard covers at four dollars per copy) and, at the other extreme, a few clericals who think that religious pressures could, if given free reign, accomplish even more than the police.

But a warning lurks in the shadow of the Detroit experience. One publisher has already begun to submit book manuscripts to the Detroit Censor Bureau for approval before printing, in order to make such changes as may be required to assure distribution in that city.[68] If the trend were to continue, the supposed needs of a thirteen-year-old girl in Detroit might determine the nation's book diet, for publishers are unlikely to prepare one edition for Detroit and another for the rest of the country.

The Government as Consumer and Distributor. To an extent only partially appreciated, the book trade is dependent for survival upon governmental purchases. Half of the hardcover books sold in this country are either bought directly by federal, state, or municipal agencies or adopted pursuant to their instructions. Public library purchases account for a very large proportion of what the children and adults of America will voluntarily read, and textbook expenditures reflect what the children will have to read regardless of their wishes. The armed forces, through the post exchanges, control the accessibility of reading matter for purchase by nearly two million military personnel. School libraries, overseas information libraries, hospital libraries, and many other government programs involve official book buying.

Obviously, there must be selectivity in administering matters like these. Public agencies are under no duty to procure everything that is printed, or to underwrite the economic success of book publishers. Discretion must be granted broadly. Being broad, it is susceptible of misuse. The large choices necessarily involved in the selection process may be exercised censorially, sometimes without reference to the intrinsic merits of the books involved; and, when this does occur, the censorial judgment is essentially unreviewable.

Instances of debatable decisions abound. The Third Air Force, which controls the post exchanges for all American armed services in Britain at one time forbade the sale in post exchanges of any books deemed objectionable by the Chicago Archdiocese Council of Catholic Women; and Dr. Kinsey's report on the alleged sexual behavior of human females was banned throughout the Army. The city manager of a large southwestern city recommended that the public library burn a large group of books (including an edition of *Moby Dick* that was suspect because it contained illustrations by the distinguished but " controversial " artist Rockwell Kent), after a " Minute Woman " had listed them as communist-connected. The Secretary of State of Illinois, responding to an indignant mother's protest that her teen-age daughter had been polluted by a book, directed a compilation of offensive volumes that should be removed from public libraries throughout the state; when the list had grown to 500 titles and had resulted in the disappearance of some six to eight thousand library volumes, suspicion arose that someone had been over-zealous or that there were imperfections in the litmus paper applied to books in Illinois, and in 1954 the volumes began to return to the shelves. In 1955 a general science textbook published by Houghton-Mifflin was dropped from the public schools of Morehouse Parish, Louisiana, because it contained passages such as: " living things which belong to recognizable kinds, which are alike in most physical traits and which breed freely with each other, are said to belong to one species." This closely parallels the definition of " species " in Webster's Collegiate Dictionary; but it was objectionable in Morehouse Parish, according to the book's critics, because it insinuates that races "breed freely with each other " and is " a dangerous socialistic trend of thought to instill into the younger generation." *

---

* Information about the Morehouse Parish episode comes from a column by Adras LaBorde, entitled " Talk of the Town," in the Alexandria (La.)

This episode illustrates in a small way one of the especially pressing problems in the publishing field. Much of the discussion in preceding pages has related to books that may be read or ignored, as each person may choose for himself. In that area, the words of the late Mr. Justice Jackson have especial pertinence: " It cannot be the duty, because it is not the right, of the State to protect the public against false doctrine. The very purpose of the First Amendment is to foreclose public authority from assuming a guardianship of the public mind through regulating the press, speech, and religion. In this field every person must be his own watchman for truth, because the forefathers did not trust any government to separate the true from the false for us." [69] Textbooks, however, are in a special category. The reader has no choice about them. They are prescribed as the authoritative sources of schoolchildren's enlightenment. Somebody has to decide which book is the best one, all things considered, for compulsory study by a child who has neither the experience nor the resources to be " his own watchman for truth."

Town Talk, November 9, 1955. Mr. LaBorde anticipated that certain " east coast " residents might accuse the local authorities of lacking the necessary capacity to appraise high-school textbooks—" To which we are happy to reply: ' Liberal intelligentsia go hang; we still have sense enough to decide what's good and what's bad for our kids. We don't need super-intelligent college professors with a leaning for pink to tell us how to go about it.' "
    Mr. LaBorde is much more moderate in his attitude toward northern educational influences than was an ante-bellum editor of Richmond, Virginia, quoted as follows in Howard K. Beale, *A History of Freedom of Teaching in American Schools* (Scribner, 1941), 148: " The South has for years been overrun with hordes of illiterate, unprincipled graduates of the Yankee free schools, (those hotbeds of self-conceit and ignorance,) who have, by dint of unblushing impudence, established themselves as schoolmasters in our midst. These creatures, with rare exceptions have not deserved the protection of our laws.—They bear, neither in person nor in mind, a very strong resemblance to human beings. So odious are some of these ' itinerant ignoramuses' to the people of the South . . . that the deliberate shooting of one of them, in the act of poisoning the minds of our slaves or our children, we think, if regarded as homicide at all should always be deemed *perfectly justifiable*. . . ."

This fact justifies a most searching analysis and appraisal of textbook contents, to assure that the educational process will be effective. It also explains why textbook publishers— who, as one of their spokesmen likes to remark, do not thrive on controversy—often encounter irresistible pressures to produce books that no one will challenge. In every community there are articulate persons who oppose school teaching that causes children to question the attitudes they particularly cherish. Since these attitudes are not always uniform throughout the country, textbook editors and publishers are sometimes hard driven to anticipate each and every objection that might be voiced.

Foresight in this respect is highly necessary because an outcry raised against a book in one place induces wariness of it elsewhere. A publisher may therefore almost welcome the opportunity to submit to external editing.[70] William E. Spaulding, former president of the American Textbook Publishers Institute, has addressed himself to the issue in blunt terms. "How many good books," he asks, "do school authorities refuse to consider for adoption just because those books have been subjected to attack? Many a superintendent of schools has quite naturally said to himself, if not to a bookman, 'I don't want a book that's been under fire. It may get me into trouble and I don't need to look for trouble these days.' He knows that attack and suspicion are enough and that no amount of vindication will positively ensure that the same book will not be attacked again. Thus, we seem to be moving closer and closer every day to a proscribing of textbooks on the basis of irresponsible and misguided criticism, to the defamation of textbook character merely by suspicion . . . As a result, teachers, authors, and publishers find themselves facing a mushroom growth of taboos. You can't say this or that any more, this or that author is out, avoid this topic, soft-pedal that, and so on." [71]

Half of the 48 states have state-wide systems of textbook

adoption, the others being "open territory." Even in those states that do require a centralized endorsement of texts, the trend is very strongly in the direction of compiling so-called multiple lists of three to five books in each subject, from which local school authorities are authorized to make their own selections. Only two states, Florida and North Carolina, adhere to the "basal book" plan, which involves prescribing a single text for state-wide use, thus entirely destroying the possibility of diversity and experimentation.

These legitimate mechanisms of book selection are readily convertible into illegitimate mechanisms of taboo-enforcement. The study of proposed texts is sometimes entrusted to professional advisers of highest standing or, at the least, to the teachers who must use the books. Often, however, the task is undertaken by persons of less apparent qualifications or by individuals who hold their posts for other than purely educational reasons.[72] Much depends on the outcome of their work, for publishers aspire to universal adoption or at least to eligibility for it. This means, in essence, that they must observe everybody's taboo. If a book could not be adopted in, say, Texas or Indiana or California, there is strong likelihood that it would not be published at all. In a realistic sense, therefore, unprofessional judgments only loosely related to pedagogical needs may sometimes determine what may be available for teaching purposes in other states—and in private as well as in public schools.

No easy solution is at hand. The aims of textbook commissioners should not be to achieve a standardized innocuity, but, rather, to encourage variety as a means of developing fresh insights into educational materials. On the whole, diversity is more likely to result from pluralism than from centralism of authority to choose suitable school books. But when the topics taught in school strike close to the community's emotions and nerves, toleration does not come easily. At those times little patience may be shown toward books that raise questions the community regards as having already been answered.[73]

Foreign Propaganda. The Foreign Agents Registration Act of 1938, as amended in 1942, requires " every person within the United States who is an agent of a foreign principal " to register with the Attorney General and to label as foreign propaganda any " communication or expression by any person which . . . influence[s] . . . any section of the public . . . with reference to the political or public . . . policies . . . of a foreign country or a foreign political party . . . [or the] foreign policies of the United States or promote[s] in the United States racial, religious, or social dissensions." [74]

As the legislative background of the statute reveals, its purpose was to protect the American people against being tricked by persons in this country who, while pretending to be disinterested, were in fact employed by foreigners " to spread doctrines alien to our democratic form of government, or propaganda for the purpose of influencing American public opinion on a political question." [75] Standing upon this narrow statutory base, and buttressed by an Opinion of the Attorney General in 1940 that certain Nazi materials were excludible from this country because of the interaction of the Foreign Agents Registration Act and the Espionage Act of 1917,[76] the Customs Bureau of the Treasury and the Post Office Department have undertaken to withhold from American addressees large quantities of books and papers shipped or mailed from abroad. During one recent month 56,500 pieces of " foreign propaganda " are said to have been seized.[77] In a single year 150,000 sacks of international mail are reported to have been specially processed through the Boston Post Office alone, and 800 different foreign publications are said to have been banned.[78]

The mechanics of suppression are less complex than the questions they raise. As printed materials enter this country from abroad, they are initially examined by customs officers. If entry is otherwise than by the mails, the Customs Bureau itself exercises a final authority of decision, subject to an importer's petition for reconsideration. If entry is by mail, the printed matter is turned over to the Post Office Department, whose legal branch decides whether or not the items in question are " foreign propaganda." If so, the Department destroys the material or gives it to other government agencies. Neither the sender nor the addressee ordinarily receives any notice whatsoever. There appears to be an increasing rigidity in effectuating the present exclusionary policies.

The constitutional doubts created by this governmental action have been fully examined elsewhere.[79] The wisdom of the action, apart from its debatable validity, warrants a few added words.

Administrative exclusion of printed matter from abroad is not necessary to protect Americans against being fooled about the origin of what they read. The foreignness of the sender is indicated at once by the geographical source of the material. As the *Harvard Law Review* puts it, " If the purpose of the Foreign Agents Registration Act is to alert recipients of political propaganda in the United States when the sender of it has foreign connections, that purpose would seem in no way circumvented by permitting the entry into this country of most, if not all, of the material currently excluded. Much of it states specifically the country of origin and the organization publishing it. In any case the very fact that it is sent from abroad presumably means that it bears a foreign postmark or shipping label. And when material is ordered or subscribed to, its recipient should be fully aware of its source." [80]

The work of the customs and postal authorities, then, is not directed at assuring that the dispatcher of printed matter shall be suitably identified (which is the declared objective of the Foreign Agents Registration Act). It is directed, rather, against the printed matter itself, with the aim of insulating Americans against books and papers coming from other countries.

Why, one may ask, should any good American be concerned about the destruction of "foreign propaganda"? The answer, of course, is that the term has no fixed meaning, and may too readily be extended to almost anything of foreign origin. Little of the printed matter now being seized is propaganda that, in the interests of a foreign government, advocates the forcible overthrow of governmental authority in the United States.[81] Much of it is descriptive, no doubt in overly sympathetic and artificially colored terms, of countries behind the Iron Curtain; some of it consists of the periodical publications that students and others read in order to remain in touch with overseas affairs; another portion consists of ideological writings (by no means exclusively communistic in character) that a customs officer thinks might raise unwelcome questions in the mind of a recipient; and some of it is objectionable for no apparent reason other than its having been printed abroad—no other explanation can readily be suggested for seizing issues of the London *Economist*, surely one of the most widely quoted and generally respected of all conservative publications.[82]

As always happens, too, the original motivations of controls in this field are easily forgotten, and then the controls broaden far beyond their expected scope.* In 1955, for example, the Post Office Department confiscated a thousand

---

* This development, in connection with restrictions upon expression, is so frequently observable that it has ceased to be regarded as phenomenal. A good example may be seen in Washington's "anti-anarchist" statute, which penalized the written encouragement of crime or disrespect for law. The statute was made the basis of prosecuting not an anarchist, but the editor of a small newspaper who, in an article entitled "The Nude and the Prudes," urged nude bathing. State v. Fox, 71 Wash. 185 (1912), affirmed 236 U. S. 373 (1915). In 1935 New Jersey enacted a statute aimed at the "German bundists" who sought to ape Hitler by attacking Jews; it forbade

copies of a pamphlet printed abroad but written by the American pacifist A. J. Muste, head of the Fellowship of Reconciliation.[83] Pacifism may be an unpopular and, in the eyes of some, even a dangerous philosophy, but it is not foreign propaganda. In 1954, to give another example, the Post Office Department ruled that an English book highly critical of the Roman Catholic Church was " foreign propaganda " and unmailable in this country because, presumably, it might " promote racial, religious, or social dissensions." [84] The book may very possibly have deserved the oblivion to which the postal authorities sought to consign it. Its merits, however, ought to be judged by its readers rather than by officials who assume " a guardianship of the public mind." After protest had been made along this line, the Post Office Department rescinded its prohibitory action.

The Foreign Agents Registration Act never purported to interpose the government between the printed page and the reader. It undertook, merely, to assure that the reader should know the source of the printed page, so that its contents

---

inciting racial or religious hatred. N. J. Rev. Stat. (1937), Tit. 2, ch. 157B. The first prosecution under the statute was directed not at pro-Nazis, but at Jehovah's Witnesses. When the statute was later used for its declared purpose, it was held unconstitutional. State v. Klaprott, 127 N. J. L. 395, 22 A. 2d 877 (1941). In 1924 Louisiana adopted a statute requiring each " fraternal, patriotic, charitable, benevolent, literary, scientific, athletic, military, or social organization " to file annually with the Secretary of State a list of its members and officers within the state. The Attorney General was authorized to seek the dissolution of any noncomplying organization. La. Stat. Ann. 12:401, 405 (West, 1951). The statute, according to common repute, was aimed at the Ku Klux Klan. On March 1, 1956, Louisiana's Attorney General filed suit to enjoin the operations of the National Association for the Advancement of Colored People because its membership lists had not been filed. New York Times, March 2, 1956, p. 24, col. 7. A state judge issued a permanent injunction against the NAACP's continued functioning in Louisiana until it turned over its membership lists. New York Times, April 25, 1956, p. 27, col. 2. So far as can be ascertained from the law reports, this was the first action brought under the 1924 law, though the Attorney General had earlier given opinions that the Society of St. Vincent de Paul and a labor union were obliged to comply with the statutory requirement.

could be appraised in the light of that knowledge. The Supreme Court has more than once reminded us that the constitutional protection of free expression is intended to safeguard the opportunity to hear or read as well as the opportunity to speak or write.[85] This opportunity vanishes when officials summarily determine the extent to which Americans may receive news and views from abroad.

Both the Post Office Department and the Customs Bureau, be it said to their credit, have begun to exercise a moderating discretion when satisfied that materials they regard as " foreign propaganda " are to be used for educational rather than propagandistic purposes.[86] Columbia University, to state one example, had experienced great difficulty during a period of fifteen months beginning April, 1953, in securing delivery of books and other publications ordered from Russia, Hong Kong, and elsewhere. These were urgently needed by the University's Russian Institute and East Asian Institute, many of whose students were preparing for the diplomatic and military services. Finally, after strenuous efforts by university spokesmen, the governmental authorities were persuaded to deliver the impounded shipments of printed materials. Since July, 1954, the University's libraries have encountered little delay in obtaining publications, though individual instructors still occasionally fail to receive materials addressed to them.

The present Solicitor of the Post Office Department, who is responsible for this aspect of its activities, has been quoted as assuring that " no qualified recipients will be denied these publications. All they have to do is satisfy us that they have a legitimate reason for reading them "—though, as he comfortably adds, " We don't have much of a problem. Most Americans don't want the stuff." [87] No doubt the Solicitor is entirely accurate in this appraisal of his fellow citizen's wishes. But individuals should be allowed to do their own discarding into wastebaskets. They should not be forced to declare in advance that they have " a legitimate reason " (or, indeed, any reason at all) for either reading or ignoring books, pamphlets, magazines, newspapers, or circulars. Whether a person reads or burns a publication is his business, not the government's.*

Postal and Customs Administration. Neither the Post Office Department nor the Customs Bureau confines its administrative attention to foreign propaganda. Both of them possess broad additional powers with respect to books and writings deemed obscene or seditious. The Postmaster General may seek to eliminate objectionable matter from the mails; [89] the Customs Bureau may seize attempted importations of offensive books.[90]

These administrative powers lose their surface resemblance when their procedural aspects are considered.

Customs seizures are no longer, as once they were, the uncontrollable reflex actions of officials poorly trained as literary critics. For years the Customs Bureau had been accustomed to find intolerably obscene what others had for generations, or even centuries, regarded as important contributions to our cultural heritage—Ovid, Boccaccio, Rabelais, and Voltaire among others. Then, in 1930, upon the initiative of senators who thought the fun had gone far enough, the law was changed to provide that the importability of books should be made finally not by customs officers, but by courts.

---

* President Andrew Jackson, 125 years ago, took a somewhat different view. He urged the Postmaster General of that time to deliver Abolitionist papers only to those southern subscribers who demanded them; "and in every instance the Postmaster ought to take the names down, and have them exposed thro the publik journals as subscribers to this wicked plan of exciting the negroes to insurrection and massacre." He believed that "few men in society will be willing to acknowledge that they are encouraging by subscribing for such papers this horrid and most wicked proceedure; and when they are known, every moral and good citizen will unite to put them in coventry, and avoid their society. This, if adopted would put their circulation down everywhere, for there are few so hardened to villainy, as to withstand the frowns of all good men." [88]

The present procedure still involves an initial customs determination, of course. But if the Customs Bureau seizes an allegedly objectionable book, the seizure must be reported to the United States Attorney, who then begins a forfeiture proceeding in the local federal court. The importer of the book is suitably notified. A jury trial can be (but rarely has been) demanded by either the importer or the government. If the federal district judge determines that the book is " obscene " or otherwise prohibited by law, the seizure is upheld; otherwise, the book is released to the one who ordered it from abroad.

The 1930 statute encouraged a little freshet of litigation to test the validity of exclusionary rulings that had for long years been beyond challenge. Charming case titles began to appear in the law reports—*United States against Married Love*, for example—as publishers and importers hastened to ask the judges whether their books really were as bad as the customs officers had believed. The judges were unable to find the vices detected by the officials. In one ruling after another, culminating in the famous *Ulysses* case in which James Joyce was held to be an author rather than a pornographer, they upset the adverse determinations of the Customs Bureau.[91]

Stung by criticism of the Bureau, the Treasury Department in 1934 began to improve its administrative vision. Now, as in the past, inspectors or other employees of subordinate rank examine imported books at ports of entry. If they are detained, the importer is notified of the detention. He may then, if he wishes, seek an overruling of the subordinate's decision by higher customs officers at the port. If he succeeds, the book enters and there is the end of the matter. If he fails, the question of admissibility must be referred to Washington. There it is considered by an exceptionally civilized censor, who, while he accords no formal hearings, is available for conference with the importer or others interested in the book.

While the work at the ports seems to be carried on with much the same obtuseness that characterized the past (Kant's *Critique of Pure Reason* and a Spanish translation of the Bible have been among the casualties of recent years), the work in Washington has taken on a new dimension of sobriety.[92]

Exclusionary rulings have not suddenly become rare. They are merely cautious. " Under-the-counter " writings, on the one hand, are identified and barred. Scientific and literary works, on the other, are identified and admitted. When the customs censor has doubt about the category in which a writing belongs, he consults the published authorities or seeks advice from acknowledged specialists in the relevant field.

Because the censorial judgment is now exercised with good sense and moderation, few adverse rulings are sought to be appealed.[93] But if an exclusionary decision is not accepted, it is subject to a full re-examination in a federal court, where no weight will be accorded the prior administrative determination. The decision of the Customs Bureau to seize a book because of its character is analogous to a prosecutor's decision to press charges against a person suspected of crime; the trial takes place subsequently to find out whether the accusation is well founded.

The postal administration is strikingly different. The Post Office Department manages a gigantic enterprise, and on the whole does it well. The mail delivery business, monopolized by the government, is the " main artery through which the business, social, and personal affairs of the people are conducted " ; [94] and, naturally enough, the Department's energies are chiefly devoted to getting material into and through the artery, rather than keeping material out. As an exceedingly minor incident of the entire operation, however, the Department does have the responsibility and power to exclude matters that are objectionable either because of their physical properties (such as explosives or corrosives) or because of their ideological content (such as obscenity or seditious utterance). In theory, the postal authorities are not in the latter case engaged in censoring writings (which the First Amendment might be thought to forbid), but are merely deciding what sort of business the government will choose to transact.

This theory, it must be conceded, has some respectable underpinnings. In 1878 the Supreme Court upheld the power to exclude lottery circulars from the mails; this was thought not to be an abridgment of free speech because the use of the mails was a mere privilege, withdrawable when Congress willed.[95] But the theory has been much weakened by critical analysis [96] and by a succession of judicially expressed doubts.[97] In 1878 the Supreme Court readily assumed that other suitable means of distribution were available to persons who were denied use of the mails. If this assumption was sound then, it is clearly not so now. All present signs point to a redirection of judicial analysis, with a probable conclusion that exclusion from the mails positively limits expression rather than merely withholds a privilege that may be granted or denied as whim may dictate.

As in other branches of this discussion, however, I wish to concentrate attention chiefly upon the merits of what is being done, rather than upon constitutional considerations. I turn therefore to the pertinent procedures, policies, and possible after-effects of postal censorship.

At the outset one must note the inaccessibility of information about the censorial practices of the Post Office Department. There are no published rules and regulations to suggest either the standards of judgment or the departmental procedures that will be followed in exclusionary cases. Even unofficial descriptions are infrequent and incomplete.[98]

In fact, the postal censorship operates very informally. Any postal matter other than first-class mail is subject to inspection for " obscenity " by any person in the department, from rural-route carrier to clerk in the central station. Anything that is thought by anybody to be non-mailable because of its contents will be rejected or, if already in the mails, will be intercepted so as to forestall its delivery. If it is intercepted, the local postmaster sends it to Washington for review by the office of the department's Solicitor. There, it is again examined by members of the Solicitor's staff, with the ultimate decision (on behalf of the Postmaster General) in the hands of an Assistant Solicitor or the Solicitor. If this decision is adverse to the mailability of the intercepted matter, the person who sought to mail it is notified that he may within fifteen days seek to show cause why it should not be destroyed. This is the first regularized notice that anything is deemed amiss, though of course the addressor may have had less formal intimations that his mail has run into difficulties. No formal hearing is granted either before or after the solicitor has ruled on mailability.[99]

Another departmental activity with censorial overtones is carried on rather more formally. Since 1950 the Post Office Department has had authority to refuse to make mail deliveries to a person who has been found to be using the mails to obtain payments for obscene matter. This is somewhat analogous to the Department's power to refuse its aid in effectuating a scheme adjudged to be fraudulent. In the latter case, the Department returns to the " suckers " the letters they have dispatched to the perpetrator of the fraud; in the former the Department issues an equivalent " stop order " against one who needs the mails in order to complete his sale of " any obscene, lewd, lascivious, indecent, filthy, or vile article, matter, thing, device or substance." [100]   In these cases, unlike exclusionary proceedings, the Department does accord the affected parties a fair hearing before branding their business as unlawful.*

* The Department came a cropper, however, in Summerfield v. Sunshine Book Co., 221 F. 2d 4 (D. C. Cir., 1954), certiorari denied 349 U. S. 921

What sorts of judgments does the Post Office Department make under these broad powers, often so abruptly exercised? Is there in fact a general acceptance of its standards? One would like to report that all is for the best in this best of all possible worlds. Alas, satisfaction must be more restrained.

In 1909 an indignant editor denounced the prevailing social standards that, he said, had led cruelly to a young girl's death because she preferred to submit to an abortion rather than bear the stigma of mothering an illegitimate child. His indignation probably grew still stronger when he was convicted of having deposited an obscene writing in the mails.[101] Few in the present Post Office Department would defend that distant prosecution commenced upon the complaint of some now forgotten predecessor. What will their successors say, however, about the judgments that are expressed today?—judgments that stigmatize Freud and Malinowski, Margaret Mead and Simone de Beauvoir, Alberto Moravia's *Woman*

(1955). Having concluded that past issues of a nudist magazine had contained obscene pictures, the Postmaster General ordered that no mail should be delivered and no money orders should be paid thereafter to the publisher. This, in effect, would have put the publisher out of business altogether, for so long as no mail at all was being delivered, payments could not be received or correspondence had with respect to future issues even though they might in fact be wholly unobjectionable (even to the Post Office Department). The court held that the "stop order" was invalid because not confined to mail relating to the issues already published and found to have been obscene.

A recent writer suggests that this decision may be defied by the Department. He quotes the following exchange with the Associate Solicitor for the Post Office Department. Question: "If you were to find that the Chevrolet Division of the General Motors Corporation had posted an obscene book, could you, as you construe your existing powers, issue an order to stop all mail sent to the Chevrolet Division?" Answer: "Yes." The significance of this, of course, is that a "legitimate" publisher of a book the Post Office Department holds to be obscene, would be subject ever afterward (if the Associate Solicitor's view were sound) to having all mail addressed to it returned to the senders as "unlawful." This would prevent all publication whatsoever, for no modern business can exist without mail service—if only to receive its bills. Edward de Grazia, Obscenity and the Mail, 20 Law & Contemporary Problems 608, at 613–14 (1955).

of Rome and Vivian Connell's *The Chinese Room* and James Jones' *From Here to Eternity?* What will they think of a determination that Aristophanes' *Lysistrata* should not be delivered to a dealer in rare editions because it "contains numerous passages which are plainly obscene, lewd and lascivious in character which are well calculated to deprave the morals of persons reading same and almost equally certain to arouse libidinous thoughts in the minds of the normal reader" ? [102]

The contrasts between the postal and customs administrations now become clear. First, the Customs Bureau avoids making as extreme decisions as those of the Post Office Department. Second, the decisions of the customs authorities are subject to an untrammeled re-examination by a judge and, if desired, by a jury. The decisions of the postal authorities, on the other hand, are not open to anyone's independent appraisals. They are reviewed, if at all, in a proceeding to set aside the administrative determination; and in such a case, some courts believe as the United States Court of Appeals said only a few years ago, "judicial review channeled within the confines of a plea for an injunction should not be over-extensive." [103] If the sender of the allegedly obscene material were prosecuted for his offense, as the statute explicitly authorizes, then he would be entitled to a trial in which the community's notions of good sense might prevail over the administrative determination of objectionability. But so long as the Post Office Department proceeds only against the published matter rather than against its publisher or seller, the postal finding of obscenity may be virtually final.[104]

When in reality there is so little opportunity for review, the importance of sound initial decisions is emphasized. In the Post Office Department a long-standing distrust of experts has prevented the sort of consultations that minimize the chance of mistakes in the administration of customs laws. Moreover, the Department has doggedly adhered to analytical methods long since in disfavor in almost all other American tribunals; for postal censors do not prove themselves capable of reading a whole work to determine its dominant purpose, but continued to be snagged by isolated words and phrases.

There is no good reason why the sort of judicial review provided in customs cases should not also obtain in postal proceedings involving the character of publications. Review of bad decisions will never take the place of good decisions in the first instance. But the possibility of review may stimulate heightened efforts to avoid arbitrariness in administration, and may thus render court proceedings unnecessary in fact. Extensive judicial re-examination of administrative factual determination is resisted in general on the ground that administrators acquire within the field of their specialization a competence that judges cannot claim. In the area of obscenity, however, this is not true.* The administrators, to begin with, are not specialists. They are lawyers or party managers or, occasionally, old postal hands whose work has probably had nothing whatever to do with literature, history, psychology, and the other disciplines that may bear upon intelligent censorship. Nor does their main work after appointment provide them with pertinent experience or information. In this respect they differ from many other adminis-

---

* The textual discussion has focused on obscenity, simply for ease of statement. What is said here about review of administrative judgments is equally applicable to other determinations of non-mailability that turn on the content of a writing. Whether or not a writing "includes matter of a character tending to incite arson, murder, or assassination," or whether, in war time, it advocates treason, insurrection, or forcible resistance to any law of the United States, is a type of question within judicial more than postal competence. About 250 books and many magazines were barred from the mails during World War I. These included religious works, a book by the president of Stanford University, and a Catholic periodical that found fault with Britain's administration of affairs in Ireland.[105] The record of suppression was much milder in World War II; the chief casualty was Father Coughlin's *Social Justice*, which was banned issue by issue until it gave up the ghost. In any case that strikes as directly as these did at the press, an opportunity should exist for a long second look.

trators who, though not especially trained at the outset of their careers, become educated through being immersed in their agency's practical affairs.

Moreover, the " fact " of obscenity is so illusory that bureaucratic methods are not peculiarly fitted to ascertain its existence. Especially when that " fact " may limit freedom of expression and may subject the press to a degree of governmental dictation, its existence should be verified by an independent examination.

Review in General. Preceding segments of this discussion have laid stress on the usual unavailability or inadequacy of procedures for testing censorial determinations. Still, a few cases do trickle into the zone of judicial cognizance. What happens to them when they do is not always reassuring.

Mention has already been made of the unduly narrow scope of review accorded to an adverse judgment of the postal authorities. Judges tend to sustain an exclusionary postal ruling so long as it lies within the outermost fringes of debatable soundness. If the administrative conclusion were the product of specialized insights denied the unspecialized judges, this deference would be not only courteous but functionally desirable. In the present context, however, no good reason appears for subordinating the judges' judgment —except that, in all likelihood, some judges prefer not to take upon themselves the responsibility for the dirty and unrewarding work of censorship. They know that if they rule against a writing, they will be accused of close kinship with Mrs. Grundy; while if they rule against censorship, Mrs. Grundy will take delight in denouncing them.

Appellate courts often exercise a similar self-restraint when called on to re-examine determinations of objectionability made by juries or by trial judges. If the finding below has a rational basis and does not obviously exhibit the application of legally impermissible tests, the reviewing judges are prone to wash their hands of the problem. Thus, for example, when a trial court in Massachusetts decided in 1944 that Lillian Smith's widely discussed and highly praised novel *Strange Fruit* [106] was obscene, the Supreme Judicial Court declined to rely upon its own evaluation of the book, but sustained the adverse determination, remarking: " The test is not what we ourselves think of the book, but what in our best judgment a trier of the facts might think of it without going beyond the bounds of honesty and reason." [107]

Professor Chafee has long espoused the view that a jury is the best tribunal, all things considered, for drawing a line between lawful and unlawful books.[108] The subjective element inevitably remains uppermost in decisions about the permissibility of writings, whether determination be made by one man or twelve. If one man makes the decision alone, however, nothing forces him to dilute his personal prejudices or to achieve awareness that his value judgments may not be shared universally. When, on the other hand, twelve jurors grapple with the issue of objectionability, the very diversity of their backgrounds and tastes drives the jurors toward a cross-sectional and somewhat de-personalized opinion.

If this results in a judgment favorable to a book, an appellate court is warranted in relying upon the jurors' conclusion as dispositive of the question. Their verdict may be taken as a sampling, albeit a highly unscientific one, of community sentiment. Judges have no special competence that enables them to say that the community will be scarred by a book the jury has deemed harmless. Since the free flow of words is essential to the proper functioning of our governmental and intellectual institutions, restrictions upon that flow should be regarded as abnormalities requiring especially convincing justifications. Hence, given a determination by jury (or, for that matter, trial judge) in favor of freedom, an appellate court need not strain to find reasons for overturning the result.

It does not follow, however, that a higher court should accord the same measure of finality to a trial tribunal's adverse judgment, if review of it be sought.

In the ordinary run of things, litigated cases deal chiefly with past episodes. These must be re-created by testimony, often conflicting, which the initial trier of the facts is peculiarly well situated to appraise. The atmospherics of the trial, including the behavior of the witnesses, can be sensed by the jury or by the trial judge who sits without a jury; the appellate court, on the contrary, has before it nothing but cold typescript, entombing the echoes of spoken words. When, however, the issue to be tried is whether a book is obscene or otherwise unlawful, obviously the chief evidence is the book itself. This can be read and appraised by the judges of an appellate court, presumably with at least as much skill as was brought to the task in the inferior court.

There are two main reasons why appellate judges should exercise that skill, notwithstanding their accustomed reluctance to re-evaluate fact findings made in the lower court.

First, the consequences of an adverse judgment upon a book reach far beyond the immediate parties to the litigation. If a jury finds as a fact that the defendant's negligently operated automobile struck and injured the plaintiff, the verdict does of course have importance for the plaintiff and for the defendant (or his insurance company) in that particular case; but the verdict against the defendant has no impact on others. By contrast, a verdict against a bookseller for selling an allegedly obscene book may well determine the availability of that book throughout a community, or even throughout a whole state. Other booksellers may decline to assume the risk of continuing sales, even though the judgment in the case at bar does not affect them in any legal sense. Thus, the rights of innumerable book buyers and readers may be determined as a practical matter by what is done in a single case in which they have not participated and of whose very existence they are probably unaware. Recognizing this, reviewing courts should not hesitate to upset seemingly mistaken (even though debatably correct) decisions about the quality of books. Where communication between writers and readers is at stake, the state's most important judges must feel free to reappraise the need for restraints.

Second, in a field where strong feeling is regularly mistaken for knowledge, "findings of fact" may readily reflect predispositions rather than evidential analysis. Jurymen are not untouched by the passions of their time; [109] and even judges may be intolerant of others' estimates of objectionability.[110] Reviewing courts should not discharge their appellate functions as though wholly unaware of these realities.

A Return to the Beginnings

The modern varieties of book censorship are not nearly so deeply rooted as most people suppose. Suppression in one guise or another is age-old. But the English obscenity law dates only from 1857, in the Victorian era, and the United States statutory framework began to be built only in 1873, when Congress was overcome by Anthony Comstock.

Before there were statutes in the Anglo-American system there was common sense—and common law. The heart of the common law approach, it seems to me, is this: No person should be deemed free to obtrude upon another an unwilling exposure to offensiveness—or, if you will, to obscenity.

The law of obscenity began, according to most legal scholars, with the case of young and bon vivant Sir Charles Sedley (or Sydlye, according to taste) in 1663.[111] Sir Charles, still drunk after a spree of several days' duration, appeared nude on a balcony overlooking London's Covent Garden, from which vantage point he flung down upon a gaping crowd not only a torrent of profane and indelicate words, but also some bottles filled with what the judges described as an " offensive liquor." No matter what one may think of the later development of obscenity law, one can muster up no sympathy for young Sedley, who was duly found guilty of a criminal offence despite the absence of any statutory definition or direct judicial precedent.

The words Sedley used were probably not wholly unfamiliar to those who heard them. I doubt that they corrupted anyone's morals or coarsened any previously delicate taste. His offensiveness lay in his imposing his words upon auditors who, being about their lawful business in the neighborhood, had no choice but to listen. Few persons over the age of ten are likely to be baffled by four-letter words, but this does not mean that every foul-mouthed ruffian is at liberty to bellow them in the town square. The courts have long held, wholly independently of statutes, that utterances of obscene language in public places, near a dwelling, or in the presence of ladies could be punished.[112] A decent regard for the sensibilities of others is all that makes communal life possible. Existence is difficult enough without the intrusions of wrongheaded nastiness upon a captive audience.

One may not with impunity dispatch letters to his political opponents, showering upon them words of a most distasteful character.[113] One may not repeatedly telephone a respectable married woman, apparently a perfect stranger, and address to her a stream of " filthy, disgusting and indecent language " while persistently proposing acts of sexual intercourse and sodomy.[114] Women may not parade unclothed on the highway [115]—not, one might suggest, because doing so will destroy the moral fabric of society, but because, as Montaigne so strongly felt, nudity in humankind is too often aesthetically offensive: nakedness exposes the defects and imperfections that otherwise remain at least partly hidden,

or remedied by the cantilever engineers who design under-
clothing. The poor wretches who suffer a compulsive need
to expose their genitals in public are forbidden to yield to
their compulsion—surely not because exposure will attract
but because it will cause a revulsion of feeling.

These diverse cases have a single common element. In
each, unwelcome conduct has been thrust by the defendant
upon fellow-citizens who cannot escape it. Choice is gone.
The community, or a part of it, is compelled to hear or see,
without reference to its own standards of acceptability. This,
in a true sense, is offensive. Many things not harmful in
themselves and, indeed, entirely tolerable in some circumstances may be utterly shocking in other contexts. It may be
only "social convention" that transforms the character of
the thing in question. But convention is the rulebook by
which the community plays the game, and the community is
entitled to write the rules.

Not long ago the city of Pascagoula, Mississippi (population, 4,000) was outraged by a local humorist who adorned
his ancient motor car with a prominently lettered sign: "All
you ladies that smoke cigarettes throw your butts in here."
The automobile, strategically parked in front of the local
post office, drew the townspeople's eyes and, seemingly,
stirred their indignation, for the owner was soon indicted for
"showing and having in his possession an obscene writing."[116] However deplorable may be the seeming mirth-
lessness of Pascagoula, is there not a good deal to be said
for upholding local tastes in matters of this sort? A civilized
being must refrain in public places from sexual or scato-
logical behavior repugnant to the citizenry, just as he refrains
in his neighbor's parlor.

Despite a strong personal preference for a society in which
the idiosyncratic is accepted calmly, I think that courts should
within rather generous limits sustain community attacks upon
"public indecency." There is always, of course, a degree of

danger that what purports to be the prevailing community sentiment may in fact itself be an idiosyncracy—as seems to be the case when, as occasionally happens, some sex-mad constable charges that a pantalooned woman is indecently exposed. In the main, however, the community is entitled to demand external respect for its mores, allowing nonconformists the right to appeal for change in prevailing attitudes but not to flout them openly meanwhile.

Trouble arises when this permissible pressure for conformity spills over into censorship, where it has no justification at all. It is one thing to say that nobody should force upon everybody's unwilling eyes or ears a communication they deem outrageous. It is quite another to say that everybody must first approve the content of the communication before it may be transmitted to anybody who is willing to receive it. Books are voluntarily read. They are not obtruded upon the passer-by, regardless of his choice. To be let alone, as Justice Brandeis said, is the most precious of all human rights. In the one case it dictates that none should be compelled to read or listen to what he abhors. In the other it dictates that none should be precluded from writing or reading as his own rather than another's taste may determine.

Perspective

Censorship is negative. It may conceivably prevent " bad " reading; but it never creates opportunities for " good " reading. Its proponents think it reduces the chances that individuals will develop antisocially; but it embodies no features that might actively enlarge their chances of developing healthily. A more positive program, though lacking the spectacular aspects of censorship, might take society farther toward the desired goals.

One's own interests are likely to determine what he reads, if anything. This man has a taste for biography, that one for adventure stories; this one for historical novels consisting mainly of bosoms, that one for Gide and Proust; that one for Spillane, this one for Saroyan. Self-selection largely controls not only the nature but the impact of reading matter. Anthony Comstock could boast of having spent forty busy years fishing for filthy literature in a sewer, without at the end being a jot or tittle worse than when he began. Why throw reformist energies into preventing the gratification of low tastes? Why not try instead to unravel the mystery of forming elevated tastes and interests, so that effective self-censorship may replace the clumsy external controls now attempted? Like any other freedom, the freedom to read can be used unwisely. But fear that freedom may be improvidently exercised does not justify its destruction. Foolish reading cannot be ended by force, but only by patient persuasion, by education rather than by edict.

A more pressing danger than bad reading is no reading at all. Many Americans, while able to read simple words and to write a decipherable signature, seem to be functionally illiterate. Another large part of the population is literarily starved. People cannot be compelled to discover the joy of books, even if, as is not the case, they should be forced. On the whole, however, little is done to entice them upon exploratory expeditions or, if the desire already exists, to gratify their wishes. Consider the plight of the public library as symptomatic of a broader problem. At a time when the cost of a " minimum " service was estimated to be $1.50 per capita, that of a " good " service was $2.25 per capita, and that of a " superior " service was $3.00 per capita, only seven states spent as much as $1.25 while twenty-nine spent less than $1.00 per capita; the average for the whole country was 96 cents.[117] In 1950 less than half of the " professional jobs " in public libraries were filled by people trained for the tasks assigned them, because inadequate budgets made professionalism impossible in one community after another. One out of six counties in the United States has no public facilities whatsoever, and most of those that do exist have insufficient reading materials and inadequate personnel. "The American public library," asserted the New York State Library, " is facing a major crisis." [118]

What we need in this country is not less reading, but more; not fewer poor books, but more good books; not repression, but liberation. After all, as President Whitney Griswold of Yale has well said, " Books won't stay banned. They won't burn. Ideas won't go to jail. In the long run of history, the censor and the inquisitor have always lost. The only sure weapon against bad ideas is better ideas." [119]

3

The Right to Make a Living

THE RIGHT to make a living," the Supreme Court of Georgia declared in 1925, "is among the greatest of human rights." [1] Two decades later Mr. Justice Douglas of the Supreme Court of the United States gave it a still higher valuation, for he called the right to work " the most precious liberty that man possesses." [2] The enthusiasm that led to these appraisals is seemingly not shared by most American legislators. In a country boastful of a free economy and of extending maximum opportunity to ambitious men, the " right " to work has been legislated into a most precarious condition.

The present discussion will deal with only one phase of the diminishing area of occupational freedom. It will not explore the federal, state, and municipal loyalty-security programs that seek to assure employee reliability—programs that have already touched in one way or another perhaps as many as one out of every five gainfully employed persons in the United States, along with many members of the families of a sizeable percentage of these. Nor will it enter into the sometimes heated debate over the emergence of labor unions as powerful regulators of employment practices—in which capacity, for better or for worse, they have eliminated choices that might otherwise be made individually. These important matters have been ably and extensively treated by others.[3] This paper will examine a less dramatic though equally significant interference with the traditional freedom to work as one wills and to be judged by the fruits of his labor, namely, the occupational license.

The Extent of Occupational Licensing

Until the end of the nineteenth century, few occupations other than those of the lawyer and the physician were subject to state licensing. There were, of course, departures from the norm. Ohio, for example, began to license insurance solicitors in 1830, a year before attorneys were reached and 66 years before physicians came under regulation in that state. By and large, however, only three learned professions—law, medicine, and the ministry—were recognized; and only the first two of these were subject to licensing.

But with the twentieth century came a veritable deluge of licensing laws. By 1952 more than 80 separate occupations, exclusive of " owner-businesses " like restaurants and taxicab companies, had been licensed by state law; [4] and in addition to the state laws there are municipal ordinances in abundance, [5] not to mention the federal statutes that require the licensing of such diverse occupations as radio operators and stockyard commission agents. As long ago as 1938 a single state, North Carolina, had extended its laws to 60 occupations. [6] One may not be surprised to learn that pharmacists, accountants, and dentists have been reached by state laws, as have sanitarians and psychologists, assayers and architects, veterinarians and librarians. But with what joy of discovery does one learn about the licensing of threshing machine operators and dealers in scrap tobacco? What of egg graders and guide-dog trainers, pest controllers and yacht salesmen, tree surgeons and well diggers, tile layers and potato growers? And what of the hypertrichologists who are licensed in Connecticut, where they remove excessive and unsightly hairs with the solemnity appropriate to their high-sounding title? [7]

The orotundity of the hypertrichological nomenclature, while inescapably reminiscent of the ditch digger who insisted that he be called a drainage engineer, is perhaps suggestive of a more significant sociological development. Differentiating the professions from mere jobs is becoming increasingly difficult, if not impossible. The Church and medicine and law were early recognized as professions because, first, " their practice is based upon the theoretical study of a department of learning " and, second, " the individuals who follow them are bound to follow a certain mode of behavior and are so regarded by the public." [8] The force of these supposedly distinguishing characteristics has much diminished through the years. Dr. Thomas Parran, former Surgeon General of the United States and now dean of the Graduate School of Public Health at the University of Pittsburgh, asserts that nurses and other " semi-professionals " must nowadays " master a body of knowledge greater in extent and usefulness for the care of the sick than all of the medical knowledge of a century ago. In addition, they have codes of ethics and possess techniques as exact as those of the brain surgeon." [9] Moreover, the expansion of cafeteria style, tax-supported universities and colleges attended by hordes of young men and women intent solely upon vocational training as funeral directors, sales executives, hotel managers, commercial artists, playground supervisors, or the like—but all of whom are deemed to be educated in the end because they are, after all, college graduates—has made it difficult to say that this occupation is " learned " while that one is not. Greater urbanization has, in addition, made for a mounting specialization.[10] Activities have been ever more narrowly defined. The expert or specialist has come into his own, respected for his grasp of the knowledge pertinent to his fragment of human activity. But because the specialist deals only with a fragment, he is not thought to deserve any particular deference outside that sphere.* Finally, the pro-

* Sir Alexander Carr-Saunders has rather sadly remarked: " No one speaks any more of the learned professions. Professional men were formerly

fessional man today only rarely exhibits the selflessness that once set him somewhat apart from the ordinary herd. If the professional man's dedication to the common weal was, as Harold Laski less generously believed, merely " the maintenance of the elaborate pretence of a very remote interest in the financial return for his work," [12] then, at any rate, a skeptical generation has found the elaborate pretence less effective than perhaps it formerly was.

All these tendencies have combined to break down what were, in the beginning, walls between separate categories and to erect, in their stead, mere differences in degree. So long as an occupation can be distinguished from the wholly unskilled or semi-skilled work that traditionally falls to those with strong backs and weak minds, persons who engage in it are encouraged to think of themselves as specialists if not as professional men.[13] And, having begun to think of themselves in that way, their very next effort is to persuade others to accord them the same recognition. Their techniques may not be readily communicable by the methods of formal education; the knowledge on which they draw may be relatively fixed rather than growing in a way necessitating continuing study; their operations may be the products of an essentially non-intellectual training narrowly focused upon immediately practical skills and information; their methods may be routinized without ever becoming exact; their business practices may more often be shaped by the traditions of the market place than by the genteel (perhaps shabbily genteel, but still genteel) traditions of professions which frown on adver-

---

regarded as possessing a broad culture, a wide special competence, and a general understanding of affairs. A measure of leadership fell into their hands, and much that we value in our society was evolved under the influence of the older professions. Today, professional men are regarded as experts— persons with high competence in a restricted sphere. Great deference is paid to them while they act within their particular range. Otherwise, they have little prestige. Outside their role, they are thought to have no more claim to be heard than the man in the street." [11] Possibly heart specialists are an exception to this general rule, since 1955, at least in the United States.

tising, price wars, and similar competitive devices. None-theless, if their vocation or employment is sufficiently distinct and self-conscious to permit the forming of an occupational organization, soon they will be knocking on legislative doors, demanding that they, too, be brought under regulation.

For let it not be thought that occupational licensing has always, or even chiefly, been imposed rather than induced. Public recognition of scandalous conditions has occasionally led to licensing against the wishes of the licensees, as when New York and New Jersey, stirred by reports of criminality on the waterfront, forbade the employment of any dock-worker who had not first obtained the Waterfront Commission's blessing; or as when stock exchanges and brokers came under federal licensing after the financial debacle of 1929. Again, the large individual responsibility borne by physicians or lawyers, whose attentions are so important to the persons they serve but so little subject to their informed judgment, created demands from outside as well as from inside the medical and legal professions that their qualifications be tested. These, however, are the rarities. In the main, those already within the occupational group clamor for licensing, always, of course, upon the stated ground that thus the public will receive protection against the incompetent or unscrupulous—but always, also, with other less emphasized purposes. One of these is to achieve a competitive advantage or an enlarged income. The other, of an emotional rather than economic nature, though in some instances of possibly even larger importance, is to achieve a formalized recognition of the knowledge, skill, and probity required of a conscientious practitioner. Be he chiropodist or chiropractor, tile layer or horseshoer, photographer or watchmaker, dry cleaner or embalmer, the sound man may yearn for professional status and social advancement.[14]

Successful campaigns to achieve licensure may in point of fact produce some gain for the community as a whole. Personal ambition, whether economic or social, does very often realize itself through creating some common good, as a sort of by-product. Moreover, swindlers and incompetents may in actuality be somewhat hindered by licensing laws, so that the public interest may to that extent be served just as the proponents of licensing asserted would be the case. It is hard to believe, however, that legislators are responding to any felt public need when they agree that florists and beauticians and naturopaths and shorthand reporters and all the other groupings must first be tested, sifted, and pasteurized—and then be protected against the competition of upstarts who might like to enter the occupation.[15]

The pattern of pressure is the same all over the country. In a single session of the New Jersey legislature calls were heard for the licensing of bait fishing-boats, beauty shops, chain stores, florists, insurance adjusters, photographers, and master painters. In no instance did the calls come from citizens who had suffered at the hands of members of those groups. They came always from the affected businessmen themselves—men who probably enjoyed cursing the government for interfering with private business, but who at the same time besought their own licensing. Typically they proposed that persons already within the occupation be licensed without examination, but they prescribed extensive tests, qualifications, and delays for those who wished to share the occupational glory after passage of the law.[16] A Wisconsin legislator, having observed the pressures at work in that state, concluded sadly that her six-year-old son could no longer reasonably aspire to become a watchmaker in Wisconsin though, fortunately, he might still hope to become President of the United States.[17]

Who is there to resist the endeavors of the " ins " to make certain that the " outs " will remain out? Obviously those who may in future find themselves excluded from an occupation, or delayed in their entry into it, are not yet aware of the difficulties they will face; unorganized and, indeed, unknown, they remain unrepresented while licensing is debated. Who can present the public's opinion of whether it will or will not be disadvantaged by recognition of yet another profession or sub-profession? The " public " has no spokesman in these matters. Occasionally a group already on the inside will rise in might to prevent others from gaining status through licensing. The medical associations of New York, for example, managed until 1956 to thwart the ambitions of that state's psychologists, who had long been agitating for the imposition of " professional standards " upon them; [18] and the osteopaths, having achieved New York licensure in 1907, now join with the physicians to beat off the chiropractors who actively seek a similar recognition. Unless there chances to be some such competition of ambitions, campaigns to become licensed are likely to be unopposed by anything other than inertia, a doughty foe indeed, but one that habitually yields to sustained pressure.

Some Social Consequences

Like most things of interest, occupational licensing is neither all good nor all bad. Some positive advantages do undoubtedly flow from it to the public at large as distinct from the licensees. For example, an individual who believes himself wronged by a licensee's poor service or sharp dealing may perhaps gain redress more simply and more cheaply through a licensing board than if he were remitted to a judicial remedy. Indeed, if only small sums of money are involved, the judicial remedy may be wholly illusory, while the administrative remedy may be quickly available. That much is clearly a gain. So, too, there may be gain for the public in discouraging the entrance into an occupation of unsuitable persons. Doomed from the start, they may, in their desperate efforts to survive, adopt unethical practices that debase their competitors as well. This possibility led

James Grafton Rogers to believe that " the public in the end will suffer, as the individual does, from the existence of misfits, failures, wasted energies and frustrated energies." [19]

Rogers spoke in 1933. The national economy was then deeply depressed. The prevailing mood favored restraints on production and competition. If more goods were being produced than were being consumed, reduce production rather than increase consumption. If professional men and occupational specialists were under-employed, restrict their number rather than release the forces that might expand the demand for their services. Those were the days when little pigs were destroyed lest they grow into the pork products for which millions of impecunious people hungered. And, by a parity of reasoning, many persons of sound mind and good will were prepared to take drastic steps to avoid the " overcrowding " of already depressed vocations. Overcrowding, they felt, could lead only to price-cutting, irregular practices, and moral decline. Escaping from those consequences was thought to warrant a somewhat rough and tough exclusionary policy.

But there is another view. The country has become great—geographically, economically, and spiritually—because Americans have refused to be static. They have embraced dissatisfaction rather than acceptance—or, at the least, unsatisfaction rather than smug belief that they had gone about as far as they could go. This has led to experiment, to mobility, to the forward rather than the retrospective view of life and its potentialities. Americans have not believed that tomorrow would inevitably be like yesterday, or even today. Their unwillingness to let the past shape their futures has made them willing to take new jobs, to start new enterprises, to aspire to a higher (or, anyway, different) achievement from that of their forbears. They have been free to try their hands at one occupation and cast it aside for another. Not all have found a comfortable niche. There have been " misfits " and

" failures " a-plenty. But the chance to choose, the right to work, the freedom to aspire—these have been the ingredients of the American dream. Now, in mid-twentieth century, question arises whether the contemporary emphasis upon occupational licensing may not tend to lead us backward from a society of hopeful movement into a society of status.

The marked resemblance between modern licensing patterns and the medieval guild system gives that question a special sharpness.[20]

The medieval guilds, whether of merchants or of craftsmen, seem originally to have been concerned with the reputations of their members. Artisans and tradesmen knew that observance of commonly accepted standards would enhance the reputation of all. At the outset the guilds readily accepted new members, seeking only to assure that all would measure up to the prescribed norms of reliability. Before the middle of the fourteenth century, however, there were thinly disguised evidences of an aim to restrict competition by restricting membership, and a century later the disguises were frankly discarded.[21] Entrance fees rose. Periods of apprenticeship lengthened. Recourse was had to law to enforce the guilds' protection of their own members against any influx of newcomers. The Statute of Apprentices in 1562, embracing a large number of earlier ordinances and enactments, required that a seven-year apprenticeship be served by all who wished entry into any of the existing " sciences, crafts, mysteries or arts." Competition between one guildsman and another all but disappeared. Each guild, in pursuit of monopoly for its members, exercised virtually complete governmental powers of a legislative, judicial, and financial character.[22] The increasingly hereditary character of occupations in that time has left us reminders today in such patronymics as Baker, Carpenter, Miller, and Sawyer.

The expansion of the European economy that began in the late-fifteenth century and was reflected in voyages of discovery and great colonial development, pressed hard against the restrictiveness of the guilds. The rise of nation states made anomalous the guilds' possession of the governmental powers they had separately exercised in their respective urban strongholds. The mercantile policies of the newly conscious national governments were impatient of the restraints on trade that the guilds so sedulously enforced. Finally, the growing philosophy of free competition—bargaining in place of regulation, questing for new markets to add to old, developing new productive and distributive methods if they were more efficient than the ones imposed by tradition—was antithetical to all for which the guilds had stood. The disintegration of the guilds, when at last it was forced, " came as a welcome release from what had become an unreasonable interference with the free play of economic forces, and their demise generally is accounted one of the principal elements in our vaunted advance from ' status ' to ' contract.' " [23]

The philosophy of free competition has dominated the economic growth of America. Of course it has never become an obsession. At no time since the first colonists set foot on this continent has there been a policy of complete laissez faire, and one shudders to contemplate any such policy today. Nonetheless, except in the case of the so-called " natural " monopolies, governmental influence has traditionally been used to support and not to limit competition, to encourage and not to restrict personal, economic, and social mobility. That tradition, whether for good or ill, is in process of drastic revision today.

The thrust of occupational licensing, like that of the guilds, is toward decreasing competition by restricting access to the occupation; toward a definition of occupational prerogatives that will debar others from sharing in them; toward attaching legal consequences to essentially private determinations of what are ethically or economically permissible practices.

State statutes sometimes allow licensed groups to govern themselves all but completely, for all the world as the guilds once did. The lawyers of California, for example, are members of an " integrated bar "—which means that they must be members of a professional association with major responsibility to examine, admit, govern, and expel them; more than half the states have similarly transformed the legal profession into an approximation of an autonomous guild.[24] Other " professions " have been eager to enjoy the same potent independence. Thus, the chiropodists of North Carolina function under the control of a board of examiners appointed by the state pedic association and, suitably, the board reports annually to the association rather than to the governor; and in Oklahoma the dentists, flattering the lawyers by imitating them, successfully campaigned for legislative recognition of The Registered Dentists of Oklahoma, who now manage their own affairs without the intrusion of the people's representatives.[25]

Price-fixing powers are often conferred on licensing bodies only nominally divorced from those whose prices are fixed;[26] not unusually the powers are to be exercised in accordance with the petition or the agreement of a stated percentage of those affected.[27] The professed reason, as a report of the Council of State Governments recently noted, is to prevent price cutting to such an extent that sanitary and health laws might be ignored in the race to show profits despite low incomes. But since only the raising of prices is allowed, and their reduction is forbidden even when the asserted occasion for their having been raised no longer exists, some question remains as to whether protection of health and sanitation is the primary objective.[28]

Moreover, one can perceive in licensing very much the same process of rigidification that infected the guilds. At the outset the reins are loose; but as time passes, the control becomes ever firmer. When, for example, Louisiana first paid heed to its "beauty shoppe" operators who wished to "protect" lady customers by reducing the competition for their patronage, the state legislature adopted a relatively mild law to regulate and define the practice of "cosmetic therapy." The "Board of Control of Cosmetic Therapy" consisted of the President of the State Board of Health, a second member drawn from that same body, and only one appointee from among the licensed cosmeticians. Within a few years the beauticians were strong enough to ask for (and to obtain) new powers of control, and to erect much sturdier defenses against competition. The governing board was expanded to six members. The President of the State Board of Health retained his seat, but the licensees captured the remaining five places for their own. In order, as the state legislature solemnly found, to assure that cosmeticians would be "well-nourished, strong and healthy," the authority to fix prices and prevent "unfair competition" was lodged in the newly constituted board. Then came closer supervision of the "beauty schools" which aspiring artistes of the profession were required to attend. A major reform was fixing a minimum tuition fee lest competition among the schools drive down their income. Extensive powers to inspect, to supervise, to direct, and to discipline were of course needed if economic as well as qualitative control were to be effective. So the powers were given.[29]

Efforts like these do not invariably succeed, but they are boldly undertaken. In one state, as an illustration, the board that licensed funeral directors adopted a regulation, later held to be invalid, requiring each licensee to keep in stock a prescribed number and variety of caskets.[30] The assigned purpose, needless to say, was to assure patrons a large range of choice. The actual effect, however, was to drive out of the business those not financially strong enough to maintain the required stock, thus narrowing the occupation still more than it already was. For each regulation that may be held invalid, however, there are dozens that succeed in curbing some licensees for the benefit of others and, perhaps more significantly still, that succeed in fending off trespassers who might otherwise compete for business.[31]

The field of operation having been marked out and surrounded by a high fence, those who did the marking and the fencing are loath to admit others into the fraternity. Extravagantly difficult entrance requirements are devised. In some states a high school graduate who aspires to be a master plumber must undergo a longer course of preparation than a classmate who wishes to be a physician or surgeon.[32] When apprenticeships must be served in order to qualify for licensed status, there is no assurance that apprentices will be accepted by the masters to whom they must be articled, or that the training they will receive will in fact be related to their needs.[33] Examination fees are set at high enough levels—sometimes as much as $100 though usually less—to discourage some who might otherwise gamble on passing an examination and being admitted.* A few atypical labor unions have been roundly and no doubt rightly criticized for raising initiation fees so steeply that prospective members have been repelled rather than attracted—the glaziers in Chicago, for example, with their $1,500 fee or the truckers in Seattle with their fee of $500.[34] As in the licensed occupations, the reason is plain. High hourly wage rates attained through collective pressure attract recruits to the trade, just as do high earnings attributable to the incomplete compe-

---

* It is not a satisfactory answer to say that any ambitious youth who wishes to enter a licensed trade may prepare for the tests, satisfy the requirements, and pay the prescribed fee without disaster. A comment made in this connection concerning a photographer's license has a broader pertinence: "A young man who might otherwise begin in a small way to take pictures or develop films for others, and gradually build up a business, is likely to be deterred by the prospect of a stiff examination and fees in excess of the few dollars in sight at the time he otherwise would begin." Frank Hanft and J. Nathaniel Hamrick, Haphazard Regimentation under Licensing Statutes, 17 N. C. L. Rev. 1, at 8–9 (1938).

tition achieved through exclusionary licensing. Hence, unless something is done to frighten these hopeful newcomers away from the favored area, the number of workers may increase disproportionately to the number of jobs. Successful efforts to attain a preferred economic position may therefore unleash the most vigorous activity to prevent others from sharing it.

The guildsmen of the middle ages would not have known what was meant by a controlled economy. Their modern counterparts (some of whom have at least heard those words) have no real desire to be a part of one. Neither the pressure groups that batter at the legislatures nor the legislators who yield to the battering wish to do anything that would alter " the American way of life." Each of the groups merely seeks to line its own nest with a few soft feathers. The occupational lobbies, one governor bitterly remarked, seem to desire free enterprise for others but not for themselves.[35] That sort of inconsistency is understandable enough, but where will it end? If dry cleaners and chiropodists and beauticians are to barricade themselves behind licenses, why not farmers and grocers and clothiers as well? Surely their work is as important, and their economic problems as urgent, as those of the licensed occupations. Americans even now have lost much of their freedom to work as they wish, to develop such skills as they may have and to use them flexibly. If they are not to lose still more, " public interest " must be perceived more broadly than it has been by the expanding list of narrowing occupations. In the end prosperity must be sought by opening economic opportunity to all, not by confining it to a protective association of insiders.

Constitutional Validity

The liberty of which one may not be deprived without due process includes, according to the Supreme Court, " the right of the citizen to be free in the enjoyment of all his faculties; to be free to use them in all lawful ways; to live and work

where he will; to earn his livelihood by any lawful calling
. . ." [36] This tells us nothing, however, about what callings
are "lawful." Statutes, ordinances, and regulations speak
to that question. Once they have spoken, it remains only to
ask whether they have embodied valid restraints on the
citizen's freedom to choose his work. A state cannot, "under
the guise of protecting the public, arbitrarily interfere with
private business or prohibit lawful occupations or impose
unreasonable and unnecessary restrictions upon them." [37]
The words resound, but they have little real bite. Legislatures, not courts, must consider in the first instance whether
a measure is reasonably needed to protect the public health,
welfare, safety, or morals; and for many years the Supreme
Court has presumed that a legislature, when it has adopted
a statute, did in fact have "knowledge of conditions supporting its judgment that the legislation was in the public
interest." [38]

That presumption is not easily overcome in an occupational licensing case. Few imaginable occupations are so
plainly unrelated to the public interest in some aspect as to
make protective statutes appear absurd on their face. True,
the real purpose of an enactment may not be revealed by
the words written in the statute book. The highest court,
however, has wisely declined to inquire into legislative
motives, but has confined its attention to what the legislature actually did. When attention is so confined, there is
little present likelihood that the Supreme Court will strike
down a program of occupational licensing.

The recent case of *Daniel* v. *Family Security Life Insurance Company* is so revealing of the Court's approach that
it warrants extended statement here. [39]

A South Carolina statute forbade life insurance companies
and their agents to operate an undertaking business, and,
similarly, forbade undertakers to serve as agents for life
insurance companies. The law was apparently aimed directly

at the Family Security Life Insurance Company, most of whose agents were undertakers. That company, which was the only one of its kind in the state, issued "burial insurance" in amounts ranging from $125 to $750. It was actuarially sound and was fully complying with all existing insurance laws and regulations. Nor was there doubt about the response to its service, for within four months of its being organized in 1948 it had issued insurance policies totaling $838,375. Then came the prohibitory legislation—legislation which the trial court believed to be invalid because it was not enacted in the public interest but "had its genesis in the desire of the existing insurance companies to eliminate the plaintiff company as a competitor."

When the case reached the Supreme Court on appeal, Mr. Justice Murphy, speaking for a unanimous court, declined to follow this lead. "It is said," he wrote, "that the 'insurance lobby' obtained this statute from the South Carolina legislature. But a judiciary must judge by results, not by the varied factors which may have determined legislators' votes. We cannot undertake a search for motive in testing constitutionality." The test, he added, must be the relationship of the statute to the public welfare. As to that, the Court felt itself "not equipped to decide desirability; and a court cannot eliminate measures which do not happen to suit its tastes . . . We cannot say that South Carolina is not entitled to call the funeral insurance business an evil. Nor can we say that the statute has no relation to the elimination of those evils. There our inquiry must stop."

This judicial self-restraint is not unseemly in a democratic system. As the Court noted in the case under discussion, the appropriate forum for the correction of ill-considered legislation is the legislature itself. In years gone by the Supreme Court too readily confused its own predilections with constitutional principle, and deemed itself justified in vetoing statutes the judges thought unwise. Today, however, the

Court rarely substitutes its preferences for those of the people's representatives. Though the intensification of occupational licensing may be deeply perturbing, one need not look to the Supreme Court of the United States to call an authoritative halt.

In the early days of licensing the state courts, as did the Supreme Court itself in those times, felt free to invalidate distasteful laws. In 1926, for instance, the Kentucky court declared unconstitutional a statutory direction that real estate brokers must obtain licenses, which could issue only upon a showing of good moral character.[40] Real estate brokerage, the court believed, was not likely to affect the public welfare more than many other activities. If this licensing statute were upheld, the court asked rhetorically, why could not the state demand a showing of good moral character before entry into all manner of businesses? Why not, indeed? Kentucky proceeded to extend the " good moral character " requirement ever more broadly; and in 1948 the court overruled its earlier decision that had cast a shadow of doubt upon the legislature's power.[41]

The Kentucky court when it took its second look at the problem reached the same conclusion as most of the state courts in recent years. They have on the whole followed the Supreme Court's lead in sustaining legislative enactments that have an arguably rational basis.[42] A few instances of judicial skepticism serve to remind us, nevertheless, that state court judges who are close to local legislatures are sometimes not very respectful of their intelligence or morals.

When the Maryland legislature, for example, yielded to the barbers' importunities that they be raised to the level of a learned profession, the judges declared that the resulting law was " an arbitrary prohibition rather than a reasonable approach to a lawful and chosen work." [43] The court was depressed rather than impressed by a legislative command that neophyte barbers must receive formal instruction in the

" scientific fundamentals for barbering, hygiene, bacteri-
ology, histology of the hair, skin, nails, muscles and nerves,
structure of the head, face and neck, elementary chemistry
relating to sterilization and antiseptics, disease of the skin,
hair, glands and nails, haircutting, shaving, and arranging,
dressing, coloring, bleaching and tinting of the hair." [44] Perhaps the court would have recognized these imposing words
for the window-dressing they are if it had known that all
the materials covered by this extensive curriculum were
embraced within the covers of a single elementary book of
300 pages.[45] At any rate, other courts have in the main left
it to the legislatures to decide whether and to what extent
the public health may require barbers to become histologists,
hygienists, and diagnosticians as well as haircutters.

A few aspirants to licensed status have run into especially
marked judicial disbelief that public welfare demands their
regulation. Thus the organized florists and watchmakers and
photographers have suffered setbacks at the hands of judges
who declined to allow legislative interference with what the
Oklahoma court described as the citizens' " inherent right to
earn their livelihood in a private field of work." [46]

Occupations like these do not have even a nominal relationship to health or to safety. If they are at all a matter of
public concern, they are so only because inept or dishonest
practitioners of these trades might bilk their customers. The
measurement of that risk, it may be argued, is a task for the
legislature, which must evaluate whether the public needs
protections other than those afforded by the criminal law and
by actions for breaches of warranty, either express or im-
plied. Some courts have simply overridden the legislative
decision, as happened in Georgia when, in striking at a
photographer's license law, the court said: " The business
of photography does not, by its nature or the usual manner of
its conduct, afford any greater or more peculiar opportunity
for fraud than do most of the other common occupations

of life. . . . It should be remembered that people generally
have some capacity for discovering fraud and otherwise
avoiding injury in business transactions; and it might not be
irrelevant to inquire whether all ingenuity in this respect
should be rendered superfluous and brought into a state of
desuetude." [47] The suggested inquiry does indeed seem relevant. But one may ask whether the court or the legislature
should make it.

A constitutional issue of considerably more substance is
suggested by the recent Illinois case of *People* v. *Brown*.[48]
Brown was prosecuted for acting as a master plumber without being licensed as required by state law. He defended by
attacking the law's validity. The Illinois statute required
every would-be plumber to serve a five-year apprenticeship
(or apprenticeship-cum-schooling) in order to become a
journeyman plumber. Apprentices and journeymen alike
were forbidden to work for anyone other than a licensed
master plumber, a status to which a journeyman might aspire
after not less than ten years in the ranks. In short, the
ancient guild structure was erected by act of the state legislature. The court, when it examined this enactment, was
especially struck by the unrestricted power it lodged in the
hands of the master plumbers themselves. " The act," observed the court, " does not load a licensed master plumber
with the obligation of employing a person who desires to
enter into an apprenticeship. The refusal to employ one as
an apprentice need not be based on any valid reason. It may
be an arbitrary refusal, it may be a refusal predicated upon
an understanding between master plumbers to limit the number of apprentices learning the trade, and it may be upon
one, or some, of the facts of race, color or creed. The act
does not allow a person to learn the trade of journeyman
plumber by acquiring the necessary instruction and training
in any way, other than as an apprentice to a licensed master
plumber. . . . The licensed plumber is in full and absolute

control of the situation, a private citizen exercising a power under the protection of the State which the State cannot lawfully exercise, i. e., the arbitrary denial to a citizen of his inherent and inalienable right to engage in a legitimate activity by his own free will and choice." [49]

This approach, which has its parallels in other jurisdictions, is attractive at first blush. The Illinois statute did in truth allow those already holding licenses to control the inflow of future competitors. It did confer a seemingly unlimited power to make discriminatory choices among aspirants to apprenticeship. And it did put all the power of the state behind enforcing the private decisions of the licensees, for none could seek to become a plumber by any other than the prescribed route of apprenticeship.

Even so, the Illinois case is not likely to have much impact on licensing laws. Apprenticeship is so time-honored a device that most judges are likely to accept it without deep questioning. As a matter of fact, they themselves sometimes prescribe it. The highest court of New Jersey, for example, has decreed that persons who wish to practice law in the state must complete a suitable course of study, must pass an examination, must give proof of good character, *and* must serve a "clerkship" of at least nine months under an attorney in good standing. Almost all the barber and beautician laws, almost all the building trades laws, and a great many of the other occupational licensing statutes as well, provide for a period of apprenticeship after completion of prescribed schooling.[50] Analytically all are defective to the same degree as the Illinois plumbing law. Conceivably they could yet fall as did the Illinois statute. But the probability is slim.

The escape route is fairly plain. The state laws will probably be interpreted as conferring on the licensing body the authority to discipline a licensee who abuses his power with respect to apprenticeships. Thus the apparent possibility of discriminatory or exclusionary policies will be said to have disappeared. The reality of their existence will remain. Youngsters who fail to become apprentices are not likely to press charges before an official body. And if they do, the official body, which is usually representative of those against whom the charges might be brought, may not proceed with crusading zeal. Nonetheless, the suggested rationalization will no doubt suffice to safeguard the licensing laws against wholesale invalidation.* Apprenticeship will fall into general disrepute only if its duration is so artifically and unreasonably prolonged as to expose beyond doubt the greediness of those who framed the apprenticeship rules.

The Intrusion of Irrelevancies

Precisely because state power is so little subject to check in this field, special care must be taken to forestall the intrusion of irrelevancies into licensing statutes. Occasionally they do creep in with a certain careless gaiety, as when Georgia enacted that each applicant for a commercial photographer's license must " submit a certificate from the board of health, showing a negative Wasserman test," [51] or when Michigan sought to compel all barbers to be American citizens,[52] a requirement that New York attempted also to impose upon masseurs and chauffeurs.[53] But even the seem-

* Note may be taken here of Kotch v. Pilot Commissioners, 330 U. S. 552 (1947), which, by a five-to-four vote, sustained a Louisiana river pilotage law giving incumbent pilots an unfettered discretion to select the apprentices who, alone, could ultimately become pilots. The discretion was exercised by choosing friends and relatives of the incumbents, a thoroughly discriminatory system if there ever was one, and yet deemed acceptable by a majority of the Court. The case has limited significance, in my opinion, because the judges were heavily influenced by the history and special needs of pilotage as distinct from the generality of occupations. The Court specifically remarked (p. 556) that admission to a trade could not be foreclosed on irrelevant grounds, as would be done if a person were denied " a right to earn a living or hold any job because of hostility to his particular race, religion, beliefs, or because of any other reason having no rational relation to the regulated activity."

ingly irrelevant may be sustained by a court reluctant to substitute its judgment for that of the legislature. The Supreme Court, for example, sustained a local requirement that pool hall operators be American citizens, saying merely that while the premise upon which this requirement apparently rests may not be well founded in experience, there might be local conditions unknown to the Court that would afford a rational basis for the legislative decision.[54] And, rational or not, citizenship has come to be an unchallenged requirement for large numbers of occupations to which it has no discernible relevance.[55] One may perhaps argue reasonably that lawyers should be citizens because their work cuts to the heart of our governmental processes and they are by definition " officers of the court," though in Britain, from which we derive so much of our professional tradition, one may be a barrister while still an alien. Not even a semblance of plausibility supports an argument that chiropodists, tree surgeons, and embalmers (among many others) must be eligible to vote before they may become eligible to seek a license.

Since 1886 race and religion have been recognized to be improper elements for consideration in connection with licensing;[56] nevertheless they may continue to be operative though concealed factors.[57]

Parochialism is also antithetical to the American tradition. Movement from place to place in pursuit of advancement or congeniality has always been an American prerogative. Observers from more static societies, noting our mobility, think of us as almost rootless. But licensing laws may soon anchor Americans to a degree not hitherto experienced. Despite occasional judicial remonstrance,[58] many statutes and ordinances require antecedent local residence as a condition of license eligibility. Restrictions of this sort are not related to the public health, safety, and welfare—the ostensible objectives of licensing laws. Rather, they are calculated to protect local interests against the competition of persons debarred from being licensed not because they lack qualifications but simply because they live on the other side of the highway.* The ultimate consequences are at once apparent. No longer can ear be given to the advice " Go west, young man "—or east or north or south. If a young man is hopeful of engaging in a licensed occupation, he must remain right where he is in order to satisfy residence requirements. Especially is this true when apprenticeship is a necessary preliminary to achieving licensed status, for the apprenticeship must be served under one who already possesses the coveted local license. Even a man already trained and licensed in one state may have to cool his heels for a long period if he has the temerity to move to another.[59]

Elements of the sort just discussed are not true qualifications to be met by a licensee. They are, rather, disqualifications. Standards of proficiency and suitability that relate to the occupation, and that can be met by a purposeful aspirant, are of course entirely defensible. Nor, indeed, is there anything wrong with establishing disqualifications that are not penal or prohibitory in purpose, but will in fact further the legitimate purposes of the licensing regulation—as does, for example, a requirement that all licensed food handlers must be free of communicable disease. Doubts do arise, however, when occupational choices are narrowed by unfunctional definitions of eligibility.[60]

---

* Consider in this connection the remarks of a Providence barber unionist quoted by Sumner H. Slichter, *Union Policies and Industrial Management* (Brookings Institution, 1941), 49–50: " I have settled more strikes for my organization by being a member of the board of state barber examiners than a dozen local unions could have done in my town, and I am secretary of my local. We have settled hotel strikes where they got scab men in there without licenses from out of town. I have gone to the police station and sworn out warrants and taken them out of the barber shops, and two hours afterward had the boss sign up. Now, those are some of the things you can accomplish by that law. . . . It keeps the bums out, and it keeps wages up, and the good barber gets a chance to earn a lot of good money."

Statutes often state, for example, that a license shall not issue to an applicant who has a " criminal record." Of course antecedent criminality may have a bearing upon fitness in some circumstances. A man who has been convicted of heroin peddling may properly be regarded as a questionable risk if he later seeks to be licensed as a physician, in which capacity he will have easy access to narcotics. A person convicted of felonious assault or robbery with fire arms may be less than an ideal recruit to the ranks of taxicab drivers. But these instances fall far short of showing that every felon should be barred from every occupation. Legislatures tend to be undiscriminating and therefore unrealistic in this respect. In Indiana, to pluck one illustration from many, a watchmaker's license may be withheld or withdrawn after " conviction of a felony." [61] Whether the conviction be for statutory rape or for receiving stolen goods, the consequences may be the same though the degree of pertinency seems decidedly different.

Such a statute may possibly be upheld on the ground that the legislature is concerned with " good moral character," which may be evidenced by the past record of law observance.[62] In practical terms, however, a blanket proscription of this sort seems more vindictively punitive than it does selectively preventive. Extension of this exclusionary policy to one licensed occupation after another may simply close every door of hope to a person once sentenced for a crime, by blocking all chances of his becoming rehabilitated in a vocation for which he may be suited. Ernst Freund wrote, years ago, that " it is certainly not the practise of criminal legislation to make permanent civil disqualification a part of punishment." [63] Modern legislatures are too often and too uncritically creating that practice by indirection.

What has just been said concerning the test of former criminality may be applied also to the much more embracive requirement that the licensee be a " person of good moral character." Good character is undoubtedly desirable in everybody, whether under license or not. But to expose everybody's occupational future to some official's appraisal of his moral soundness is quite another thing. Unless the question has a distinct relevance to the subject matter, it ought not to be asked.

Relevance is fairly plain where the licensee will bear heavy responsibilities of a fiduciary character. This is the case with lawyers, securities dealers, and livestock commission merchants, among others. The issue of character is also worth exploring when the occupation is tightly regulated in the public interest, and temptation to ignore the regulations may be especially acute; this may be the case with liquor dealers. Separate investigation of good moral character may be warranted, too, where an occupational category has demonstrably been infiltrated by persons of a lawless bent, with consequent injury to the more law-abiding elements; this seems to have occurred among the longshoremen of the port of New York. Even in these types of cases, great care should be taken to avoid adverse determinations about so imponderable a matter as character; and in no event should a summary procedure be allowed to cut off an individual's opportunity to meet the issues that may be raised.[64] Judgment in this area is inevitably largely subjective, and special pains are therefore required to prevent decisions based on hunch, speculation, or gossip.

In very recent years "loyalty" has come to bulk large in licensing matters. Troubled as most other Americans have been by the issues of Communism and international conflict, licensing authorities have sometimes allowed loyalty oaths and investigations to enter by strange doors. A Texas statute of 1952 requires each applicant for a pharmicist's license to swear that "he is not a member of the Communist party or affiliated with such party, and that he does not believe in and is neither a member of nor supports any group or organization that believes in, furthers or teaches the overthrow of the United States Government by force or any illegal or unconstitutional methods." [65] The relationship between this oath on the one hand and, on the other, the public health which is the interest purportedly protected by the licensing of pharmacists, is somewhat obscure. No more apparent is the justification for requiring professional boxers and wrestlers in Indiana to swear that they are not subversive; [66] if one had consciously wished to manufacture a reductio ad absurdum, one could not have wrought better than did the state athletic commission in this instance. A junior high school teacher of music, having been forced to resign after being identified as a Communist, had difficulty becoming a piano tuner in the District of Columbia because, forsooth, he was " under Communist discipline." [67] Veterinarians in the state of Washington may not minister to an ailing cow or cat unless they have first signed a non-Communist oath, thus assuring that they will not indoctrinate their four-legged patients.[68]

These official actions, while somewhat more bizarre than most, are by no means exceptional.[69] One may confidently predict that they would be held unconstitutional if challenged. Expurgatory oaths and loyalty investigations may sometimes be justifiable, but there is not yet a place for them in every phase of existence.[70] In circumstances like those just suggested, they are totally irrelevant to the objective of the licensing controls. Nor can they be defended on the ground that if a " subversive " is denied an occupational license, he will have no earnings to contribute to organizations of communist orientation. That possibility will exist so long as " subversives " have any income at all, whether or not derived from a licensed occupation. We cannot protect against subversive spending by forbidding " subversives " to attempt to make a living.

The fact is, of course, that the importation of security and loyalty concepts into all the myriad activities now covered by licensing would create risks far greater than could be traced to " disloyal " morticians, opticians, and physicians—if, indeed, any there are. An official finding concerning a disqualifying disloyalty is more likely to reflect a deduction from the licensee's alleged beliefs and rumored associations than a proof of reprehensible deeds. Constant expansion of officials' concern with what private persons think and whom they know is not the way to preserve a free society against being subverted. It is, instead, a step toward self-destruction. We need to remind ourselves from time to time that " every adherence to our moral professions reinforces our strength and therefore our security." [71]

But to say that official concern with " loyalty " is often unwarranted is not to say that it is never warranted. Because their duties bring them into close contact with matters of military significance, maritime workers are subjected to security tests by the Coast Guard, without whose approval they may not obtain purely private employment. The methods and standards used in administering the port security program have been criticized, but, apart from procedural infirmities, the validity of the program itself has not been widely challenged. [72] In that case the damage to individuals who may wrongly be judged " security risks " is plausibly deemed offset by a heightened protection against potential dangers.

A more debatable use of loyalty tests occurs in the legal profession. A number of statutes, rules, and decisions point in the direction of excluding Communists from the practice of law. [73] The theory underlying this has recently been stated by a committee of the Association of the Bar of the City of New York as follows:

In opportunity for direct influence on the minds of youth, sabotage, or espionage, a Communist lawyer is not in as sensitive a position as a school teacher, public employee, or private employee working on defense projects. However, because of his position of public trust, his knowledge of law and procedure, his right to appear for others in court, a Communist lawyer has inherent power to exercise more subtle but possibly equal or greater influence in the carrying out of such unlawful purposes.

But irrespective of number or influence, the intensity of the feeling against Communist lawyers within the bar is based generally upon ethical considerations. Every person upon admission to the New York Bar takes an oath to uphold the Constitution. Upon admission he becomes an officer of the Court. He assumes the responsibility of advising private citizens as to their rights and duties under the law. The very essence of his profession is contrary to the overthrow of the Government by force. Since the two aims are incompatible, any lawyer who purposes a violent revolution should be disbarred.[74]

Some years earlier the Association of American Law Schools had declared that a man's freedom to believe as he sees fit " does not mean that his attitudes toward his chosen profession are irrelevant to his qualifications for that profession." Hence, it continued, " A belief in lawful procedures may properly be demanded of one who undertakes to be a teacher of law. Whatever ideals he may cherish, he must be willing to work for them within the framework of orderly, lawful and democratic processes. The teacher of law with no real belief in the principle of legality is a contradiction in terms." [75] Much this same feeling underlies the conviction that Communists have no proper place in a profession dedicated to the preservation of order. Professor Ralph Brown, in a notably calm and painstaking study of the matter, commented: " Since constitutions are our fundamental source of legality, a willingness to support and defend our constitutional system (which includes procedures for its orderly alteration) would seem to be a prerequisite for a lawyer's faithful performance of his duties *as a lawyer*." [76]

These views have, however, been caustically criticized. One writer, himself a professor of law at the time, exclaimed: " This seems to me to be as large a piece of nonsense as saying that a man who advocates forcible overthrow of government can be excluded from the plumber's trade because he may break the pipes. The analogy highlights the error. Our hypothetical plumber believes in force as a method of altering government, not as a method of plumbing. So a lawyer may believe in force as a method for governmental change without believing in it as a method of practicing law. The fact that he believes in, and advocates, such a method of governmental change cannot be rationally made to show that he will ever represent the interests of any client, in court or outside of court, by any other than peaceful and legal means." A lawyer's license, he added, is solely to practice law. If a lawyer advocates a revolution, he does so not as a lawyer, but " in the same capacity as political scientists, plumbers and other citizens," and should be treated no differently.[77]

Whatever may be the merits of these opposed opinions, concern about " subversive " lawyers is likely to wax larger rather than to diminish. This is not because their number is great or their influence keenly felt. By April, 1956, the Department of Justice had obtained indictments under the Smith Act against not only the varsity team of the Communists, but also the junior varsity, the scrubs, and some of the water boys; only one lawyer was listed among all those indicted for having conspired to advocate and teach the overthrow of the government by force and violence. But the law is a disputatious profession, and lawyers are not going to permit a few cold facts to stop their enjoyably heated dispute about whether Communists should be allowed to belong to the club. The central theme of the debate has attracted so much attention that some very important subsidiary issues have been slighted.

1. Too little distinction is being made between the past and the present. In the State of Washington, for example, the admission oath includes: " I am not now and never have been a member of any organization having as its pur-

pose and object the overthrow of the United States government by force or violence." [78] The insistence on past as well
as present spotlessness raises a question whether an applicant
may not thus be subjected to a punishing disqualification.
The ineradicable stain theory has not been well received in
our jurisprudence. *Ex parte Garland*, one of the post-Civil
War cases, held that a former participant in an armed
rebellion against the government (let alone a mere advocate
of rebellion) could not be punished by eternal banishment
from the legal profession; [79] the wisdom of the holding was
happily confirmed by the subsequent career of Augustus H.
Garland, who ultimately became Attorney General of the
United States. In 1955 the Supreme Court of New Mexico
denied admission to an applicant who had terminated Communist membership in 1940, a dozen years before he became
a law student.[80] Doubt very reasonably exists as to whether
this is a reasonable purification of the bar or a retroactive
punishment for conduct that was not violative of any law in
1940 or of the applicant's obligations as they then existed.

2. When eligibility to obtain or retain professional status
is made to turn solely upon the individual's organizational
connections, no consideration at all is given to the individual's guilty knowledge of or participation in the objectionable purposes of the organization with which he is linked.
One may suppose that by now all the world must know the
widely publicized characteristics of the Communist Party.
But the membership disqualification is by no means confined
to membership in the Communist Party as such. The phrase
commonly in use is "*any* organization that advocates or
believes in the overthrow of the government by force or
violence." Opinions differ concerning the nature of organizations and the propriety of their purposes. The Supreme
Court suggested in *Weiman* v. *Updegraff* in 1952 that caution
must be exercised in ascribing to each member of a group

an awareness or support of all its objectives.[81] Even more clearly, disqualification should not be allowed to hinge on some purely personal relationship; it must not be assumed, without specific proof, that wickedness has rubbed off onto a lawyer from someone else with whom he has been associated.[82] A decade ago New York refused to grant a lawyer's license to an applicant who was a member of Father Coughlin's Christian Front.[83] He was found disqualified because he believed " in the resort to force to overthrow the existing form of government of the United States." In that instance, however, the belief was brought home to him personally through his own words and deeds; it was not simply imputed to him because of his organizational identification or his association with other men.

3. Philosophical beliefs, even obnoxious beliefs, ought not to be given the same disqualifying force as conduct. The Supreme Court, in a five-to-four decision, has said that a state may, if it wishes, regard a conscientious objector as unable or unwilling to support the state constitution by bearing arms in its defense; and for that reason he may be excluded from the bar even though in fact he might never be called upon for military service.[84] The New York Court of Appeals has been more tolerant of conscientious disagreement with the prevailing view concerning arms-bearing.[85] One who will not serve in the militia, though the state constitution authorizes his being conscripted, may perhaps as a matter of cold logic be unable to swear in good faith to support that constitution. Still, in practical analysis, a man who believes in lawful procedures while being utterly repelled by the idea of violence, seems thoroughly suited for a career at the bar. At any rate, wrongheadedness ought to be carefully differentiated from bad character, evidences of which should ordinarily be sought in behavior alone.

4. An applicant's declination to co-operate with an inquiry

should not be regarded as the equivalent of unsatisfactory answers. Of course where an applicant holds relevant information not otherwise readily available to a licensing board, the board may be justified is asking that he disgorge it. But cases are likely to arise in the " loyalty " field in which, for one reason or another, an applicant may conscientiously refuse to answer the bar examiners' questions about political affiliations or opinions.

One such case is *In re George Anastaplo*.[85] Anastaplo, a University of Chicago honor graduate, appeared to believe sincerely that no inquiry should be made into political beliefs or Communist ties. He therefore declined to respond directly to questions touching these matters. At no time did he rely on the Fifth Amendment, containing the privilege against self-incrimination; he rested his case solely on the First and Fourteenth Amendments, with their protection of freedom of belief. Specifically, he would not say whether or not he was a Communist. His examiners, however, were not wholly without information on this point. Anastaplo had himself stated in his application papers, under oath and without any mental reservations, that he supported and would in the future support both the state and the federal constitutions. Moreover, his record was irreproachable; his testimonials from teachers, political and community leaders, and his clergyman were most impressive; there was no breath of scandal about him, so far as appears in the record, unless it be scandalous to think—as Anastoplo did—that Communists should be allowed to practice law if they wished and that " the right to revolt by force of arms if necessary is an inherent and traditional American political theory, as embodied in the Declaration of Independence . . ." [86]

Emerging from all the testimony is a picture of an opinionated, tenacious, and perhaps even over-scrupulous young man who would not hobble his ideas when they began to run ahead of his examiners' opinions. These qualities are not unprecedented among reputable lawyers, and sometimes they are not regarded as positive misfortunes. The examining committee in Anastaplo's case had no patience with them, nor did the Supreme Court of Illinois, which curtly said that it might attach to the " privilege " of practicing law whatever conditions the court might reasonably select—" and if an applicant does not choose to abide by such conditions he is free to retain his beliefs and go elsewhere."

Anastaplo was probably wrong in insisting that revolution is a right. Of course it is true that Jefferson and Lincoln said the same thing; and lawyers often boast of the fact that twenty-six members of their profession were among the fifty-six delegates to the Second Continental Congress, from which issued the revolutionary Declaration of Independence. In reality, nevertheless, the right to revolt comes into being only after a revolution has succeeded, at just about the same moment that its leaders receive garlands as the heroes of " the glorious revolution," instead of being beheaded as the treacherous instigators of a wretched plot. Still, Anastaplo's incomplete grasp of the realities did not wholly unfit him for a profession that has its full share of dreamers, quixotic and otherwise. One may doubt, too, whether the Illinois authorities were wise in resting their decision on an unanswered question when they possessed so much independent evidence that, in effect, provided the answer they sought.

As a matter of fact, the admitting authorities ought to develop more concern about the questions they propound than about the answers they do not obtain.[87] Applicants, it is reported, are very often asked whether they believe that Communists are, or should be, eligible to practice law; in at least one jurisdiction a youngster who gives the " wrong " answer is likely to find himself in trouble. In other instances, the examiners' rather than the applicants' idiosyncracies and colorations are revealed by questioning concerning Americans for Democratic Action, United World Federalists, the American Civil Liberties Union, and other allegedly "pinkish" organizations. In Hawaii the ultimate is perhaps attained. An applicant is interrogated about his connection with every organization among the two hundred odd listed by the Attorney General as subversive, Communist, or otherwise objectionable; then he is asked catch-all questions about past or present membership in baneful organizations; and finally he is confronted with this poser: "If you were to be listed as a 'Communist' in the records of any federal investigative agency, what past actions or organizational affiliations of yours not already listed by you might be used by such investigative agency to support its conclusion? In answering this question, assume that all of your past actions and organizational affiliations are known to such investigative agency." [88]

5. Expulsion from the legal profession rests on different considerations from those that operate in admissions cases. When a lawyer faces discipline, he is being called to account for his record; when an applicant is denied admission, he is being subjected to a predictive judgment. Clearly enough, purging a profession of those who have by their own conduct dishonored it is a social obligation of highest order.

In their enthusiasm to detect and disbar Communists, however, lawyers have sometimes advanced rather dubious programs.

The American Bar Association in 1950 proposed that each member of the bar should periodically swear that he has never been a member or a "supporter" of an organization that espouses governmental overthrow and that he has never been "affiliated" with the Communist Party.[89] This idea was not well received, partly because of the indefiniteness of the terms in which it was framed. Leading lawyers, including John W. Davis, Owen J. Roberts, and Harrison Tweed, joined in deprecating it. The Association of the Bar of the City of New York endorsed the opinion of its Committee

on Law Reform (which included Herbert Brownell, Jr., the
present Attorney General) that a non-Communist oath requirement "might lessen the freedom of the bar to accept
the responsibility of representing unpopular causes." Opposition to the American Bar Association idea was vigorously
voiced in Massachusetts and elsewhere.[90] The proposal was
taken up in two or three states, but seems to have died a
deserved death otherwise.

A current favorite, also sponsored by the American Bar
Association, is a suggestion that an attorney who pleads the
Fifth Amendment in declining to testify in any lawful inquiry, shall be at once investigated by the local bar association.[91] If the attorney does not answer inquiries put to him
during that investigation, then disbarment is advocated.
Thus far this program, well debated within the profession
itself, has not made great headway. The Supreme Court of
Florida in 1955 reversed a disbarment order based entirely
on refusal to answer rather than on positive proof of disqualification, thus following the lead of the New York Court
of Appeals in somewhat comparable cases that arose in less
agitated times.[92]

Lawyers unquestionably have a high obligation of candor,
an obligation that comes into conflict with the constitutional
privilege to remain silent. Some members of the bar believe
most earnestly that, whatever may be the case as to members
of other occupational groups, the attorney's privilege must
not be allowed to take precedence over the attorney's obligation. Their attitude reflects a commendably high resolve
that the legal profession shall not only be free of taint but
shall be above even the suspicion of taint.

Running counter to that view, however, is the lawyer's duty
to defend rather than diminish the nation's constitutional
heritage. That heritage would undoubtedly lose some of its
richness if exclusion from the bar were to be predicated on
invocation of a constitutional protection. No matter how

frequently the courts and legal writers point out that a Fifth Amendment plea is not a confession of guilt, the lay public (and, indeed, some lawyers as well) persist in regarding the exercise of constitutional privilege as a proof of unworthiness. The bar should be able to recognize other people's insensitivities and misconceptions without sympathetically absorbing and, as it were, legitimatizing them. The Fifth Amendment, Dean Erwin Griswold has said, is " a symbol of our best aspirations and our deep-seated sense of justice." [93] Cherished for generations as a safeguard against ancient abuses—abuses that have their contemporary expression in the police states Americans abhor—the Fifth Amendment is now challenged in the name of security. Lawyers can not afford to join in an emotional hunt for perfect security at the expense of traditional liberties. The incautious discarding of one constitutional protection cheapens others as well, for the erosion of values is a process not easy to halt.

The Problem of Administration

Earlier pages have suggested that decisions in the licensing field may be affected by the character of the agencies that regulate an occupation—ostensibly in the public interest. A further word deserves to be said on that score.

Seventy-five per cent of the occupational licensing boards at work in this country today are composed exclusively of licensed practitioners in the respective occupations. These men and women, most of whom are only part-time officials, may have a direct economic interest in many of the decisions they make concerning admission requirements and the definition of standards to be observed by licensees. More importantly, they are as a rule directly representative of organized groups within the occupation. Ordinarily they are nominated by these groups as a step toward a gubernatorial or other appointment that is frequently a mere formality. Often the formality is dispensed with entirely, appointment being made directly by the occupational associations—as happens, for example, with the embalmers in North Carolina, the dentists in Alabama, the psychologists in Virginia, the physicians in Maryland, and the attorneys in Washington. This virtual capturing of the licensing bodies has been justified on the ground that thus political patronage and partisanship have been excluded, while expert and informed administration has been assured.

A less enthusiastic view would be that thus general consideration of the public interest has been effectively subordinated to particularized consideration of group advantage. The latter is not invariably opposed to the former, but the possibility of conflict arises frequently enough to warrant more detachment than the present system assures.

Constricting an appointing authority's choice of personnel to carry out statewide policies has been severely criticized by political scientists,[94] as has the transfer of administrative power directly into the hands of those who are to be regulated.[95] Experience has confirmed the theoretical objections. Minorities within an occupation tend to be ignored when the regulators are chosen by or are sympathetically associated with the dominant element.[96] Agencies composed of public servants, according to one investigation of public administration, " are, for the most part, making an intelligent and conservative use of their Rule-Making Power—while on the other hand, those agencies which are manned, not by State employees, but by members of the vocation and occupation which they purport to regulate, are, for the most part, using the Rule-Making Power far in excess of that which could have been reasonably contemplated by the General Assembly." The investigators reported among their " most prominent discoveries " that " the rules promulgated in many instances unreasonably curtail the free exercise of competition and unreasonably fetter the initiative of persons engaged in the profession or vocations involved; and that admission itself to some of the professions and vocations is unreasonably restricted." [97]

Similar observations have been made in every part of the nation. At the Governor's Conference in 1951 the Governor of Arkansas complained of the large number of virtually autonomous authorities in his state, where they functioned without uniformity, with small assurance of efficiency, and with utter "lack of responsibility to the Chief Executive, to the Legislature, or to the people." [98] He urged a consolidation of boards, a minimization of monopolies by an infusion of lay membership into the administrative body, and an enlarged control over licensing by the governor and legislature. His complaints and his proposals were endorsed by many other governors, some of whom had already had encouraging experiences with centralized license agencies.[99] The chief criticism of the autonomous boards was their tendency to close the doors of opportunity. This tendency was not subject to effective check by the conventional organs of government because, though in fact the licensing boards were exclusionists, they effectively disguised themselves as experts to whose judgment deference must be paid.

The point has not wholly escaped judicial notice. In invalidating a license law for dry cleaners, one court rested its decision in part upon the transfer of governmental power into the hands of a private group. Licensing boards, the court declared, are " legislatively launched and put on their own. . . . Without the aid of the statute these groups would be mere trade guilds, or voluntary associations; with it they become State agencies, retaining, however, as far as possible, distinctive guild features. An exclusive self-governing status is achieved by the device of securing a majority membership on the administrative boards or commissions, and in aid of this the power of the State is heavily involved by way of prosecution in the criminal courts of those who are unable to secure the approval of the Board and obtain license to engage in the occupation." [100] But this clarity of perception is rare; most American courts accept the boards as what they purport to be, that is, governmental rather than occupational agencies. In any event, the problem is not primarily one for judicial so much as for legislative concern.

It is not necessary to think of occupational boards as selfish, venal, or arrogant in order to think of them as inept, inefficient, and costly. Government is surely as serious and complicated a profession (or art or trade) as, say, chiropody, manicuring, or horseshoeing. Accordingly, there is no more reason to imagine that a horseshoer can be a good bureaucrat than to imagine that a bureaucrat can be a good horseshoer. A man may be a master at paring a callus without achieving competence to conduct the formal disciplinary proceedings of a regulatory body dealing with chiropodists. The proliferation of separate boards, each staffed with experienced craftsmen who are wholly inexperienced in statecraft, gives little assurance that laws will be executed effectively. Nor does duplication of files, staffs, facilities, and offices reduce the costs of state government.

The argument is made, however, that only a board drawn from the regulated occupation can have the technical proficiency required for evaluation of license applicants. [101] The solution of this difficulty lies not, as is supposed, in creating more and more trade-minded boards. It lies, rather, in creating a responsible administrative body that, if need be, may employ vocationally experienced staff members and that should in all instances recruit suitable advisory groups from within the affected occupation. A searching and fair chiropodist's examination cannot be drafted by a lawyer or a clergyman or a statistician; but if a licensing agency were made up of such a trio, they need not divorce themselves from the insights others can contribute.

Among the needed insights would unquestionably be those of persons versed in the work of the immediately affected occupational category. In point of fact, however, the examinations given by most licensing boards today are unsatisfactory because the examiners confine themselves too narrowly to their own technical experience. This is only one, and not the sole, source of relevant wisdom. " Proper construction and administration of tests," the Council of State Governments has said, " require the services of experts who can apply the knowledge and techniques gained from numerous investigations conducted in the testing field in recent years." [102] Illinois and Michigan reorganization commissions and other students of the matter have found that " many licensing boards have not had the services of testing experts, and consequently most licensing examinations have not reflected recent advancements in this field. These studies recognize that the practical knowledge of licensing board members is essential in the examining process, but they suggest that the skills of testing experts are also necessary. Finally, they assert that the purposes of the examinations need to be evaluated carefully and that tests then should be constructed to provide the information needed to attain these purposes."

In short, expertness is needed in administering licensing programs as well as other regulatory programs. In the complex modern world, the needed expertness is that of the generalist who can weave together into a workable whole the separate expertness of the specialists.

A Possible Reorientation

Occupational licensing has gone too far. It compresses rather than liberates the economy, stratifies society instead of furthering its democratization. Nevertheless, the excesses and abuses of licensing do not entirely obscure its utility. It does in fact afford protection against suffering at the hands of the blatantly inept or patently corrupt. The question to be considered is whether such protection as is truly necessary (for, after all, there is such a thing as over-protection) can be obtained with less social risk.

First. Occupational licensing must return to first principles. It is—or, rather, should be—a prophylactic measure, intended to save the public from being victimized. It is not—or, rather, it should not be allowed to continue to be—an economic weapon intended to strengthen the licensees.

If prophylaxis and not aggrandizement be the aim, we can struggle along with much less licensing than we have—and certainly without the additional licensing of caterers, canopy and awning installers, cider makers, coal merchants, dancing masters, egg breakers, frog dealers, music teachers, and beer coil cleaners who have recently sought to be regulated. There is always a chance that a customer may be cheated in any money transaction. Nonetheless, the dimensions of the remedy ought to be largely influenced by the size of the problem. Surely there is no evidence at hand that Americans are being subjected to a larger scale ruination of peace of mind, pocketbooks, or physiques than are, let us say, the English, the Germans, or the Canadians. These peoples survive without the plethora of protective laws that are mistakenly regarded in this country as a token of achievement. No doubt they suffer occasionally at the hands of unscrupulous merchants, craftsmen, tradesmen, and semi-professionals. But they believe that a poultice instead of major surgical procedures may suffice to reduce what is, after all, only a small pain in the neck.

Occupational licensing should be reserved for special cases. One special case arises when an occupation of critical public importance has been overrun, and not merely occasionally infected, by persons insensitive to their responsibilities. When the range of effective choice by patrons is wide—as it is, for example, with respect to most of the service trades—the argument for licensing is likely to be weak. When the patron may readily become the victim—when he cannot choose who will serve him (longshoremen) or when he is too distant to know the facts about his servant (stockbrokers and livestock commission agents)—the argument for licensing may be stronger. Even then, the existence of evils ought to be demonstrated, not supposed, before resort to licensing.

A second special case may arise where theoretical training is a necessary step toward achieving occupational competence. The word " necessary " deserves special emphasis. Schooling ought to be prescribed when needed to equip a person for a career, but not when needed chiefly to discourage him from launching one. Intimidation rather than illumination seems to be the objective of some of the present educational requirements. Of eighteen representative states included in a study of barbering regulations in 1929, not one then commanded an aspirant to be a graduate of a " barber college," though apprenticeship was necessary in all.[103] Today, the states typically insist upon graduation from a barbering school that provides not less (and often much more) than 1,000 hours of instruction in " theoretical subjects " such as sterilization of instruments, and this must still be followed by apprenticeship. Opinions may differ about the motives that underlie this striking shift from in-service to in-school training; but at least one man whose memory runs as far back as 1929 doubts that barbering has risen to new heights because of it.

Still, schooling does have its sound uses. In instances when fitness turns upon the acquisition of theoretical insight, the occupation is very likely to have large public importance. The scope of mischief will probably be broader, and the consequences of its occurrence more disturbing, than in cases involving the usual arts and crafts. Sometimes judgments will conflict as to whether an activity is a science concerning which theoretical training is feasible or, by contrast, a bit of masquerade. Phrenology and astrology gulled some sincere persons in the past, and chiropractic and naturopathy have their supporters today. The legislature may have to make hard choices, but it should not issue the credentials of a learned profession to every inventor of a pseudo-scientific jargon who would like to own a money-making school or call himself doctor.

Second. In place of indiscriminate licensing when no urgent need exists for so restrictive and regimenting a device, new thought should be given to the utility of certification. The impersonality of modern life being what it is, many persons are uninformed about the training or qualifications of those with whom they deal. This difficulty can be lessened if a differentiation be made within an occupational category between those who possess certain desired characteristics and those who do not.

Thus, for example, the designation of a nurse as a " registered nurse " gives her a titular distinction that at once identifies her as a person schooled in her calling. In many states anyone may nurse the infirm for pay, but if a *trained* nurse is wanted, the certification of those who are registered serves to indicate the individuals of supposedly greater worth. Similarly, the laws of some states forbid the use of the title of " architect " except by those who have been registered upon proof of training and skill. Anyone may perform architectural planning and design, but he may not lay claim to a designation reserved for persons possessing defined qualifications. Elsewhere, the title of " registered professional engineer " may be used by persons who have met stated standards, but others may discharge engineering functions so long as they do not misrepresent their qualifications by pretending to be registered (and, thus, approved) when in fact they are not.

The distinction between optional certification and compulsory licensing is obvious. The former does not exclude anyone from a calling or business; it simply precludes his mislabeling himself. Occupational licensing does more. It prevents anyone's engaging in the regulated activity until a somewhat inaccessible license has first been obtained, and thus narrows the numbers of those who, under whatever name, may share in the business to be done. For this reason, the occupational organizations prefer the compulsory rather than the optional system. The registered nurses, for example, fight tooth and nail in state after state to obtain passage of laws that will exclude from nursing work anyone who is not a licensed practitioner. The architects have largely succeeded in monopolizing not only the title but the activity as well.

Optional certification meets the public need fairly in a great many fields. Officially declared standards of skill and training serve to separate the genuine from the soi-disant experts; and the permissive use of an appropriate title enables the public to know which is which. At the same time, these steps do not foreclose the development of skills by newcomers; they do not artificially limit the movement of persons within the United States; and they leave the door of opportunity open for men who are occupationally gifted though not conventionally schooled.

Third. Reduced emphasis on the present forms of restrictive licensing does not require return to the horse-and-buggy days of law administration. If private actions at law to recover damages and penal actions to recover fines or, in gross cases, to effect imprisonment were the only weapons in the public arsenal, the bad actors within an occupational group might steal the show as well as the customers' money. Litigation is too slow and too costly to be practical as a remedy. And a fine, which is the usual penalty where mala prohibita are involved, comes to be regarded by the lawless as merely one among other business costs rather than as a deterrent of misconduct.

Fortunately, a more effective control is available. Its model

is a little noticed provision of the Emergency Price Control
Act of 1942. That statute, it will be recalled, authorized
the regulation of prices to counter the inflationary pressures
created by wartime expansion of demands and curtailment of
supplies. Enforcement of regulations could be achieved by
various devices. Violators were subject to the sanctions of
the criminal law. The courts were empowered to enjoin
continued disregard of the economic controls. Individuals
who were overcharged were given the right to sue for treble
damages, plus reasonable fees for their lawyers. Finally, the
Act provided that whenever the Price Administrator felt the
step necessary to effectuate the control program, he could
require the licensing of any person " as a condition of selling
any commodity or commodities." Then, whenever he thought
there had been a violation, the Administrator was to send
the licensee a warning notice. And " if the Administrator
has reason to believe that such person has again violated any
of the provisions . . . the Administrator may petition any
. . . court . . . for an order suspending the license of such
person for a period of not more than twelve months." [104] In
less stilted terms, this meant that dealers in price-controlled
goods and providers of price-controlled services could be
made licensees by operation of law. Their licenses, like those
issued more conventionally in response to a specific application, could then be suspended. Without a license, a person
could not legally remain in business. This sanction was
little used in enforcing price regulations,[105] though a not
dissimilar suspension power was extensively relied upon to
obtain observance of rationing controls.[106]

A comparable plan could be developed in areas of occupational activity that cause especially large public concern.
The legislature could in those areas validly provide for registration of all who wished to be licensed. The license would
issue without more ado upon registration. Doing business
without the required automatic license could be made an

offense, thus encouraging an accurate register of those engaged in the occupation. Then, in order to maintain high levels of rectitude, provision could be made for a decree of suspension or revocation upon a finding, after suitable judicial proceedings, that the licensee had misrepresented his skill or training, had demonstrated his incompetence, or had engaged in dishonorable conduct relevant to his occupation.*

This proposal envisages the creation of an appropriate administrative agency to receive and investigate complaints, to negotiate informal settlements (including consent suspensions), to initiate actions in court by the filing of duly detailed complaints, and to present evidence and argument in the subsequent hearings before the court. While judges cannot be saddled with purely administrative functions lest they be unable to discharge their own judicial responsibilities, none of the tasks here suggested would be other than those appropriate to the courts. The judges would sit in their usual capacity as triers of factual controversies, with power in the end to determine the consequences. Their judgments would resemble in part the penalties they may now impose after infractions of law have been proved, and in

---

* " Dishonorable conduct relevant to the occupation " is a much more meaningful phrase than " good moral character " or similar locutions. The trouble with these is their utter abstraction. In Repouille v. United States, 165 F. 2d 152 (C. A. 2, 1947), for example, a petitioner for citizenship was rejected because he had not had " good moral character " during the five years preceding his petition. He had chloroformed his blind, mute, deformed, and idiot child in circumstances so heartrending that the jury before whom he was tried for first degree murder brought in a verdict of manslaughter in the second degree, with a recommendation of " utmost clemency," and the trial judge had stayed execution of sentence. Nevertheless, in the citizenship proceeding, the court felt that since the practice of euthanasia probably did not conform to " the generally accepted moral conventions current at the time," an adverse finding was necessary as to moral character. Now suppose that Repouille had been a licensed assayer or harbor pilot or boiler inspector, and the question was whether his license should be revoked because he was not a person of good moral character. In such a case, the " bad character " should bear some relationship to the activity under license, or, if it has none, it should be ignored for that purpose whatever its significance might be in other aspects of the licensee's life.

part the equitable decrees of injunction they may issue in appropriate cases.

The advantages of this over the present form of occupational licensing are manifold. In the first place, it would expunge with one stroke the whole complex of problems stemming from selfish efforts to narrow occupational opportunities. It would eliminate the maladroit administration that comes from abdicating effective public control over licensing boards. It would assure fair hearings for licensees under a cloud, by requiring the careful formulation of charges and the presentation of evidence in open court. It would prevent captious findings about an applicant's character, while at the same time giving assurance that the unworthy would be stricken from the rolls if their unworthiness ever became demonstrable.*

In occupational licensing, the choice is not between some regulation and none. The choice is between licensing for the sake of the occupations and, on the other hand, licensing for the sake of the public at large. As matters stand, the citizen's right to use his faculties in a freely chosen career has been squeezed beyond justification. What we need now is fewer but better designed bindings on that right.

---

* It is worth noting in this connection that "character tests" are not likely to screen out any very large number of initial applicants, because at that time few of the applicants will yet have been exposed to the situations in which character defects are brought to light. Thus, it is estimated that in New York, Illinois, and California less than one-half of one per cent of the candidates for admission to the bar are held up by the character committees. During ten years, from 1938 to 1948, only eight out of 3,805 applicants were rejected on recommendation of the character committee in the First Appellate Court District of Illinois. Ralph S. Brown, Jr., and John D. Fassett, Loyalty Tests for Admission to the Bar, 20 U. Chi. L. Rev. 480, at 497 (1953). One may reasonably believe, however, that perhaps a larger number of ill-suited persons might have applied for admission if there had been no screening device at all. Nevertheless, a full record on which to base a judgment about character is not likely to exist at an early stage of a man's career.

Epilogue

THE PRECEDING pages do not tell an altogether cheering or comforting story. They reflect a mounting legislative and administrative insensitivity to the dignity of man as an individual. They show a revival of readiness to hobble minds under the guise of mending morals. They depict the gradual closing of the occupational doors through which energetic Americans have traditionally been free to pass in pursuit of their ambitions.

For all that, catastrophe is not on our doorsteps—or even just around the corner. Only a few—far too many, but relatively only a few—are the victims of legislatively endorsed crudities in the administration of loyalty and security measures; concentration camps are maintained in readiness for the politically suspect, but in fact they are still empty; entrance into and egress from the country are hedged about with cruel traps, but, even so, our nation is far from being hermetically sealed off from the world; the invasion of privacy through excessiveness of policing is a present reality, but not an ever-present one; books of strikingly profuse variety are still published and read despite censorial efforts to dictate their contents; the postal and customs authorities blunder in administering laws aimed at domestic deceptions in the distribution of "foreign propaganda," but notwithstanding their blundering, Americans are perhaps better informed about world affairs than ever before; the stratification of society may be seen as the ultimate consequence of multiplied limitations upon the individual's freedom to choose his occupation, but American economic organization is as yet far from having lost its effervescence.

These reassurances must be stated lest a recital of grievances be taken as a rounded description of the whole. This book deals with defects, not disasters; with flaws, not with failures.

Defects, however, are serious enough. The time for dealing with them is before they do become disasters. No sensible physician delays treating a patient's ailments until he has become moribund.

Freedom is not a monolith, to be possessed altogether or not at all. It is, rather, a mosaic of many tiles. The design may not be noticeably marred by removal of a single tile here, and another one there. Nonetheless, the whole effect may be lost if enough " unimportant " pieces are pried loose.

The danger lies in this: if the change is achieved bit by bit, rather than by sledgehammer blows, the fact of change may be ignored. In a country accustomed to freedom, a citizen can overlook the existence of un-freedom so long as he is not touched personally and the trammels rest only on the other fellow.

Human beings are extraordinarily adaptable to their environment. This quality, so important to physical survival and material advancement, becomes a peril in the realm of the spirit. Individuals acclimatize themselves to an atmosphere of repression as readily as to the malodorous effluvia of the cities in which they live. Restraints too quickly come to be viewed as normalities, illiberality gains too ready acceptance as a way of life, suspicion and hostility too easily supplant trust and friendliness as the dominant elements of man's relationship to his fellow man. Evils must be attacked before they achieve familiarity if toleration of them is to be defeated.

A few years after the end of World War II Los Alamos

clearly illustrated the process of environmental submergence. Perched on a striking mesa in New Mexico not far from Frijoles Canyon and the Bandelier National Monument, Los Alamos and its surroundings might well delight a traveler with an eye for sunlit scenery. When I first visited there, however, my eye was caught not by scenery but by security guards. Machine gun towers and light tanks were more impressive novelties than were the rocks and rills, the woods and templed hills. My credentials were in good order, the officials of the atomic energy installation expected me, the wayfarer was warmly welcomed. Nevertheless my stay was much too brief to habituate me to the differences between an artificially (though no doubt necessarily) restricted community and the open cities in which Americans customarily move. My discomfort, I readily observed, was not shared by those of longer residence in that place. The apparatus of security was unnoticed by eyes grown used to it. The ladies gossiped over their marketing chores, the men went about their affairs with the insouciance or the intensity that would have marked similar activities anywhere. Most of all, the young children (of whom there were many, for Los Alamos was then preponderantly a community of youthful families) grew up with the carefree acceptance of their surroundings that always marks those who have experienced no other. Within the guarded circumference of Los Alamos are smaller enclaves that can be entered only by persons with special clearances. The youngsters rode their tricycles to the boundaries of the forbidden zones, or played cops and robbers around their gates and fences, with complete indifference. They were untouched by the peculiarities of the Los Alamos atmosphere because, for the children, the pecularities were the conventionalities of life.

Just so could long exposure inure most of us to a change in the climate of liberty. An American way of life is conceivable that holds much less expansiveness, much less spontaneity, much less diverse richness than the American way of life we cherish today. Sensitivity to the process of alteration must be manifested before the alteration is completed; afterward, un-freedom would soon find allies in lethargy and custom as well as in the repressive forces that can always be marshalled as its supporters. To remain muscularly free, we must see to it that freedom receives constant exercise.

The mightiness of some issues that shake the modern world tends to shrink the significance of others. If civilization cannot succeed in avoiding its own incineration, the sorts of problems this book has discussed might as well be forgotten now as later. But the essential values of human life and of national character ought not to be abandoned without a struggle—as they are very likely to be if one despairs of being able to preserve them. If we are in fact to survive not merely as a few blobs on a damaged planet but as a society of free men, we must take pains to keep freedoms as well as men alive and vigorous. Today is a perfectly good day for reminding ourselves that the blessings of liberty have been hard won in the past and should not be softly lost in the present through slothfulness, inattention, or doubt.

Notes to Chapter One

[1] James M. Landis, " The Development of the Administrative Commission," an address before the Swarthmore Club of Philadelphia, February 27, 1937; printed in Walter Gellhorn, *Administrative Law* (Foundation Press, 1940), 18.

[2] Kenneth C. Davis, Development of the Administrative Agency, in University of Chicago Conference on Freedom and the Law (1953), 56. Professor Davis also points out that emphasis on " positive government " is reflected in thirty of the thirty-seven national constitutions adopted since 1940, in the form of protection of employment, living standards, health, education, or social insurance.

[3] The " thrill and chill " phrase comes from Louis L. Jaffe, The Effective Limits of the Administrative Process, 67 Harv. L. Rev. 1105, 1107 (1954). Professor Jaffe, be it noted, has for twenty years been one of the coolest and most effective analysts of the administrative process, having viewed it with exemplary detachment amidst the more prevalent stridencies of praise and damnation.

[4] For discussion of the retreat from enthusiasm for central planning, see Michael Polanyi, *The Logic of Liberty* (University of Chicago Press, 1951), 125.

[5] Robert H. Jackson, The Administrative Process, 5 Journal of Social Philosophy 143, 149 (1940).

[6] The bar's pronouncements appear in the report of the American Bar Association's Special Committee on Administrative Law, 59 A. B. A. Rep. at 544, 549 (1934).

[7] The legislative efforts to " improve " the administrative process culminated in the so-called Logan-Walter Bill, vetoed by President Roosevelt on December 18, 1940. House Doc. No. 986, 76th Cong., 3d Sess. The vetoed bill was the latest in a succession that was notable for its variety of form (though not of purpose) and for the absence of any detailed underlying study. For a good review of the developing legislative picture, see Louis L. Jaffe, Invective and Investigation in Administrative Law, 52 Harv. L. Rev. 1201, at 1221–36 (1939).

[8] Former Dean Pound's strictures appeared in the 1938 Report

of the American Bar Association's Special Committee on Administrative Law, 63 A. B. A. Rep. at 346 et seq. (1938). For critical evaluation of this report, see the Jaffe article cited in note 7 above.

[9] Roscoe Pound, For the "Minority Report," 27 A. B. A. J. 664 (1941). During World War II Pound continued to develop the same theme. See his The Challenge of the Administrative Process, 30 A. B. A. J. 121 (1944). Compare Richard H. Field, Rationing Suspension Orders: A Reply to Dean Pound, 30 A. B. A. J. 385 (1944).

Kenneth C. Davis published a stinging critique of Pound's assertions in Dean Pound and Administrative Law, 42 Colum. L. Rev. 89 (1942). Davis was in turn attacked by Edward W. Bailey, Dean Pound and Administrative Law—Another View, 42 Colum. L. Rev. 781 (1942), to which Davis replied with Dean Pound's Errors about Administrative Agencies, 42 Colum. L. Rev. 804 (1942). For another critical evaluation of Pound's contributions to the administrative law debate, see Jerome Frank, *If Men Were Angels* (Harper, 1942), Ch. 5 and Appendix VII.

[10] The Ohio broadside against the administrative process came from E. F. Woodle (then president of the Bar Association in Cleveland), Let's Decide Every Case on Its Merits, 28 J. Am. Jud. Soc'y 118–19 (1944); also printed under the title, We Cannot Have Two Systems of Doing Justice, Ohio L. Rep. (October 9, 1944).

[11] The Administrative Procedure Act is 60 Stat. 237, 5 U. S. C. A. 1001.

[12] For Congressional splutterings of indignation about "the subversion of the administrative process," see, e. g., addresses of Senators Lehman, Morse, Humphrey, and O'Mahoney, 101 Cong. Rec. 11053, 11065, 11066, 11072 (August 2, 1955). For scholarly demonstrations tending to support the Lehman thesis, see The NLRB under Republican Administration: Recent Trends and Their Political Implications, 55 Colum. L. Rev. 852 (1955); The "Eisenhower" Board: Taft-Hartley under a Republican Administration, 4 Utah L. Rev. 380 (1955); Clyde W. Summers, Politics, Policy Making, and the NLRB, 6 Syracuse L. Rev. 93 (1954); and compare J. Kaczmarek, Change in Labor Relations: Progress or Pendulum, 43 Geo. L. J. 477 (1955); The Disputed Policies of the New Labor Board—A Symposium, 43 Geo. L. J. 335 (1955).

[13] Among academic advocacies of stronger judicial action see Kenneth C. Davis, Development of the Administrative Agency, University of Chicago Conference on Freedom and the Law (1953), 58,

61, and the same author's Standing to Challenge Governmental Action, 39 Minn. L. Rev. 353 (1955); Louis B. Schwartz, Legal Restrictions of Competition in the Regulated Industries: An Abdication of Judicial Responsibility, 54 Harv. L. Rev. 436 (1954). And compare Eugene V. Rostow, The Democratic Character of Judicial Review, 66 Harv. L. Rev. 193 (1953).

[14] Wong Yang Sung v. McGrath, 339 U. S. 33, modified 339 U. S. 908 (1950).

[15] As to commingling of administrative functions, see Walter Gellhorn, *Federal Administrative Proceedings* (Johns Hopkins, 1941) 23–24.

[16] The Secretary of Labor's Committee on Administrative Procedure, The Immigration and Naturalization Service (mimeo. 1940), 77, 81–82. The members of the committee were Professor Marshall Dimock of the University of Chicago, Professor Henry M. Hart, Jr. of the Harvard Law School, and Professor John McIntire of George Washington University.

[17] Legal periodical commentary on Wong Yang Sung v. McGrath may be found in 25 Notre Dame Law. 723; 11 Ohio St. L. J. 570; 98 U. Pa. L. Rev. 920; 18 Geo. Wash. L. Rev. 557; 48 Mich. L. Rev. 1127; 25 N. Y. U. L. Rev. 638.

[18] The overruling of the Federal Administrative Procedure Act by the McCarran-Walter Act is recognized by the Supreme Court in Marcello v. Bonds, 349 U. S. 302 (1955). On January 6, 1956, the Attorney General announced new regulations, 21 Federal Register 97, modifying 8 C. F. R. 242.53. Despite the statutory authorization of commingling of functions, the new regulations look in the direction of discouraging the performance of " prosecuting " functions by the officer who presides over a deportation hearing. The new regulations have been praised as an improvement, but have been criticized as not going far enough. See Will Maslow, Recasting our Deportation Law: Proposals for Reform, 56 Colum. L. Rev. 309, at 350–53 (1956).

[19] For a recent comprehensive discussion of attitudes toward the foreigner, see John Higham, *Strangers in the Land* (Rutgers, 1955), esp. pp. 186, 194 et seq. And see also William C. Van Vleck, *The Administrative Control of Aliens* (Commonwealth Fund, 1932), Ch. 1.

[20] For allusions to the security of judicial as compared with administrative action affecting aliens, see, e. g., Ng Fung Ho v. White, 259 U. S. 487 (1922); White v. Chin Fong, 253 U. S. 90 (1920).

[21] As bearing on suppression of information at the source, see, among other things, a report on government news suppression by a very experienced and conscientious journalist Allen Raymond, *The People's Right to Know* (American Civil Liberties Union, 1955); Kent Cooper, *The Right to Know* (Farrar, Straus and Cudahy, 1956), esp. pp. 193 et seq.; and, generally, Harold L. Cross, *The People's Right to Know* (Columbia University Press, 1953). As to complaints by scientists that acute preoccupation with protecting "scientific secrets" has led governmental authorities to withhold from our own research workers data that would facilitate their producing still more secrets, see Norbert Weiner, *The Human Use of Human Beings* (Houghton Mifflin, 1950), Ch. 8, esp. 135; and see also Walter Gellhorn, *Security, Loyalty, and Science* (Cornell, 1950), 9–75. At hearings before the House Committee on Government Operations in March, 1956, restrictions on information were severely criticized by men of science including Lloyd V. Berkner, president of Associated Universities, Inc. (Brookhaven National Laboratory), Harold C. Urey, University of Chicago, a Nobel laureate, and Detlev W. Bronk, president of the National Academy of Sciences. Representative John E. Moss, chairman of the subcommittee before which their testimony was given, declared that application of research results "to important technological developments has been delayed and even prevented altogether because of a fetish for extreme secrecy imposed on the scientific community." He added: "There is every indication that the more information there is made available, the greater will be the nation's security." *New York Times*, March 10, 1956, p. 35, col. 3; March 11, 1956, p. 21, cols. 1–2.

Valuable comments will also be found in Robert Cutler, The Seamless Web, 57 Harvard Alumni Bulletin 663 (1955) (pro-news suppression), and in Carroll Binder, Secrecy vs. Security in a Free Society, 57 Harvard Alumni Bulletin 666 (anti-news suppression). For other suggestive comments on the problem, see David Riesman, "Civil Liberties in a Period of Transition," *Public Policy, 1942* (Friedrich and Mason, eds.; Harvard, 1952), 48; Paul Blanshard, *The Right to Read* (Beacon Press, 1955), 120; William A. Robson, *Justice and Administrative Law* (3d ed.; Stevens & Sons, 1951), 573–75.

[22] The comment on registration of Communist presses is by J. R. Wiggins, executive editor of the *Washington Post* and *Times-*

Herald, in an address entitled "On Making Martyrs," delivered at Colby College, Waterville, Maine, November 4, 1954.

[23] Hamilton's comments, which were made in connection with the possible necessity of a standing army, appear in *Federalist Papers* (Modern Library ed.), No. 8, p. 42.

[24] The quoted phrase about the clash of rights comes from a letter addressed to Justice Harlan F. Stone by his colleague Justice Felix Frankfurter, May 27, 1940, concerning the flag salute case (Gobitis) then before the Supreme Court for decision. The letter is printed in full in Alpheus T. Mason, *Security Through Freedom* (Cornell, 1955), 217-18.

[25] Our country has rightly emphasized its Christian origins and its underlying doctrine that all men are brothers; yet there has always been among Americans a latently powerful element of hatred of fellow men who happened to be Catholics or Jews or Negroes or foreigners. Persons prejudiced against one ethnic or cultural group are prone, according to the evidence of recent extensive studies, to be hostile to others as well. Liking "their own sort of people," they reject those who are "different." Chauvinism— or, to use a more flattering and thoroughly misdescriptive term, One Hundred Percent Americanism—is a projection of this attitude. It represents not so much a critical admiration of one's own country and people as an uncritical distaste of the rest.

The studies of prejudice referred to above are those of T. W. Adorno *et. al.*, *The Authoritarian Personality* (Harper & Bros., 1950). For criticism and evaluation, see Richard Christie and Marie Jahoda, eds., *Studies in the Scope and Method of "The Authoritarian Personality"* (Free Press, 1954). For a layman's "distillation" of the Adorno group's studies, see Selma G. Hirsch, *The Fears Men Live By* (Harper & Bros., 1955); and see also Gerhart Saenger, *The Social Psychology of Prejudice* (Harper & Bros., 1953), esp. Ch. 9.

[26] The able historian Hofstadter links ethnic prejudice with pseudo-conservatism, believing that "it is merely the expediencies and the strategy of the situation today that cause groups that once stressed racial discrimination to find other scapegoats"—to move on "from anti-Negroism and anti-Semitism to anti-Achesonianism, anti-intellectualism, anti-nonconformism, and other variants of the same idea." Richard W. Hofstadter, The Pseudo-Conservative Revolt, 24 American Scholar 9, at 24, 25 (Winter 1954–55).

[27] Edmond Cahn, in *The Moral Decision* (Indiana University

Press, 1955), 178, identifies "allegiance through principled recalcitrance" as a paramount manifestation of true allegiance, and
notes that "throughout the nation's history it has been closely
associated with our finest political figures."

[28] Judge Hand's words appear in an address delivered before
the American Jewish Committee, printed in the *New York Times*,
January 30, 1955, p. 68, col. 4. The address was published by the
American Jewish Committee in 1955 under the title "A Fanfare
for Prometheus." The quoted portion appears on pp. 4–5 of that
publication.

[29] John Stuart Mill, *On Liberty* (reprint; Oxford University Press,
1952), Ch. 3, 81.

[30] Walter Bagehot, *The Metaphysical Basis of Toleration* (1874),
printed in Vol. III of his *Literary Studies* (new ed., 1895), reprinted
in Howard Mumford Jones' *Primer of Intellectual Freedom* (Harvard, 1949), 80.

[31] Judge Prettyman's discussion of "guesstimates" appears in
American Airlines v. Civil Aeronautics Board, 89 U. S. App. D. C.
365, 192 F. 2d 417 (D. C. Cir., 1951).

[32] The reminder about St. Paul's stone throwing comes from
John Stuart Mill, *On Liberty*, Ch. 2, 33. Mill also points out that
Marcus Aurelius, certainly one of the most enlightened and most
ethically motivated men of his age, felt it proper to authorize the
persecution of Christians because he "knew" their teaching was
false and ruinous. "Unless any one who approves of punishment for
the promulgation of opinions, flatters himself that he is a wiser and
better man than Marcus Aurelius—more deeply versed in the wisdom
of his time, more elevated in his intellect above it—more earnest in
his search for truth, or more single-minded in his devotion to it when
found; let him abstain from that assumption of the joint infallibility
of himself and the multitude. . . ." (p. 35.)

[33] The power to withhold deportation is granted by section 243
(h) of the Immigration and Nationality Act of 1952, 60 Stat. 212,
8 U. S. C. A. sec. 1253(h). A similar power existed under sec. 20
of the Immigration Act of 1917, as amended in 1950. The earlier
section, however, did not so clearly make the Attorney General's
mere *opinion* decisive; under the preceding law, the Attorney
General had to *find* that a deportee would not be persecuted, and
this finding was presumably to be based on recorded evidence.

[34] As to the discretionary nature of the power to withhold deportation, and the propriety of exercising that power on the basis of

secret evidence, see Namkung v. Boyd, 226 F. 2d 385 (C. A. 9, 1955) ; United States ex rel. Dolenz v. Shaughnessy, 206 F. 2d 392 (C. A. 2, 1953) ; and see also United States ex rel. Leong Choy Moon, 218 F. 2d 316 (C. A. 2, 1954) ; Chiu But Hao v. Barber, 222 F. 2d 821 (C. A. 9, 1955), certiorari granted Nov. 7, 1955, but subsequently remanded to dismiss judgment as moot, 350 U. S. 878. Cf. Maeztu v. Brownell, 132 F. Supp. 751 (D. C. D. C., 1955), in which District Judge Morris was shocked that a discretionary power to suspend deportation had been exercised on the basis of secret evidence: " To say that these plaintiffs, the parents of three American children, should be deported, which also means in effect the deportation of such American children, upon the basis of ' confidential information,' which may be no more than anonymous hearsay rumors, or even unexplained membership in some organization listed by the Attorney General as subversive, is to deny that the Government is competent to function in such fashion as to give every one with which the Government deals the right to know upon what basis such action is taken. There is no place in this Government, in its legislative, judicial or executive departments, for arbitrary action, and there is no way to know whether such action is arbitrary or not, unless the basis upon which it is taken is revealed." Contrary to the Maeztu case are Jay v. Boyd, 224 F. 2d 957 (C. A. 9, 1955), affirmed by the Supreme Court on June 11, 1956, in a 5–4 decision, 76 S. Ct. 919, and United States ex rel. Matranga v. Mackay, 210 F. 2d 160 (C. A. 2, 1954), certiorari denied 347 U. S. 967 (1954). Administration of the discretionary power to suspend deportation is critically discussed in the Rights of Aliens in Deportation Proceedings, 31 Ind. L. J. 218, at 227 et seq. (1956).

[35] The Korean Communist's case is that of Namkung, cited in note 34 above. Inquiry to the representative of a foreign government is said not to be a general practice. " In a single instance a subordinate official made such an inquiry without so far as appears any authorization to do so." United States ex rel. Dolenz v. Shaughnessy, 206 F. 2d. 392, at 395 (C. A. 2, 1953).

[36] The case of the trembling Titoist first appeared as United States ex rel. Dolenz v. Shaughnessy, 200 F. 2d 288 (C. A. 2, 1952), certiorari denied, 345 U. S. 928 (1953) (Black and Douglas, JJ., dissenting). Judge Clark, dissenting in the Court of Appeals, said (p. 292) that upon " reading this record—containing nothing to challenge the alien's contention—hardly any of us would doubt the

fate awaiting this renegade Communist if returned to the communist
country where he had joined the party as a boy." He deplored his
court's quickness to hold that a person was entirely "subject to
the unreviewable and uncontrollable doom of a governmental
official."

"Doom" is not too strong a word. In at least one known case
a defector who was deported to an Iron Curtain country was
promptly executed upon his arrival there. See Hearings before the
Subcommittee of the Senate Appropriations Committee, 83rd Cong.,
2d Sess., Part 1, pp. 167–68 (1954).

[37] The Chinese case is that of Chiu But Hao, 222 F. 2d 821
(C. A. 9, 1955).

[38] The criticisms of the administrative judgments about withholding of deportation come from Report on the Administration
of the Immigration and Nationality Act (U. S. Government Printing
Office, 1955), 68–70. The task force was created in 1954 by the
then chairman of the Judiciary Committee, Representative Chauncey
W. Reed. It functioned under the direction of Walter M. Bester-
mann, Legislative Assistant to the Committee on the Judiciary.

Drawing for his information on studies made for the Hoover
Commission and other governmental bodies, Will Maslow, in Recasting our Deportation Law: Proposals for Reform, 56 Colum.
L. Rev. 309 (1956), has shown (pp. 350–51) that of the ninety
hearing officers who acted in these matters in 1954, only twenty-four
had had any legal training at all and only nineteen were attorneys;
in 1952, only 40 per cent of the group had college degrees; they
lacked tenure and received lower salaries than were paid to hearing
officers in other government agencies.

[39] Information about visa officers in the consular corps comes
from Report of the President's Commission on Immigration and
Naturalization, Whom We Shall Welcome (U. S. Government
Printing Office, 1953), 132. The report states, among other things,
that only three per cent of our consuls have had schooling in law,
though modern visa issuance requires skill in handling multitudi-
nous and complex legal materials. The figure comes from information supplied by the Department of State, appearing in Hearings
before the President's Commission (House of Representatives Committee Print, 82d Cong., 2d Sess., 1952), 1864, 1865. And see
also Charles P. Schwartz, American Immigration Policy, 55 Colum.
L. Rev. 331, at 338 (1955).

[40] Mr. Berle's remarks about consuls appear in hearings before

the House Committee on Un-American Activities, Proposed Legislation to Curb or Control the Communist Party of the United States, 80th Cong., 2d Sess. (1948), 259.

The most thorough discussion of the consular visa-veto power will be found in Harry N. Rosenfield, Consular Non-Reviewability: A Case Study in Administrative Absolutism, 41 A. B. A. J. 1109 (1955).

[41] The question of consular veto power came up in connection with discussion of whether visa issuance should be transferred from the Department of State (consuls) to the Department of Justice (Immigration and Naturalization Service). The Senate Judiciary Committee, then making the studies that preceded the McCarran-Walter Act, favored retaining the existing " multiplicity of control " because, as indicated, it built " additional fences of protection which the alien must surmount." Sen. Rep. No. 1515, 81st Cong., 2d Sess. (1950), 332.

[42] For discussion of the untoward effects of diminished good will as a consequence of visa administration, see Report of the President's Commission on Immigration and Naturalization, Whom We Shall Welcome (U. S. Government Printing Office, 1953), 66. Professor Edward A. Shils, of the University of Chicago, is quoted as saying (Report, 69) that the handling of visas " is not only injurious to American science and injurious therefore to American development and welfare and to American intellectual achievement; it is injurious to the achievement of the ends of foreign policy. Every time a visa is refused to an eminent European scientist or scholar, and many times when it isn't, it gets into the Communist press. Of course. . . . Communists believe what they believe and . . . [we] can't do much about that, but there are a large number of people in Europe who are not Communists, who are pro-American and want to be, and they find it difficult to defend American policy when America behaves in this way."

[43] The cancellation of scientific congresses is indicated in the same report on p. 67. Some of the drastic implications for American science are reflected in a special issue on American Visa Policy and Foreign Scientists, 8 Bulletin of the Atomic Scientists 209 ff. (1952) ; and see also American Visa Policy: A Report, 11 Bulletin of the Atomic Scientists 367 (1955).

[44] The comment about consular shyness may be found in Report on the Administration of the Immigration and Nationality Act (U. S. Government Printing Office, 1955), 83.

[45] The American Bar Association recommendation about a Board of Visa Appeals appears in 7 Administrative Law 235 (1955), commenting on bills introduced by Senators Lehman and Ives in 1955, which would provide, among other things, for such a board. The Department of State has itself established an informal body to which cases may be referred for advice; but power of ultimate decision still rests with the consul, so that the body can scarcely be deemed a " review board " or a " board of appeals." In many instances its chief effect has been to delay favorable decisions that the consul was hesitant to make without first " passing the buck " to headquarters. See Eliot B. Coulter, Visa Work of the Department of State and the Foreign Service, 28 Dep't State Bull. 195 (1953).

[46] Justice Brandeis characterized deportation orders in Ng Fung Ho v. White, 259 U. S. 276 (1922).

[47] The " banishment or exile " phrase comes from Fong Haw Tan v. Phelan, 333 U. S. 6, 10 (1948); and see also Jordan v. De George, 341 U. S. 223, 231 (1951).

[48] The case of the hapless ex-Communist is Galvan v. Press, 347 U. S. 522 (1954). The words quoted from Mr. Justice Black are found in his dissent on p. 533. See also, as showing the Court's seemingly reluctant but nonetheless firm upholding of Congressional power to authorize extreme administrative action in this general area, Harisiades v. Shaughnessy, 342 U. S. 580 (1952). President Eisenhower has recommended to Congress that it re-study the question of whether deportation should be allowed in the case of former " subversives," because this may result in the ouster of an alien who has more recently " conducted himself as a model American." Letter to Senator Watkins from the President, dated April 6, 1953, in 99 Cong. Rec. 4321 (1953).

[49] Recognition of the increasing severity of the expulsion power is stated in the Harisiades case, cited in note 48 above, on p. 588.

[50] The figures concerning departures of aliens during 1931–40 and 1950 come from Milton R. Konvitz, *Civil Rights in Immigration* (Cornell, 1953), 207. The figure for 1952 comes from the Annual Report of the Attorney General for that year, p. 27; the 1954 figure comes from the Attorney General's report for the year which ended June 30, 1954, pp. 46–47. A substantial reservoir of potential deportees remains. It has been estimated that when the McCarran-Walter Act became effective on December 24, 1952, there were between three and five million illegally resident aliens who might be deported regardless of their length of residence.

Sidney Kansas, Immigration and Nationality Act (4th ed.; Immigration Publications, 1953), 40.

[51] The 1945–54 total of deportations for "subversive or anarchistic" activities comes from the Immigration and Naturalization Service Annual Report for 1954, Table 33. For further discussion of the significance of these figures, see Will Maslow, Recasting Our Deportation Law: Proposals for Reform, 56 Colum. L. Rev. 309, at 334 (1956). Despite the small number of cases involving "subversives" that are brought to the hearing stage, the Department of Justice has announced that 14,500 "subversive investigations" involving aliens were pending on June 30, 1955. Department of Justice Press Release, July 20, 1955.

[52] The case of the former marihuana delinquent is Marcello v. Bonds, 349 U. S. 302 (1955).

[53] As to employment beyond our borders, Executive Order 10459, June 4, 1953, created an International Organizations Employees Loyalty Board which passes on the loyalty of American nationals who are being considered for work on the staffs of international agencies. One rather rum consequence of the delays in "clearing" Americans for these employments is that the international agencies simply turn to other quarters in order to recruit personnel who will be available when needed, so that American job applicants increasingly lose out in competition with nationals of other countries who make no bones about their lack of loyalty to the United States. See article by C. L. Sulzberger, "When Security Defeats Its Own Purpose," *New York Times*, September 26, 1955, p. 22, col. 5.

[54] As to the time lag between arrest and decision, one informed writer says that "From 1946 to 1951 the Immigration and Naturalization Service was so far behind in adjudicating cases that it required from four to eight years before a case was finally determined. . . . At the present time [1953] about two years are required; unless it is a suspension case in which event it may require four years . . . eventually it may only require one year to terminate a case from the time the alien is taken into custody for deportation; much sooner if the alien is detained." Sidney Kansas, Immigration and Nationality Act (Immigration Publications, 1953), 43.

[55] Zydok's case is reported sub nom. Carlson v. Landon, 342 U. S. 524 (1952). The Court's description of him appears on pp. 532–33.

It is important to stress that the decisions now under discussion are made by the hearing officers whose limited qualifications are described in note 38, above. The Attorney General's judgment is rarely brought to bear on these matters or, indeed, on any other individual cases in the deportation process. The chairman of the Board of Immigration Appeals has testified that the Attorney General reviews about a dozen cases a year. Hearings before the House Appropriations Committee on Justice Department Appropriation for 1956, 84th Cong., 1st Sess. (1955), 37. A recent writer puts the number even lower, having found only 35 cases during a seven-year span that were reviewed by the Attorney General. Will Maslow, Recasting Our Deportation Law: Proposals for Reform, 56 Colum. L. Rev. 309, at 358 n (1956).

[56] United States ex rel. Knauff v. Shaughnessy, 338 U. S. 537 (1950).

[57] For the post-Supreme Court developments in this case, see Ellen Knauff, *The Ellen Knauff Story* (Norton, 1952).

Light has recently been shed on the meaning of " confidential information." Mr. Justice Black, dissenting in Jay v. Boyd, 76 S. Ct. 919, at 930 (1956), writes: " According to officers of the Immigration Service it may be ' merely information we received off the street '; or ' what might be termed as hearsay evidence, which could not be gotten into the record . . .'; or ' information from persons who were in a position to give us information that might be detrimental to the interests of the Service to disclose that person's name . . .'; or ' such things, perhaps, as income-tax returns, or maybe a witness who didn't want to be disclosed, or where it might endanger their life, or something of that kind. . . .' Hearings before House Subcommittee on Legal and Monetary Affairs of the Committee on Government Operations, on Practices and Procedures of the Immigration Service, 84th Cong., 1st Sess., 18, 67, 138, 207."

[58] Shaughnessy v. United States ex rel. Mezei, 345 U. S. 206 (1953).

[59] Archibald MacLeish, " The Alternative," a lecture delivered at Columbia University, March 21, 1955, under auspices of the Roger N. Baldwin Civil Liberties Foundation; printed in 44 Yale Review 481 (1955).

[60] Carl Becker, *Freedom and Responsibility in the American Way of Life* (Knopf, 1945), 18.

[61] For a discussion of the British legislation, see Sir Cecil T. Carr, Crisis Legislation in Britain, 40 Colum. L. Rev. 1309 (1940) ; and compare Cornelius P. Cotter, Constitutionalizing Emergency Powers: The British Experience, 5 Stan. L. Rev. 382 (1953) ; Paul B. Rava, Emergency Powers in Great Britain, 21 B. U. L. Rev. 403 (1941).

For a retrospective examination of the matter, reflecting considerable relief that things did not turn out so badly as one might have expected, see Rule of Law, A Study by the Inns of Court Conservative and Unionist Society (Conservative Political Centre, 1955). The committee that prepared this study was chaired by Sir Patrick Spens, K. B. E., Q. C., M. P.; J. E. S. Simon, Q. C., M. P. was its vice-chairman.

[62] Ralph S. Brown, Jr., Loyalty-Security Measures and Employment Opportunities, 11 Bulletin of the Atomic Scientists 113, at 117 (1955).

[63] Chief Justice Warren's estimate appears in " The Law and the Future," *Fortune Magazine* (November, 1955), 106, 229. The editors of that magazine advanced the estimate of 20,000,000 as did Harry P. Cain in an address, " Strong in Their Pride and Free," delivered at the 1955 Conference of the National Civil Liberties Clearing House and printed in pamphlet form by the American Civil Liberties Union in June, 1955.

[64] *National Science Foundation, Fifth Annual Report (U. S. Government Printing Office,* 1955) at 18–19; summarized in 34 Chemical and Engineering News 928 (February 27, 1956).

[65] Among the sober and effective critics of cancelling open, unclassified research projects has been been John T. Edsall, of the Biological Laboratories at Harvard, whose Government and the Freedom of Science appears in 121 Science 615 (1955). See also *Medical Research: A Midcentury Survey* (Little, Brown, 1955), Vol. I, 185 et seq.; Edward A. Shils, *The Torment of Secrecy* (Free Press, 1956), esp. 178 et seq. And see a statement of the board of directors of the American Association for the Advancement of Science, Strengthening the Basis of National Security, 120 Science 957 (1954). An eminent presidential committee reported to President Eisenhower in 1956 that " loyalty " questions should not be allowed to enter into the making of grants for unclassified research. " So long as the scientific integrity of an individual is unaffected by political, moral, ideological, loyalty or other attitudes or commitments," the committee declared, " those attitudes and commitments have no bearing on the merits of his research. Lack of scientific integrity from whatever cause will be revealed inevitably by the normal critical scrutiny to which the free and open work of every scientist is subjected throughout his career by fellow scientists." Disloyalty is not to be condoned in any citizen, the committee said, but " We do believe that the proper objectives of government in

sponsoring basic research will be best served by concentration on scientific competence alone." Progress in the attack on cancer, for example, "would be no less beneficial to all humanity for having been made by a Communist." *New York Times*, April 5, 1956, p. 5, col. 1; the full text is also printed in 123 Science 660 (April 20, 1956); 12 Bull. of the Atomic Scientists 227 (1956). The Public Health Service, through which many medical research grants are made, moved quickly toward adoption of the committee's views. 123 Science 651 (April 20, 1956); *New York Times*, April 22, 1956, p. 1, col. 2.

⁶⁶ The Zwicky story is reported by Herbert Brucker, Editor of the Hartford Courant, in Public Libraries Division Reporter (October, 1955), 6. Zwicky, who has resided in this country since 1925, is quoted by Brucker as saying: "I would apply for American citizenship tomorrow if you did not have two classes of citizens. If you are a naturalized citizen, you are a second-class citizen. My friend Professor Herman Weyl, the great mathematician, became an American citizen without studying the class rule. So his citizenship was taken away because he went to Zurich to lecture and stayed abroad too long. If I am more free as a Swiss than as an American, I stay Swiss."

⁶⁷ The Supreme Court's reminder about the history of liberty is contained in McNabb v. United States, 318 U. S. 332, 347 (1943), per Frankfurter, J.

The late Mr. Justice Robert H. Jackson, in *The Supreme Court in the American System of Government* (Harvard, 1955), 71, wrote: "I believe that the safeguard of our liberty lies in limiting any national policing or investigative organization, first of all to a small number of strictly federal offenses, and secondly to nonpolitical ones.

"The fact that we may have confidence in the administration of a federal investigative agency under its existing heads does not mean that it may not revert again to the days when the Department of Justice was headed by men to whom the investigatory power was a weapon to be used for their own purposes."

⁶⁸ The estimate about informants' unreliability was made by Eleanor Bontecou, Due Process in Security Dismissals, 300 The Annals of the American Academy of Political and Social Science, at 107 (July, 1955).

⁶⁹ Greene v. Secretary of State for Home Affairs, [1942] A. C. 284. See also Liversidge v. Anderson, [1942] A. C. 206. For an able and comprehensive discussion, see Cornelius P. Cotter, Emer-

gency Detention in Wartime: The British Experience, 6 Stan. L. Rev. 238 (1954).

The power to detain under Regulation 18B of the British Defence Regulations is similar to the power conferred upon the federal government by the Internal Security Act of 1950, 65 Stat. 1021, 50 U. S. C. §§ 812, 813, to seize and detain an individual as to whom, in time of war or national emergency, there is a belief that he may engage in, or conspire to engage in, espionage or sabotage. During 1953 five detention facilities, with a capacity of close to 15,000, were " activated " by the Department of Justice, to be ready to receive persons in preventive detention if there were an internal security emergency. The Department of Justice had disclosed two years earlier that it had already compiled a list of 14,000 persons to be taken into custody if war were declared. See The Internal Security Act of 1950, 51 Colum. L. Rev. 606, at 646, n. 380 (1951). During World War II, the United States detained (without charges of penal offense) some 70,000 citizens and 42,000 non-citizens. Arnold Brecht, The Concentration Camp, 50 Colum. L. Rev. 761, at 766 (1950). This figure may be contrasted with the more moderate British totals during the five critical war years 1939–1944: 1,810 altogether, of whom 24 were aliens and 812 were citizens of enemy alien origin. (These figures are derived from the Cotter article cited in the preceding paragraph, p. 258.)

[70] Miss Bontecou, in the paper referred to in note 68 above, p. 105, gives specific examples of known miscarriages of justice in the loyalty-security program. The Knauff case discussed in the text above, pp. 35–36, is of course a prime illustration.

[71] Rule of Law—A Study by the Inns of Court Conservative and Unionist Society (Conservative Political Centre, 1955), 13.

[72] The Chinese " Security Hero " award is reported by Robert Franklin in a dispatch to *The Observer* (London), August 21, 1955.

[73] Alexis de Tocqueville, *Democracy in America* (Knopf, 1945), Vol. I, 263.

Notes to Chapter Two

[1] The economic differentiation between book publishing and the mass media is discussed in Robert W. Frase, The Book Trade, in 14 Current Economic Comment (May, 1952), No. 2, pp. 47, 55. And see also Kurt Enoch, The Mass Media: Challenge / Chimera?, 1 Essential Books, No. 5, p. 10 (1956).

[2] For statement of the view that freedom may be advanced by censorship, see, for example, Pope Leo XIII, *Libertas Humana* (Paulist Press ed., 1941), 18: " Men have a right freely and prudently to propagate throughout the State *what things soever are true and honorable*, so that as many as possible may possess them; but *lying opinions*, than which no mental plague is greater, and vices which corrupt the heart and moral life, *should be diligently repressed* by public authority, lest they insidiously work the ruin of the State. The excesses of an unbridled intellect, which unfailingly end in the oppression of the untutored multitude, are no less rightly controlled by the authority of the law than are the injuries inflicted by violence upon the weak." (Italics added.)

And see also Francis J. Connell, Censorship and the Prohibition of Books in Catholic Church Law, 54 Colum. L. Rev. 699 (1954). Father Connell is Dean of the School of Sacred Theology, The Catholic University of America.

[3] More extended analysis of the philosophical implications of censorship appears in a report entitled " The Freedom to Read," made to the National Book Committee in February, 1956, by Richard N. McKeon, professor of philosophy at the University of Chicago, Robert K. Merton, professor of sociology at Columbia University, and myself. The remarks in the text are derived from this report.

[4] The Society for the Diffusion of Useful Knowledge is described by Sir Cecil Carr, A Victorian Law Reformer's Correspondence, Selden Society Annual Lecture (London, 1955), 6.

[5] The early developments in low-price publishing are treated in Freeman Lewis, Paper-Bound Books in America, Bulletin of the New York Public Library (February, 1953), 3. Mr. Lewis' paper is the main source of factual statements in the text concerning the paper-

bound book industry. Among the features of Mr. Lewis' paper to which I should like to call especial attention is an appendix, pp. 17 ff., containing a list, never before available, of paperbound best sellers.

[6] Sales of paperbound books are estimated in *Publishers' Weekly*, (January 21, 1956), Vol. CLXIX, 214.

[7] Discussion of the elite reading public of the past as compared with the present appears in Paul Lazarsfeld and Robert K. Merton, " Mass Communication, Popular Taste and Organized Social Action," *The Communication of Ideas* (Lyman Bryson, ed.; Harper, 1948), 95, 109.

[8] Lord Chief Justice Cockburn spoke in Queen v. Hicklin, L. R. 3 Q. B. 360 (1868). For the fullest account of the developing law in this field, see William B. Lockhart and Robert C. McClure, Literature, The Law of Obscenity, and the Constitution, 38 Minn. L. Rev. 295 (1954); and the same author's Obscenity in the Courts, 20 Law & Contemporary Problems 587 (1955). And see also J. E. Hall Williams, Obscenity in Modern English Law, 20 Law and Contemporary Problems 630 (1955); Norman St. John-Stevas, *Obscenity and the Law* (Secker and Warburg, 1956), 66 et seq.

[9] James Pickett Wesberry, Every Citizen Has a Right to Know: A Report of the Georgia Literature Commission (1954), 3.

[10] See *The Portable D. H. Lawrence* (Viking, 1950), 656 et seq. In some Ameircan Indian societies direct conversation between father-in-law and daughter-in-law is taboo; the equivalent of our " smutty stories " has developed in Indian circles, involving the shocking, shameless, and sniggeringly funny situation of their speaking to one another. See Weston La Barre, Obscenity: An Anthropological Appraisal, 20 Law & Contemporary Problems 533, at 539 (1955).

[11] Reichenbach's triumphs are described in Curtis D. MacDougall, *Hoaxes* (Macmillan, 1940), 252. A different and less dramatic version of the " September Morning " incident appears in Heywood Broun and Margaret Leech, *Anthony Comstock: Roundsman of the Lord* (Boni, 1927), 238–39. According to these authors, Comstock noted a newly published reproduction of the painting on display in a New York art dealer's window. On his own initiative he ordered its removal. His order was defied; but ultimately the dealer did displace the picture because the publicity brought such crowds that his customers were unable to enter the shop.

[12] James Pickett Wesberry, Every Citizen Has a Right to Know: A Report of the Georgia Literature Commission (1954), 58.

[13] References to the Geneva conference on obscene literature appear in William B. Lockhart and Robert C. McClure, Literature, The Law of Obscenity, and the Constitution, 38 Minn. L. Rev. 295, at 323 (1954); compare Norman St. John-Stevas, *Obscenity and the Law* (Secker & Warburg, 1956), 96–97.

[14] Eric Larrabee, "Morality and Obscenity," in *Freedom of Book Selection* (F. J. Mosher, ed.; American Library Association, 1954), 37.

[15] The quoted effort to define "obscenity" appears in Harold C. Gardiner, S. J., Moral Principles Towards a Definition of the Obscene, 20 Law & Contemporary Problems 560 at 569, 570 (1955). Compare Father Gardiner's thoughtful book, *Norms for the Novel* (The America Press, 1953), esp. Chs. 4 and 5.

[16] Information about these non-erotic stimuli may be found in Glenn V. Ramsey, The Sexual Development of Boys, 56 American Journal of Psychology 217, at 222–23 (1943); and see also Alfred C. Kinsey, *Sexual Behavior in the Human Male* (W. B. Saunders Co., 1948), 164–65, where references appear to the commotion-producing effects of skiing, swimming, and sitting in hot sand, among other apparently innocent pursuits. My attention was initially directed toward these sources by Gershon Legman's *Love and Death: A Study in Censorship*, privately published by the author in 1949.

The unanticipated impact of the seemingly unexciting has application in the field of book-reading. In Commonwealth v. Gordon, 66 D. & C. 101, 137–38 (1949), aff'd 166 Pa. Super. 120, 70 A. 2d 389 (1950), the learned Judge Curtis Bok commented that if a person "reads an obscene book when his sensuality is low, he will yawn over it or find that its suggestibility leads him off on quite different paths. If he reads the Mechanics' Lien Act while his sensuality is high, things will stand between him and the printed page that have no business there."

John Milton, in the *Areopagitica* (1644), made somewhat the same point when he said: "Wholesome meats to a vitiated stomach differ little or nothing from unwholesome; and best books to a naughty mind are not unapplicable to occasions of evil."

[17] The study of erotic stimuli noted by college women is described by Morris L. Ernst and William Seagle, *To the Pure* (Viking, 1928),

239 et seq. Compare, however, Alfred C. Kinsey, *et al.*, *Sexual Behavior in the Human Female* (Saunders, 1953), 669–72.

[18] The reference to "sacrosanct institutions" comes from Larrabee, "Morality and Obscenity," in *Freedom of Book Selection* (F. J. Mosher, ed.; American Library Association, 1954), 37.

[19] Compare Judge Jerome N. Frank's remark, concurring in Roth v. Goldman, 172 F. 2d 788 (C. A. 2, 1949), at 792: ". . . no sane man thinks socially dangerous the arousing of normal sexual desires. Consequently, if reading obscene books has merely that consequence, Congress, it would seem, can constitutionally no more suppress such books than it can prevent the mailing of many other objects, such as perfumes, for example, which notoriously produce that result."

[20] Judge Tolin's researches are recorded in Bonica v. Oleson, 126 F. Supp. 398 (S. D. Cal., 1954). For further discussion of factors courts have considered important in determining obscenity, see Criminal Law: Obscene Literature Statutes, Wis. L. Rev. 492 (1955).

[21] William B. Lockhart and Robert C. McClure, Literature, The Law of Obscenity and the Constitution, 38 Minn. L. Rev. 295, 320 (1954).

[22] "The Deadwood Coach" met its fate in Fox Film Corp. v. Collins, 236 Ill. App. 281, at 291 (1925).

The variability of appraisal of "violence" and "horror" finds current illustration, according to the *New York Times*, September 17, 1955, in an action of the Swedish film censors, who banned the showing of Walt Disney's "20,000 Leagues Under the Sea" to children under the age of fifteen, because they would be excessively frightened by an underwater fight between a man and an octopus. American children are apparently made of sterner stuff than their Swedish coevals, for they suffered the picture without a murmur of protest.

[23] The "comics code" is discussed by Charles F. Murphy, A Seal of Approval for Comic Books, 19 Federal Probation (June, 1955) 19, 20. And see also Paul S. Deland, Battling Crime Comics to Protect Youth, 19 Federal Probation (September, 1955) 26.

[24] The assumption that stimulated thoughts lead to anti-social results is explicitly indicated in the Report of the Select Committee on Current Pornographic Materials, the so-called Gathings Committee, H. Rep. No. 2510, 82nd Cong., 1st Sess. (1952), which tells on p. 2 of writings "promotive of obscenity, immorality, and

other matters of an offensive nature," "subversive of morals, allegiance, or faith," and having a content "believed to exercise a debasing and degrading influence on susceptible youth."

The Gathings Committee's report is analyzed (unfavorably) in Will Oursler, Books on Trial, 78 Library Journal 173 (1953).

[25] Mr. Hoover's words are quoted by Bishop John F. Noll in Manual of the National Organization for Decent Literature, p. 122, and re-quoted in Obscene Literature, 34 Marq. L. Rev. 301, at 302 (1951).

[26] Dr. Wertham has written extensively in popular magazines. The most frequently quoted of his works is *Seduction of the Innocent* (Rinehart, 1953).

Compare the report of the Senate Judiciary Committee's Subcommittee to Investigate Juvenile Deliquency, S. Rep. 62, 84th Cong., 1st Sess. (1955), 12: ". . . majority opinion seems inclined to the view that it is unlikely that the reading of crime and horror comics would lead to delinquency in a well-adjusted and normally law-abiding child." The New York State Joint Legislative Committee to Study the Publication of Comics, on the other hand, took a strongly Werthamist view, saying: " Crime comics are a contributing factor leading to juvenile delinquency. . . . The reading of crime comics stimulates sadistic and masochistic attitudes and interferes with the normal development of sexual habits in children and produces abnormal sexual tendencies in adolescents." N. Y. Legis. Doc. (1954), No. 37, pp. 34–35.

[27] Sheldon and Eleanor Glueck, *Unraveling Juvenile Delinquency* (Commonwealth Fund, 1950), 273 et seq. The Gluecks also inquired into the recreational preferences of delinquent and nondelinquent children; 7.8 per cent of the non-delinquent children preferred " non-active" ways of spending their time (including reading and movie-going), but only 2.7 percent of the delinquent group had that preference (pp. 160–61).

[28] The testimony of Judge Smyth is reported in the *New York Times*, September 2, 1955, p. 19, col. 1.

[29] For a recent report upon delinquents' reading problems see Melvin Roman, Joseph B. Margolin, and Carmi Harari, Reading Retardation and Delinquency, 1 National Probation & Parole Association Journal 1 (1955). An earlier study of nearly 150 maladjusted boys had reflected the same close relationship between delinquency and reading difficulty. Henry Feinberg and Clyde L. Reed, Reading Level of a Group of Socially Maladjusted Boys, 12

Journal of Social Psychology 31 (1940). A few years before that, a survey of the sixteen- to nineteen-year-old boys then in the New York State reformatory had shown that not a single one of the 187 inmates had reading capacity commensurate with his mental age. Paul Fendrick and Guy Bond, Delinquency and Reading, 48 Journal of Genetic Psychology 236 (1936).

[30] The dangers of miscalculating the origins of juvenile delinquency are effectively developed by Herbert A. Bloch, in The Inadequacies of Research in Delinquency Causation, 1 National Probation and Parole Association Journal 31 (1955). On p. 36 Professor Bloch writes: " As one example of untested judgments which are so common, consider the current outcry that comic books are the cause of delinquency. When the public temper shifts, popular condemnation then focuses on television programs, or some other facet of our culture chosen as a scapegoat upon which we can vent our frustration. Recurrently, we fall back upon the nostrum of the well-meaning citizens' committee: ' Lack of playgrounds is really the reason for youthful lawlessness.' The inclination toward ready-made formulas, based upon untested observation and experience, is still the rule."

[31] Marie Jahoda, *The Impact of Literature*: *A Psychological Discussion of Some Assumptions in the Censorship Debate* (American Book Publishers Council, 1954), 23. The quoted principle is supported by studies in such widely varied fields as drug-using, voting habits, race prejudice, and sexual excitation. Dr. Jahoda was assisted in her study by the staff of New York University's Research Center for Human Relations.

[32] See Frederic Wertham, *Dark Legend* (Duell, Sloan & Pearce, 1941), 201: " It seems to me just as inexact to say fiction has no influence at all on people's actions as to blame crime on such fiction. Apparently anti-social impulses do not originate that way. But when they once exist, added impetus may be given them by way of identification with a fictional scene."

[33] The Aristotelian view is described by Mortimer Adler, *Art and Prudence* (Longmans, Green & Co., 1937), 46, as follows: " The situations of life which excite emotions make action both possible and necessary; but imitations [art] excite emotions and make action for a time, at least, both impossible and unnecessary. The soul is thus relieved. This relief is its catharsis."

[34] Dr. Benjamin Karpman, chief psychotherapist of Saint Elizabeths Hospital in Washington, discusses the relation between reading

and sexual action in his *The Sexual Offender and His Offenses* (Julian Press, 1954), 485, saying: "Contrary to popular misconception, people who read salacious literature are less likely to become sexual offenders than those who do not, for the reason that such reading often neutralizes what aberrant sexual interests they may have."

[35] As to television, for example, the Family Service Association of America asserts, according to the *New York Times*, September 15, 1955, p. 37, col. 1, that television "family comedies" may prove to be more damaging to youngsters' attitudes toward life than crime and adventure stories. The latter, say the association's specialists in child psychology, "are accepted by most viewers as pure entertainment with little personal reality." But the depiction of the family has relationship to the child's experience. If the TV father "is constantly visualized as a dunce or the mother as a social climber, watchers may eventually be infected with the idea that this is normal, and therefore acceptable, family life."

And see also Television and Juvenile Delinquency, an interim report of the Senate Judiciary Committee's Subcommittee to Investigate Juvenile Delinquency, 84th Cong., 1st Sess. (1955), 31: "There is reason to believe that television crime programs are potentially much more injurious to children and young people than motion pictures, radio, or comic books. Attending a movie requires money and the physical effort of leaving the home, so an average child's exposure to films in the theater tends to be limited to a few hours a week. Comic books demand strong imaginary projections. Also, they must be sought out and purchased. But television, available at a flick of a knob and combining visual and audible aspects into a 'live' story, has a greater impact upon its child audience."

[36] The comment on the reading of Aristophanes and Juvenal may be found in *The Works of Lord Macaulay* (Longmans, Green, 1879), Vol. VI, 491. The words appear in an essay on the comic dramatists of the Restoration, written in 1841.

[37] G. K. Chesterton, *Selected Essays* (Collins, 1939), 234–35, quoted more extensively in Jahoda, *The Impact of Literature* (American Book Publishers Council, 1954), 10–11.

[38] As to limits on expression, compare Mr. Justice Frankfurter, concurring in Pennekamp v. Florida, 328 U. S. 331, at 356 (1946): "Freedom of the press is not freedom from responsibility for its exercise. That there was such legal liability was so taken for granted by the framers of the First Amendment that it was not spelled out.

Responsibility for its abuse was imbedded in the law." And see also the testimony given before the Hennings Committee (the Senate Judiciary Committee's Subcommittee on Constitutional Rights) in November, 1955, by the doughtily libertarian Alexander Meiklejohn: " Speech, as a form of human action, is subject to regulation in exactly the same sense as is walking, or lighting a fire, or shooting a gun. To interpret the First Amendment as forbidding such regulation is so to misconceive its meaning as to reduce it to nonsense." Hearings pursuant to S. Res. 94, Security and Constitutional Rights, at 8 (1955).

[39] References to the books on polygamy and the Scottsboro case appear in House Report 2510, 82d Cong., 2d Sess. (1952), 14–15; and the minority statement on p. 122. See also Charles G. Bolté, Security Through Book Burning, 300 Annals of the American Academy of Political and Social Science 87, 92-93 (1955).

[40] Reflecting the fear of new ideas is, for example, People v. Berg, 241 App. Div. 543, 544-545, 272 N. Y. Supp. 586, 588 (2d Dept., 1934), affirmed 269 N. Y. 514, 199 N. E. 513 (1935), where the court said that obscenity could be determined by considering whether a book has a tendency to " lower the standards of right and wrong, specifically as to the sexual relation."

[41] The Lenin statement, said to have been made in 1920, is quoted in Alan Barth, *Government by Investigation* (Viking Press, 1955), 183.

Sir Richard Livingston, of Oxford, effectively characterizes the Soviet attitude as follows, in *Some Tasks for Education* (Oxford, 1946), 75: " In Russia we have a secular version of the medieval church. The citizen may criticize details but he ' must keep his mouth shut about the higher policy.' . . . No doubt interference with free speech is not the same as falsification of facts. Liberty is not truth; and its denial is not identical with falsehood. But in effect liberty is essential to truth; and liberty is refused in order to set propaganda free."

[42] Compare Walter Bagehot's appraisal of the use of state power to extirpate error: " I think the effect has often been to eradicate a heresy among the few, at the cost of creating a skepticism among the many; to kill the error, no doubt, but also to ruin the general belief. And this is the cardinal point, for the propagation of ' truth ' is the end of persecution; all else is only a means." *The Metaphysical Basis of Toleration* (1874), reprinted in Howard Mumford Jones, *Primer of Intellectual Freedom* (Harvard, 1949) 79, 81.

[43] Description of the newspaper situation appears in Paul Blanshard, *The Right to Read* (Beacon Press, 1955), 58.

[44] Paperbound sales are compared with *Life's* in Freeman Lewis, Paper-Bound Books in America, Bulletin of the New York Public *Library* (1953), 11.

[45] The indicated circulation figures come from N. W. Ayer & Son's *Directory of Newspapers and Periodicals* (1955).

[46] David Riesman, "Civil Liberties in a Period of Transition," in *Public Policy* (Friedrich and Mason, ed.; Harvard, 1942), 35.

[47] The Briton who commented on our "girlish attitude" is William Empson, quoted by Lazarsfeld and Merton, "Mass Communication, Popular Taste and Organized Social Action," in *The Communication of Ideas* (Lyman Bryson, ed.; Harper, 1948) 95–96.

[48] For the findings of students of communication, see, e. g., Eunice Cooper and Marie Jahoda, The Evasion of Propaganda, 23 Journal of Psychology 15 (1947). And see also Carl I. Hovland, Arthur A. Lumsdaine, and Fred D. Sheffield, *Experiments on Mass Communications* (Princeton University Press, 1949), esp. Ch. 3.

[49] The importance of face-to-face contacts is emphasized by, among others, Paul F. Lazarsfeld, Bernard Berelson, and Hazel Gaudet, *The People's Choice* (2nd ed.; Columbia University Press, 1948), 75, 150–58; Gerhart Saenger, *The Social Psychology of Prejudice* (Harper & Bros., 1953), Ch. 14; Eugene L. Horowitz, The Development of Attitude Toward the Negro, Archives of Psychology, No. 194 (1936), 30, 35. These matters are reviewed in Jahoda, *The Impact of Literature* (American Book Publishers Council, 1954), esp. pp. 24–35.

[50] The comment on the unadhesiveness of ideas comes from Lazarsfeld and Merton, "Mass Communication, Popular Taste and Organized Social Action," in *The Communication of Ideas* (Lyman Bryson, ed.; Harper, 1948) 95, 99. As to the circumstances in which the mass media are most effective, see the same work at p. 117.

[51] George F. Kennan in a letter dated January 24, 1953, to William S. Dix (Librarian of Princeton University), printed in 47 American Library Association Bulletin 470 (1953). Mr. Kennan sagely adds to the quoted sentences that a great deal more is involved, in any event, than merely a matter of political expediency. "If we were to assume that our students and our public were incapable of arriving at the truth by free inquiry, we would place ourselves, by that very assumption, a good distance into the realm

of genuine totalitarianism. To take this position implies that, since the students and the public cannot pursue the truth by free inquiry, there must be some other persons or authorities to tell them what the truth is, and we all know what the implications of that would be."

⁵² The Report of the Secretary of Defense's Advisory Committee on Prisoners of War was made on August 17, 1955, and is printed by the U. S. Government Printing Office under the title " POW." The quoted passage appears at p. 63 of the report.

⁵³ Ortega's remark appears in a speech delivered during the bicentennial celebration of Goethe's birth, at Aspen, Colorado, on July 2, 1949, as reported in the *New York Times*, July 3, 1949, p. 28, col. 1.

⁵⁴ Learned Hand, Address at the Harvard Tercentenary Observance, printed in 49 Harvard Alumni Bulletin 37 (September 30, 1936), reprinted in *The Spirit of Liberty* (Irving Dilliard, ed.; Knopf, 1952), 115, 152, 153. Two other notable flashes of Judge Hand's skepticism that the last true word has already been said, may well be cited here. " The spirit of liberty," he says, " is the spirit which is not too sure that it is right." " How tentative and provisional are our attainments, intellectual and moral; how often the deepest convictions of one generation are the rejects of the next . . ." The first of these statements appears in the Dilliard collection on p. 190; the second, in the *Saturday Review of Literature* (November 22, 1952), Vol. XXXV, 55.

⁵⁵ The Eisenhower letter was addressed to the American Library Association on June 24, 1953. Its text appears in 28 Wilson Library Bulletin 59, 60 (1953), and in the *New York Times*, June 27, 1953, p. 16, col. 5.

⁵⁶ Zechariah Chafee, Jr., Censorship of Plays and Books, 1 Bill of Rights Rev. 16, 18 (1940).

⁵⁷ As to the strain of neuroticism in the hunter of eroticism, see Heywood Broun and Margaret Leech, *Anthony Comstock, Roundsman of the Lord* (Boni, 1927), and Alec Craig, *The Banned Books of Britain* (Geo. Allen & Unwin, 1937), 105 et seq. There is of course a very real possibility that some (not all) of the censorially minded persons in a community are discharging a subconscious need to demonstrate their own moral rectitude by denouncing the lack of it in others. Compare Selma G. Hirsch, *The Fears Men Live By* (Harper, 1955), 53; Gerhart Saenger, *The Social Psychology of Prejudice* (Harper, 1953), 116 et seq.

[58] A marked exception to the general rule that censors are culturally underdeveloped is Huntington Cairns, who became special legal adviser to the Secretary of the Treasury in 1934 and has continued since that time to advise the Treasury in debatable customs cases. Cairns, an able and sensitive lawyer, is at present secretary of the National Gallery of Art. His work in the Treasury is described in a monograph of the Attorney General's Committee on Administrative Procedure, Administration of the Customs Laws, Sen. Doc. No. 10, 77th Cong., 1st Sess. (1941), Part 14, pp. 49–52. And see also Zechariah Chafee, Jr., *Government and Mass Communications* (University of Chicago Press, 1947), 254 ff. See Huntington Cairns, Freedom of Expression in Literature, 200 Annals of the American Academy of Political and Social Science 76 (1938), for a statement of his own views.

[59] As to the direction of censors' energies, compare the somewhat harsher judgment of Professors William B. Lockhart and Robert C. McClure, Obscenity in the Courts, 20 Law & Contemporary Problems 586, at 604 (1955): "The censor is rarely a well-balanced and literate person; he usually is compulsively interested only in finding what he seeks and in its merciless and indiscriminate suppression once he finds it. To put a writer's months or even years of creative work and a publisher's capital investment in a new publication at the mercy of such a person without an obligation on the courts to evaluate the book as a whole is to invite timidity and restraint in both author and publisher—a sure way to destroy the value to society of free literature."

[60] Minnesota's grandmotherly censor is described in James P. Wesberry, Every Citizen Has A Right To Know: A Report of the Georgia Literature Commission (1954), 44.

[61] For discussion of NODL methods, see John E. Twomey, The Citizens' Committee and Comic-Book Control: A Study of Extragovernmental Restraint, 20 Law & Contemporary Problems 621, at 626–28 (1955).

[62] The Georgia statute creating the Literature Commission is 26 Ga. Code Ann. (Harris, 1955 Supp.) ch. 63A.

[63] Sunshine Book Co. v. McCaffrey, 112 N. Y. S. 2d 476 (Sup. Ct., N. Y. Co., 1952), involved an unsuccessful effort by a publisher of several nudist magazines to enjoin New York City's Licenses Commissioner from interfering with their circulation by writing to newsstand operators as follows: "In the event you display or offer for sale any of the above identified publications . . .

steps will be taken looking to the suspension or revocation of your license."

On February 27, 1956, the then Licenses Commissioner of New York announced that he and a group representing the newsstand operators had agreed on a " self-policing " program under which the dealers would remove " obscene " magazines " voluntarily and at their own discretion." Twenty-four " nudist " and " girlie " magazines had thus far been " voluntarily " banned after having been listed by a special committee that meets with the commissioner at his office each month. The committee's members are drawn from the American Legion, the Veterans of Foreign Wars, the Disabled American Veterans, and the Lighthouse of the New York Association for the Blind. *New York Times*, February 28, 1956, p. 33, col. 8.

For an extended and able discussion of the efficacy of police and licensing pressures, see Censorship of Obscene Literature by Informal Governmental Action, 22 U. Chi. L. Rev. 216 (1954).

[64] An example of official exhortation to limit circulation of printed matter appears in American Civil Liberties Union Weekly Bulletin No. 1739 (1956): " Mayor Thomas A. D'Alesandro of Baltimore asked dealers and distributors to ban 500 books and magazines from newsstands as a means of combatting juvenile delinquency. The only objection to this attempted censorship was raised by ACLU's Maryland Branch, which charged the mayor with exceeding his legal powers."

[65] As to journalistic moralizing about " obscene " books, Gershon Legman, *Love and Death* (privately published, 1949), comments on p. 61 on a book chronicling the career of a character named Duchess Hotspur (she " runs through so many men she cannot remember their names, examines them in the nude before admitting them to her bed-chamber, can keep track of them only by cutting their initials on the leaves of her fan "). The book was offered free in a full-page, four-color advertisement in the comic-section of a national newspaper chain—" more exciting than Scarlett O'Hara . . . Yours as a gift." The newspaper owner, says Legman, arranged to run Duchess Hotspur as a daily comic-strip, " by way of climaxing his successful campaign for the suppression of Edmund Wilson's ' filthy ' and ' indecent ' *Memoirs of Hecate County*."

[66] The Georgia figures appear in James P. Wesberry, The People's Right To Know: A Report of the Georgia Literature Commission (1954), 8, 41.

[67] The Detroit test of illegality is reported in an article under the by-line of Louis Tendler, headed " Tightest in Nation—Detroit Book Censorship a Model for Other Cities," *Detroit News*, May 5, 1955.

[68] Inspector Herbert W. Case, head of the Censor Bureau until February, 1955, testified about manuscript reading, before the House Select Committee on Current Pornographic Materials, H. Rep. No. 2510, 82d Cong., 2d Sess. (1952), 60. In response to a question as to whether he rejected an entire manuscript, or merely suggested deletions or changes, Inspector Case added: " Both, depending upon the seriousness of the continuous amount of deletions that are in it. . . . take the book I had here, where we had 12 pages continuously through, we simply say that it was unacceptable in its complete form, it would have to be rewritten. However, if there were only six or seven pages, and certain paragraphs on those pages they could revise it and change it."

In his column in *Newsweek* (March 21, 1955), 95, John Lardner sardonically remarks that the pre-publication submission of manuscripts " does not mean, as yet, less work for the cops. They still have to read, in order to advise the publisher what to do. The chances are, however, that under their firm but kindly discipline, the publisher—and other publishers, as they, too, begin to avail themselves of Case's literary tips—will cut down their output considerably, and eventually cure themselves of publishing altogether. Like smoking or drinking, it's just a habit."

[69] Justice Jackson spoke in Thomas v. Collins, 323 U. S. 516, at 545 (1945) (concurring opinion).

[70] Examples of textual changes (sometimes involving a slight tinkering with history) in order to satisfy local critics, are given by Paul Blanshard, *The Right to Read* (Beacon Press, 1955), Ch. 4, esp. pp. 88 ff. In an instance well known in the book trade but apparently not publicized, a textbook that pointed out dangers as well as advantages of home ownership was changed (by forgetting the dangers) after criticism by a real estate board.

[71] William E. Spaulding, Can Textbooks be Subversive? 34 Educational Record 297, at 303 (1953). Mr. Spaulding adds warning that the measures he complains of " will not go far toward strengthening our defenses against communism. . . . The result can be an enforced moratorium on all real progress in textbooks."

[72] As to the appraisal of texts, one may note, in passing, that the Indiana State Superintendent of Public Instruction announced in

1951 that he had invited a group of nineteen Catholic priests to assist him in "screening" school textboks for what he described broadly as "traces of communism or subversive influences"; Catholics were chosen as advisers, he explained, because they are "considerably versed in being able to spot Communist or subversive influences." *The Nation* (December 15, 1951), p. 511. A member of the Textbook Commission of that same state announced her belief two years later that *Robin Hood* should be banned from school libraries because it reflected a "communistic" philosophy. *New York Times*, November 14, 1953, p. 1, col. 7. In 1956 the West Virginia Textbook Advisory Committee requested the Americanization Committee of the National American Legion to examine social science textbooks to be used in elementary schools. Censorship Bulletin, American Book Pub. Council, May 1956.

The Board of Education in Georgia in 1955 overruled its professional advisers, and rejected three books as not in accord with the southern way of life. "One, a songbook, changed Stephen Foster's 'darkies' to 'young folks' or 'brother'; the publisher offered to go back to the original, but the Board refused the book in either form." American Civil Liberties Union, Clearing the Main Channels (35th Annual Report, 1955), 11.

[73] As to toleration of contrary opinions, compare Howard K. Beale, *A History of Freedom of Teaching in American Schools* (Scribner, 1941), xii–xiii: "Men usually 'tolerate' opposing views on subjects that they do not regard as important, and then rationalize 'intolerance' into necessity when disagreement involves a matter vital to them . . . the seventeenth century cared tremendously about religion and was unconcerned about capitalist economics or nationalistic patriotism, while the twentieth century has lost its interest in theology and is vitally interested both emotionally and materially in capitalist economics and nationalistic patriotism. . . . Thus teachers in each century and locality have been allowed freedom to discuss subjects that did not seem to matter and denied freedom on issues about which men did seriously care."

[74] The Foreign Agents Registration Act, 56 Stat. 250, 255 (1942), 22 U. S. C. §§ 611(c)(3), 611(j) (1952).

[75] For legislative history of the Foreign Agents Registration Act, see House Report No. 1381, 75th Cong., 1st Sess. (1937), 2: "This required registration will publicize the nature of subversive or other similar activities of such foreign propagandists [that is, those who pretend to be American but are in actuality the subsidized

representatives of foreign interests], so that the American people may know *those who are engaged in this country by foreign agencies* to spread doctrines alien to our democratic form of government." Senate Report No. 1783, 75th Cong., 3d Sess. (1938), 2, also makes clear that the Foreign Agents Registration Act was to apply to people operating *in this country*.

[76] The opinion about the excludibility of Nazi materials is 39 Op. Atty. Gen. 535 (1940).

[77] Information about the seizure of 56,500 pieces of "foreign propaganda" is drawn from Government Exclusion of Foreign Political Propaganda, 68 Harv. L. Rev. 1393n (1955), a careful exploration of administrative practice in this field, containing considerable information not otherwise readily obtainable. Statements in the text concerning the exclusionary mechanisms are largely derived from this able law review discussion, esp. pp. 1394–95.

[78] The annual haul of propaganda in Boston is mentioned in ACLU Weekly Bulletin No. 1712, August 22, 1955, p. 3, summarizing investigation conducted by Boston *Post*.

[79] The constitutional issues are well discussed in 68 Harv. L. Rev., esp. pp. 1402 ff.

[80] 68 Harv. L. Rev. at 1399.

[81] Interestingly enough, existing statutory law provides as to insurrectionary material that only the courts, and not the Customs Bureau, shall have power to order exclusion (after a jury trial, if desired). The elaborate procedural safeguards of the law in this respect were not accidental, but reflected a clearly expressed congressional fear of placing censorial authority in bureaucratic hands. See 46 Stat. 688 (1930), 19 U. S. C. § 1305 (1952); Zechariah Chafee, Jr., *Government and Mass Communications* (University of Chicago Press, 1942), 252.

[82] News of the seizure of the *Economist* appears in Civil Liberties (December, 1955) No. 137, p. 1.

[83] Information about the Muste pamphlet comes from ACLU Weekly Bulletin No. 1712, August 22, 1955, p. 3.

[84] The book in question is *Catholic Imperialism and World Freedom*, by Avro Manhattan, published in London in 1952 by Watts and Company. The book circulated freely in the United States from 1952 until the autumn of 1954, when the Post Office Department decided to declare it non-mailable as foreign propaganda. ACLU Weekly Bulletin No. 1700, May 30, 1955.

[85] The rights of hearers or readers are suggested, for example, by

Marsh v. Alabama, 326 U. S. 501 (1946); Tucker v. Texas, 326 U. S. 517 (1946); Martin v. City of Struthers, 319 U. S. 141 (1943). In the Struthers case, which seems to me to be especially strong for present purposes, an ordinance had forbidden ringing doorbells and knocking on doors by uninvited persons who wanted to press leaflets upon householders. The Supreme Court thought that each householder should be free to decide for himself whether he wishes to receive calls from leaflet-distributors; freedom of speech (p. 143) "embraces the right to distribute literature . . . and necessarily protects the right to receive it . . ."

[86] As to postal discretion in support of educational programs, see, e. g., 68 Harv. L. Rev. at 1394n: "In November of 1954 the Post Office Department held up shipment of 75 copies of *The State and Revolution* by V. I. Lenin, ordered by Brown University for use in a history course. The Solicitor notified the University, requesting a statement as to whether it desired to receive the books, ' the nature of its utility to the University and the restrictions placed upon its accessibility.' Upon assurance by the University that the booklets were to be used only for study purposes and ' not to promote the dissemination of propaganda ' the Solicitor allowed delivery. Letter from John K. McIntyre, Assistant to the President, Brown University, to the *Harvard Law Review*, Feb. 23, 1955."

ACLU Weekly Bulletin No. 1740, March 5, 1956, reports that Jeremiah Feingold, the owner of a small bookstore in San Francisco, had been aided in overcoming postal and customs censorship of imported books. Feingold, according to the ACLU, " imports books in Russian for such customers as the U. S. Army Language School at Monterey, the University of California, Stanford University, and the Library of Congress." Shipments consigned to him, however, were confiscated time after time by customs officials, so that several foreign suppliers had refused to continue sending him books. Occasionally he received books, while other copies of the very same work were confiscated. This happened, it is said, with books by Shakespeare, Gorky, De Maupassant, Chekhov, Dickens, Tolstoy, and Pushkin. Apparently this occurred when the books were packed in cartons with other material which was deemed to be " propaganda " rather than literature. In January, 1956, the Post Office Department was persuaded to instruct the San Francisco postmaster to release " any books still being held by his office which were found not to be non-mailable per se, but were withheld because contained in a parcel with books of a non-mailable character." Further, in an unusual move, the Post Office Department agreed to notify Feingold if any materials were confiscated in the future, and to give him an opportunity to argue for their delivery to him.

[87] The Post Office Department Solicitor is quoted by Dorothy Kahn, " Abe Goff, Our Chief Censor," *The Reporter* (May 19, 1955), p. 27.

[88] The Jacksonian attitude toward postal distribution appears in *Correspondence of Andrew Jackson* (J. S. Bassett, ed.; Carnegie Institute, 1931), Vol. V, 360–61, partly quoted in Clement Eaton, *Freedom of Thought in the Old South* (Peter Smith, 1951), 143 n. For subsequent developments, especially the first formal barring of abolitionist " propaganda sheets " from the mails beginning in 1857 and, in 1861, the barring of papers sympathetic to the Confederacy, see E. P. Deutsch, Freedom of the Press and of the Mails, 36 Mich. L. Rev. 703, 723 (1938).

[89] The Postmaster General's pertinent powers are set forth in 18 U. S. C. §§ 1341 (fraudulent matter), 1461 and 1463 (dealing chiefly with obscene matter, information about contraception, and incitements to various heinous crimes), and 1717 (seditious matter).

The Postmaster General also has power, under 39 U. S. C. § 232, to revoke the second-class mail privileges of periodical publications, a matter of tremendous moment to them because the mail rate differential in their favor is an important economic subsidy. United States ex rel. Milwaukee Social Democratic Publishing Co. v. Burleson, 255 U. S. 407 (1921), upheld the withdrawal of second-class privileges from future issues of a publication some of whose past issues had been found to contain seditious matter. In Hannegan v. Esquire, 327 U. S. 146 (1946), the Court said, however, that the Postmaster General could not withhold second-class privileges from a publication whose contents were believed by him to be un-meritorious though still mailable. The procedures in second-class mail matters are for the most part reasonably calculated to allow consideration of the pertinent questions. See Monograph of the Attorney General's Committee on Administrative Procedure, Post Office Department, Sen. Doc. No. 186, 76th Cong., 3d Sess. (1940), Part 12, pp. 2–15. And see also Frank Thayer, *Legal Control of the Press* (3d ed.; Foundation Press, 1956), 183 et seq. The second-class mail problems are not included in the present discussion because they pertain exclusively to periodicals rather than books, which are the special focus here.

For the basic study on which almost all later writers have heavily relied, see Lindsay Rogers, *The Postal Power of Congress* (Johns Hopkins, 1916).

[90] The seizure powers of the Customs Bureau appear in 19 U. S. C. § 1305.

[91] United States v. Ulysses, 72 F. 2d 705 (C. C. A. 2d, 1934). The Married Love case, referred to in the text, is reported at 48 F. 2d 821 (S. D. N. Y., 1931); it held that Dr. Marie C. Stopes' book was an aid to conjugal success rather than an obscene writing.

[92] Professor Chafee reported in 1947 that a copy of Kant's *Critique of Pure Reason* and a Spanish translation of the Bible had been seized by inspectors. *Government and Mass Communications* (University of Chicago Press, 1947), 255.

[93] The few reported challenges of the present customs censor's decisions, stretching over a quarter of a century, include Parmelee v. United States, 113 F. 2d 729 (D. C. Cir., 1940) (*Nudism in Modern Life* was held to be importable); United States v. Two Obscene Books, 92 F. Supp. 934, 99 F. Supp. 760 (N. D. Cal., 1950, 1951), affirmed sub nom. Besig v. United States, 208 F. 2d 142 (C. A. 9, 1953) (the books in question where Henry Miller's *Tropic of Cancer* and *Tropic of Capricorn*; their seizure was upheld); United States v. One Unbound Volume, 128 F. Supp. 280 (D. Md., 1955) (portfolio of prints of archeological artifacts held to be obscene rather than a work of scientific merit).

[94] The mail delivery business is described in Pike v. Walker, 121 F. 2d 37, 39 (D. C. Cir., 1941), certiorari denied, 314 U. S. 625 (1941).

[95] The lottery circular case is Ex parte Jackson, 96 U. S. 727 (1878).

[96] The privilege theory is analyzed by, among others, Zechariah Chafee, Jr., *Government and Mass Communications* (University of Chicago Press, 1947), 277 ff.; E. P. Deutsch, Freedom of the Press and of the Mails, 36 Mich. L. Rev. 703 (1938). And see also William B. Lockhart and Robert C. McClure, Literature, the Law of Obscenity and the Constitution, 38 Minn. L. Rev. 295 (1954); Comment, Constitutional Law—Censorship of Obscene Literature, 52 Mich. L. Rev. 575 (1954).

[97] For judicial doubtings of the privilege theory see, e. g., Hannegan v. Esquire, 327 U. S. 146, 156 (1946): "But grave constitutional questions are immediately raised once it is said that the use of the mails is a privilege which may be extended or withheld on any grounds whatsoever." See also Cates v. Haderlein, 342 U. S. 804

(1951) (reversing, on government's confession of error, a lower court holding that there was no constitutional requirement of a hearing before issuance of a postal fraud order) ; Door v. Donaldson, 195 F. 2d 764 (D. C. Cir., 1952) ; Walker v. Popenoe, 149 F. 2d 511 (D. C. Cir., 1945) ; Doehla Greeting Cards, Inc. v. Summerfield, 116 F. Supp. 68 (D. D. C., 1953).

[98] For information about postal procedures, reference may be made to Monograph of the Attorney General's Committee on Administrative Procedure, Post Office Department, Sen. Doc. No. 186, 76th Cong., 3d Sess. (1940) ; Zechariah Chafee, Jr., *Government and Mass Communications* (University of Chicago Press, 1947), 324 ff. ; Charles R. Cutler, The Post Office Department and the Administrative Procedure Act, 47 Nw. U. L. Rev. 72 (1952) ; and, recently and compactly, Edward de Grazia, Obscenity and the Mail: A Study of Administrative Restraint, 20 Law & Contemporary Problems 608 (1955). And see also Postal Sanctions: A Study of the Summary Use of Administrative Power, 31 Ind. L. J. 257 (1956).

[99] Walker v. Popenoe, 149 F. 2d 511 (D. C. Cir., 1945), held that the Department was not entitled to withhold delivery of allegedly obscene material without notice and hearing; if this would take too long, the Department was advised instead to institute criminal proceedings against the mailer, under a penal statute making it a crime to deposit obscene (or otherwise objectionable) publications in the mails. The present statute to that effect is 62 Stat. 768 (1948), 18 U. S. C. § 1461 (1952 Supp.). Mr. de Grazia, in the article cited in the preceding note, remarks (p. 610) that " the Department proceeds as though *Walker* v. *Popenoe* were but a bad dream, continuing to seize all mail conceived by it to be obscene— without prior notice and hearing." The United States Court of Appeals for the District of Columbia on May 31, 1956, again rebuked the Post Office Department for continuing the very same conduct that had been " expressly condemned " in the *Popenoe* case. See Sunshine Book Co. v. Summerfield, 24 Law Week 5260.

[100] The " stop order " statute is 64 Stat. 451 (1950), 39 U. S. C. § 259(a) (Supp. 1952).

[101] The indignant editor's case is Knowles v. United States, 170 Fed. 409 (C. C. A. 8, 1909).

[102] In 1955 the Solicitor seized Lysistrata as being obscene on the grounds quoted, to which he added: " The effect of the book is intensified and heightened by the indecent and lascivious character of the illustrations "—by Norman Lindsay, the well-known Aus-

tralian artist. The purchaser of the book began an action to compel the Postmaster General to deliver the book. Levinson v. Summerfield, Civil Action No. 976–55 (D. Dist. Col., 1955). After a little preliminary sparring, the Postmaster General delivered the book to the plaintiff, thus rendering the case moot and avoiding a judicial determination on the merits.

[103] The quotation about judicial review comes from Roth v. Goldman, 172 F. 2d 788, 789 (C. A. 2, 1949), certiorari denied 337 U. S. 938 (1949). Judge Frank, concurring, felt (p. 790) that the court's ruling about the suitable scope of review "vests immense administrative censorship authority in one fallible man, makes him an almost despotic arbiter of literary products." He added (p. 795): ". . . it is arguable that with a statute which, at best, skirts unconstitutionality, the finding of fact that such [i. e., socially undesirable effects on normal readers] will be the probable results must be supported by evidence of an unusually clear and convincing kind—in other words, it is arguable that the evidence ought to be of a far stronger character than is required as the basis of ordinary administrative action."

[104] For illustrations of virtual finality, see Masses Publishing Co. v. Patten, 246 Fed. 24, 31–33 (C. C. A. 2d, 1917); Donaldson v. Read, 333 U. S. 178 (1948). But compare Bonica v. Oleson, 126 F. Supp. 398, 401 (S. D. Cal., 1954): "It appears that the only controverted issue at the administrative level was whether or not the films were 'obscene, lewd, or lascivious,' and the only evidence on this crucial issue was the films themselves. Thus, the court is in a particularly advantageous position to evaluate the evidence."

[105] Information about World War I censorship comes from Blanshard, *The Right to Read*, 114. For further treatment of the events of that period see James R. Mock, *Censorship 1917* (Princeton, 1941), esp. pp. 153 et seq.; and see also Zechariah Chafee, Jr., *Free Speech in the United States* (Harvard, 1941), 98 et seq.

[106] A sampling of the reviews of *Strange Fruit* reveals the following: ". . . absorbing . . . I find nothing in the novel that is pornographic . . ." Edward Weeks in *Atlantic Monthly* (May, 1944), Vol. CLXXIII, 127; "One of the finest, most sensitive novels of the season." A. C. Spectorsky in the *Chicago Sun*, March 5, 1944, p. 3; ". . . innate integrity . . . honesty of portrayal . . ." *Christian Science Monitor*, May 1, 1944, p. 14; "One of the most rewarding first novels to come out of the South in years . . ." William Du Bois in the *New York Times*, March 5, 1944, p. 1; ". . . a major novel

. . . Firmly and convincingly written . . . The atmosphere is superb
. . ." Struthers Burt in the *Saturday Review of Literature* (March
11, 1944), Vol. XXVII, 10.

[107] The *Strange Fruit* decision is Commonwealth v. Isenstadt, 318
Mass. 543, at 556 (1945). The approach there taken is not, how--
ever, universal. See especially the contrasting attitude of the Illinois
Supreme Court in American Civil Liberties Union v. City of Chicago,
3 Ill. 2d 334, 121 N. E. 2d 585 (1954); and see also Attorney
General v. Forever Amber, 323 Mass. 302, 81 N. E. 2d 663 (1948).
Cf. Brown v. Kingsley Books, 1 N. Y. 2d 177, 134 N. E. 2d 461
(1956) (upheld statute authorizing injunction against sale and
distribution of printed matter adjudged to be obscene; appellate
court may fully review trial judge's findings of fact).

[108] As to the jury's virtues, see Zechariah Chafee, Jr., *Government
and Mass Communications* (University of Chicago Press, 1947),
220; and see also the same author's Censorship of Plays and Books,
1 Bill of Rights Rev. 16, 19 (1940). I should note, however, that
many experienced trial lawyers do not share the Chafee view. They
prefer to try obscenity cases before a judge sitting without a jury,
because they believe that jurors tend to shame one another into
returning a finding of obscenity.

But compare Halsey v. New York Society for the Suppression
of Vice, 234 N. Y. 1 (1922): A bookseller who sold Theophile
Gautier's *Mademoiselle de Maupin* was hounded by the Society's
agent, but was ultimately acquitted of the charge of having trafficked
in obscenity. He then sued the Society for malicious prosecution,
and recovered damages. The Court of Appeals was divided as to
whether the Society had had reasonable cause to think the book
obscene. As to this, Andrews, J., said (p. 6): " The conflict among
the members of this court itself points a finger at the dangers of a
censorship entrusted to men of one profession, of like education
and similar surroundings. Far better than we, is a jury drawn from
those of varied experiences, engaged in various occupations, in close
touch with the currents of public feeling, fitted to say whether the
defendant had reasonable ground to believe that a book such as this
was obscene or indecent."

[109] It was a jury, rather than judges, who found Theodore
Dreiser's *American Tragedy* to be obscene. See Commonwealth v.
Friede, 271 Mass. 318 (1930). A survey made by the American
Institute of Public Opinion (Gallup poll) and the National Opinion
Research Center (Chicago University) under the direction of Pro-

fessor Samuel A. Stouffer of Harvard and reported by him in *Communism, Conformity, and Civil Liberties* (Doubleday, 1955) shows among other things that 68 per cent of the population would not allow speeches by Communists and 66 per cent would favor removal from libraries of books written by Communists (pp. 40–41). The percentages go down when other deviations from accustomed patterns are suggested, but, even so, 35 per cent of the population is apparently ready to remove from public libraries a book by a Socialist in favor of public ownership, and another 13 per cent are still undecided; comparable percentages would not allow a speech in favor of government ownership of railroads and "big business"; and 54 per cent (another 13 per cent being undecided) would not allow a Socialist to teach in a college or university (pp. 29–31). Professor Stouffer concludes (p. 223) that "most of the seemingly intolerant people are good, wholesome Americans," though of course the country "also has its share of hopelessly bigoted, even vicious people." The findings of this extensive and carefully conducted study do not suggest to me that jurymen (who are also for the most part "good, wholesome Americans") will certainly reflect intolerance in their verdicts if any tinge of "leftism" is attached to a book or its author. But the findings do suggest a predisposition that deserves to be recognized and discounted by perceptive reviewing courts. Those who may have occasion to select jurymen in matters of this sort may well note Chapter 4 of the Stouffer study, showing that tolerance of nonconformity of all sorts seems greatest among the youthful and the well educated. Persons who have had a great deal of schooling have had the largest opportunity to observe what has been called "the infinite capacity of the human mind to resist the introduction of learning." This may explain why they tend to be the least fearful of the effectiveness and the effects of words.

[110] An example of judicial self-assurance: When the quality of Henry Miller's writing was to be determined in United States v. Two Obscene Books, 92 F. Supp. 934 (N. D. Cal., 1950), the trial judge remarked that what was "salacious or filthy" could not become "clean and wholesome upon the mere statement of some alleged or so-called critic." Hence, the testimony of "19 persons alleged to be experts in the field of literary criticism" was deemed "wholly irrelevant and immaterial." The judge, unaided by experts, gave full vent to his indignation at the books when the case came before him

on the merits, 99 F. Supp. 760 (N. D. Cal., 1951), affirmed 208 F. 2d 142 (C. A. 9, 1953).

Note, by contrast, the present Massachusetts statute, enacted in 1945, Mass. Laws Ann. (Michie, 1955), vol. 9, ch. 272, sec. 28F, which in terms provides that when the issue is obscenity, experts may properly give evidence about " the literary, cultural or educational character " of the book.

¹¹¹ Sir Charles Sydlyes Case, 1 Keble 620 (King's Bench, 1663). See Leo M. Alpert, Judicial Censorship of Obscene Literature, 52 Harv. L. Rev. 40 (1938); Sidney S. Grant and S. E.Angoff, Massachusetts and Censorship, 10 B. U. L. Rev. 36, at 52 (1930). Sedley's place in the literature and society of his time is mentioned in *The Cambridge History of English Literature* (Putnam, 1912), Vol. VIII, 158, 226.

¹¹² For non-statutory denunciations of vulgarity see, e. g., State v. Appling, 25 Mo. 315 (1857); Barker v. Commonwealth, 14 Pa. 412 (1852). And see William L. Prosser, *Insult and Outrage*, 44 Calif. L. Rev. 40 (1956).

¹¹³ The " dirty letters " case is United States v. Limehouse, 285 U. S. 424 (1932).

¹¹⁴ The case involving telephonic indecency is Commonwealth v. Mochan, 177 Pa. Super. 454, 110 A. 2d 788 (1955). This case is discussed in 16 U. Pitt. L. Rev. 397 (1955). In 1954 Louisiana enacted a statute providing fine and imprisonment for local telephone calls of an anonymous nature involving the use of " obscene, profane, vulgar, lewd, lascivious or indecent language, suggestions, or proposals." Act of July 7, 1954.

¹¹⁵ As to nudity on the highway, compare King v. Gallard, W. Kelynge 163 (King's Bench, 1733): The court quashed an indictment brought against a woman for " running in the common way, naked down to the waist "—because " nothing appears immodest or unlawful."

¹¹⁶ City of Pascagoula v. Nolan, 183 Miss. 164, 184 So. 165 (1938). And see Holcomb v. State, 5 Ga. App. 47, 62 S. E. 647 (1908), for another illustration of extreme sensitivity to any reference to the posterior.

¹¹⁷ The figures on library expenditures come from Office of Education Bulletin No. 9, Public Library Statistics (U. S. Dept. of Health, Education & Welfare, 1953), 15:

Per capita expenditure	Number of states
less than 27 cents	1
27–49 cents	10
50–74 cents	7
75–99 cents	11
$1–$1.25	12
$1.25 and over	7

[118] The New York State Library's report, "Public Library Study," is printed in 78 Library Journal 1608 (1953). The authors are Virginia L. Moran, L. Marion Moshier, Irving Vershoor, and William Blom.

[119] A. Whitney Griswold, *Essays on Education* (Yale University Press, 1954), 96.

Notes to Chapter Three

[1] Schlesinger v. Atlanta, 161 Ga. 148, 159, 129 S. E. 861, 866 (1925).

[2] Justice Douglas spoke in Barsky v. Board of Regents, 347 U. S. 442, 472 (1954) (dissenting).

[3] As to the loyalty-security programs see, e. g., Eleanor Bontecou, *The Federal Loyalty-Security Program* (Cornell, 1953); Ralph S. Brown, Jr., Loyalty-Security Measures and Employment Opportunities, 11 Bulletin of the Atomic Scientists 113 (1955). As to the role of labor unions, see, e. g., Sumner H. Slichter, *Union Policies and Industrial Management* (Brookings Institution, 1941), esp. pp. 9–97; Ralph A. Newman, The Closed Union and the Right to Work, 43 Colum. L. Rev. 42 (1943); Clyde W. Summers, The Right to Join a Union, 47 Colum. L. Rev. 33 (1947); Philip Taft, *Economics and Problems of Labor* (Stackpole Co., 1955); and see also Arthur Lenhoff, The Right to Work: Here and Abroad, 46 Ill. L. Rev. 669 (1951).

[4] Council of State Governments, Occupational Licensing Legislation in the States (1952), 7–8, contains a seemingly incomplete but probably the most comprehensive single list of the licensed occupations. It omits a number of instances that were located independently. William Beard, in *Government and Technology* (Macmillan, 1934), 494, refers to a study that discovered 250 trades and professions subject to license restrictions in one or more localities.

⁵ W. Brooke Graves, Professional and Occupational Restrictions, 13 Temp. L. Q. 334, 346 n. (1939), refers to studies of municipal licensing in representative states including Reid, *Municipal Business and Occupational License Taxes* (Alabama League of Municipalities, 1936); Graves, *Report on Study of Business License Ordinances*, (League of California Municipalities, San Francisco, Los Angeles, 1936); Municipal License Fees in Washington, U. of Wash. Bur. of Gov. Research (1938). See also Malcolm B. Parsons, *The Use of the Licensing Power by the City of Chicago* (University of Illinois Press, 1952), 1–64; *License and Permit Fees in Iowa Cities* (Institute of Public Affairs, U. of Iowa, 1952); Ernest H. Campbell and Sidney Coleman, *Licensing by Washington Cities* (University of Washington Press, 1951), 8, 49–58.

⁶ The North Carolina situation is well discussed in Frank Hanft and J. Nathaniel Hamrick, Haphazard Regimentation under Licensing Statutes, 17 N. C. L. Rev. 1, 21 (1938).

⁷ Hypertrichology, as defined in Conn. Gen. Stat. (1953 Supp.), sec. 1760(c), involves " the removal of superfluous hair by electrical or other methods approved by the state board of examiners of hypertrichologists."

⁸ As to the early characteristics of professions, see Sir Alexander Morris Carr-Saunders, " Metropolitan Conditions and Traditional Professional Relationships," in *The Metropolis in Modern Life* (Robert Moore Fisher, ed.; Doubleday, 1955), 280.

⁹ Quoted from Dr. Parran's comments in *The Metropolis in Modern Life* (Robert Moore Fisher, ed.; Doubleday, 1955), 305.

¹⁰ As to the impact of urbanization on specialization, R. E. Park, *Human Communities* (The Free Press, 1952), 24, takes the point a step farther: " In the city every vocation, even that of a beggar, tends to assume the character of a profession, and the discipline which success in any vocation imposes, together with the associations that it enforces, emphasizes this tendency—the tendency, namely, not merely to specialize, but to rationalize one's occupation and to develop a specific and conscious technique for carrying it on."

¹¹ Carr-Saunders' lament about the lowered prestige of professional men appears in his paper cited in note 8 above, p. 286.

¹² Harold Laski, *The American Democracy* (Viking, 1948), 568. The more orthodox view is reflected in State ex rel. Steiner v. Yelle, 174 Wash. 402, 25 P. 2d 91 (1933): " A profession is not a money getting business. It has no element of commercialism in it. True, the professional man seeks to live by what he earns, but his

main purpose and desire is to be of service to those who seek his aid and to the community of which he is a necessary part."

[13] For encouragement of the belief that almost everyone is a " professional man," see, e. g., Donald Young (president of the Russell Sage Foundation), " Universities and Cooperation among Metropolitan Professions," in *The Metropolis in Modern Life* (Robert Moore Fisher, ed.; Doubleday, 1955), 290: " In the United States, the word profession denotes almost all occupations which require more training than those activities vaguely designated as unskilled or semi-skilled. For general purposes, there is no apparent advantage in distinguishing between a business, a trade, a vocation, and a profession. Such a distinction inevitably becomes invidious and is often made without logical basis."

A valuable review of definitional efforts can be found in Morris L. Cogan, Toward a Definition of Profession, 23 Harv. Educ. Rev. 33 (1953).

[14] As to the yearning to achieve social recognition through " professional " identification, compare Carr-Saunders, cited in note 8 above, p. 281: Manual workers are conscious of their indispensability because they see the results of their work, but non-manual workers feel a need to show that they, too, are important. " In effect, they attempt to demonstrate that they are experts without whose services society cannot get along, and that they are generally not so very far removed from doctors and the fully recognized professions. But the non-manual workers exaggerate the degree and quality of their expertness in an attempt to make good their claims. They say little about the ends which they hope to reach by professional recognition; namely, social upgrading and improved remuneration. In practice their associations act as trade unions in the matter of collective bargaining and in their efforts to restrict a particular way of making a living to their members." Compare *New York Times*, June 22, 1956, p. 20, col. 1, under headline, " Policemen Weigh Status in Society—Convention Delegates Here Debate Seeking a Rating as Professional Men." An official of the National Conference of Police Associations is quoted as exclaiming, " We aren't watchmen, that's for sure. The Army officer has professional recognition, so why not the police officer? "

[15] As to the " public need " for licensing, compare Frank Hanft and J. Nathaniel Hamrick, Haphazard Regimentation under Licensing Statutes, 17 N. C. L. Rev. 1, 4 (1938): " Did the legislators after examination of the needs of society come by themselves to the

conclusion that trained and qualified chiropodists are vital to the public interest? . . . Or that boughten photographs are so closely connected with the general welfare that only licensed photographers should be allowed to take photographs for a price, whereas anyone may take them for himself?" The authors reach a negative conclusion, suspecting that many of the laws "are procured by men already in these occupations in order to keep others out."

[16] The New Jersey situation has been well described by Dayton D. McKean, *Pressures on the Legislature of New Jersey* (Columbia University Press, 1938), esp. p. 56.

[17] The Wisconsin licensing pressures are discussed by Ruth B. Doyle, The Fence-Me-In Laws, 205 Harpers 89 (August, 1952). For a description of developments in Nebraska, see Richard A. Knudsen, Licensing of Professions and Occupations in Nebraska, 29 Neb. L. Rev. 146 (1949).

[18] The definition and examining of psychologists was finally achieved in New York by N. Y. Laws 1956, ch. 737. For reflections of the struggle to become licensed, see The Bulletin of New York State Psychological Association, Vol. I (1948), No. 1, p. 1; Vol. I (1948), No. 2, p. 1; Vol. II (1949), No. 2, p. 1; Vol. III (1950), No. 1, p. 3; Vol. III (1950), No. 2, p. 3.

[19] James Grafton Rogers is quoted by Frances P. DeLancy, *The Licensing of Professions in West Virginia* (Foundation Press, 1938), 139.

[20] The striking parallelism between guilds and occupational licensing has been especially well observed by Professor J. A. C. Grant of California in The Gild Returns to America, 4 Journal of Politics 303 and 458 (1942).

[21] For restrictive aims of medieval guilds, see William J. Ashley, *Introduction to English Economic History and Theory* (4th ed.; Longmans, Green, 1906), Vol. I, 72.

[22] For the managerial aspects of the guilds, see Edward P. Cheyney, *Industrial and Social History of England* (rev. ed.; Macmillan, 1922), 52–55; Council of State Governments, Occupational Licensing Legislation in the States (1952), 10–13. And see also Charles Gross, *The Guild Merchant* (Oxford, 1890), 36–52, 61–76; George Clune, *The Medieval Guild System* (Brown & Nolan, 1943), 21–43, 48–83, 111–24.

[23] The comment about the welcomed demise of the guilds comes from J. A. C. Grant, The Gild Returns to America, 4 Journal of Politics 303 (1942).

[24] The California "integrated bar" is provided for by the California Business and Professions Code (Deering, 1951), secs. 6018 et seq. The progress of integration is described by Glenn R. Winters, *Bar Association Organization and Activities* (American Judicature Society, 1954), 9–10. The "integration of the bar" has been sustained in Petition of Florida State Bar Association, 40 So. 2d 902 (Fla., 1949) ; and compare In re Disbarment of West, 212 N. C. 189, 193 S. E. 134 (1937).

[25] The North Carolina "pedics" can point with pride to N. C. Gen. Stat. (Michie, 1950), secs. 90–190, 90–192.

The triumph of the Oklahoma dentists is reflected in Okla. Stat. Ann. (West, 1949), tit. 59, secs. 231–49.

[26] In Louisiana, for example, the barbers' prices are regulated by a very sympathetic board. See La. Stat. Ann. (West, 1951), tit. 37, sec. 420.

[27] As to price-fixing upon petition of those whose prices are fixed, see David Fellman, A Case Study in Administrative Law— The Regulation of Barbers, 26 Wash. U. L. Q. 213, 222 ff. (1941).

[28] Council of State Governments, Occupational Licensing Legislation in the States (1952), 44, casts doubt upon the primary objective of price fixing.

[29] The progress of cosmetic therapy control "in the public interest" may be traced from Louisiana Laws 1924, Act 135 to Louisiana General Statutes (Dart, 1949 Supp.), secs. 9484 et seq., showing the economic developments achieved by a 1940 statute. The present laws are shown in Louisiana Revised Statutes (West, 1951), art. 37, secs. 491 et seq.

[30] The requirement about keeping caskets in stock was held invalid in Golden v. Bartholomew, 140 Neb. 65, 299 N. W. 356 (1941).

[31] An excellent example of success in "fending off trespassers who might otherwise compete for business" may be seen in Daniel v. Family Security Life Ins. Co., 336 U. S. 220 (1949). And compare Dentists, Dental Laboratories, and the Public Interest, 51 Nw. U. L. Rev. 123 (1956). See also Delaware Optometric Ass'n. v. Sherwood, 24 Law Week 2520 (Delaware Chancery Court, April 27, 1956) (optometrists' attempt to restrain opticians from fitting contact lenses).

[32] Of course a plumber's training is prolonged as an ostensible protection of the citizenry against the ill health that might be caused by faulty drains. Oddly enough, however, the stated grounds

for revoking a plumber's license may include such sins as aiding unlicensed persons in any task defined as plumbing, while omitting any mention of performing plumbing work so unsatisfactorily as to endanger public health and safety. Council of State Governments, Occupational Licensing Legislation in the States (1952), 42.

33 Apprenticeship practices are discussed by Sumner H. Slichter, *Union Policies and Industrial Management* (Brookings Institution, 1941), 9–45. Professor Slichter's discussion deals particularly with apprenticeship programs unrelated to licensing requirements, but is clearly pertinent to the latter. And compare Apprenticeship in Building Construction, Bureau of Labor Statistics Bull. No. 459 (1928), which, on p. 9, quotes a St. Louis contractor: "A boy has as good a chance to get into West Point as into the building trades unless his father or his uncle is a building craftsman."

34 For discussion of union initiation fees, see Clyde W. Summers, Admission Policies of Labor Unions, 61 Quarterly Journal of Economics 66, 80 (1946). For a compendium of union practices, see National Industrial Conference Board, Handbook of Union Government Structure and Procedures (1955), 33–42; and see also N. I. C. B., Sourcebook of Union Government Structure and Procedures (1956).

35 The governor's comment on occupational lobbies appears in Examining and Licensing Boards, 24 State Government 280, 281 (1951).

36 The citizen's right "to be free in the enjoyment of all his faculties" is discussed in Allgeyer v. Louisiana, 165 U. S. 578, 589 (1897).

37 The comment about "unreasonable and unnecessary restrictions" was made by Mr. Justice Butler in Burns Baking Co. v. Bryan, 264 U. S. 504, 513 (1924), quoted approvingly by Mr. Justice Sutherland in Liggett Co. v. Baldridge, 278 U. S. 105, 113 (1928).

38 The presumption that the legislature knows facts is stated in Hardware Dealers Mutual Fire Insurance Co. v. Glidden, 284 U. S. 151 (1931).

39 Daniel v. Family Security Life Ins. Co., 336 U. S. 220 (1949).

40 The licensing of real estate brokers was held unconstitutional in Rawles v. Jenkins, 212 Ky. 287, 279 S. W. 350 (1926). And see also Howard v. Lebby, 197 Ky. 324, 246 S. W. 828 (1923) (licensing of house painters declared unconstitutional).

41 Rawles v. Jenkins was overruled sub silentio by Shelton v. Mc-

Connel, 308 Ky. 280, 214 S. W. 2d 396 (1948). Four years later, in Miller v. State Real Estate Commission, 251 S. W. 2d 845 (Ky., 1952), the court said that Rawles v. Jenkins had not been brought to its attention when the Shelton case was argued; but the Shelton case was acknowledged as the then controlling authority in Kentucky. Sims v. Reeves, 261 S. W. 2d 812 (Ky., 1953), put the matter to rest by following the Shelton rather than the Rawles case, in a square holding.

⁴² The prevailing attitude of the state courts is exemplified by Biddles, Inc. v. Enright, 239 N. Y. 354, 363, 146 N. E. 625, 628 (1925): "Any trade, calling or occupation may be reasonably regulated if ' the general nature of the business is such that unless regulated many persons may be exposed to misfortunes against which the legislature can properly protect them.' "

⁴³ The Maryland barbering case is Schneider v. Duer, 170 Md. 326, 184 Atl. 914, 917 (1936).

⁴⁴ The curriculum for barbers was set forth in Md. Acts 1935, c. 371, sec. 282 L.

⁴⁵ See David Fellman, A Case Study in Administrative Law, 22 Wash. U. L. Q. 213, at 240 n. (1941), describing the Associated Master Barbers of America's "Standardized Textbook of Barbering."

⁴⁶ As to florists, see Kresge Co. v. Couzens, 290 Mich. 185, 287 N. W. 427 (1939).

As to watchmakers, see State ex rel. Whetsel v. Wood, 207 Okla. 193, 248 P. 2d 612 (1952).

As to photographers, see State v. Gleason, 277 P. 2d 530 (Mont., 1954); State v. Cromwell, 72 N. D. 565, 9 N. W. 2d 914 (1943); Sullivan v. DeCerb, 156 Fla. 496, 23 So. 2d 571 (1945).

The Oklahoma court that invalidated the licensing of watchmakers has approved stringent control over barbers as a sanitary and health measure, and the licensing of dry cleaning establishments because their activities, if carelessly pursued, might affect health or create fire hazards. Herrin v. Arnold, 183 Okla. 392, 82 P. 2d 977 (1938); Jack Lincoln Shops, Inc. v. State Dry Cleaners' Board, 192 Okla. 251, 135 P. 2d 332 (1943), appeal dismissed for want of a substantial federal question, 320 U. S. 208 (1943). Photography, by contrast, " is one of the innocent, usual occupations in which everybody who so wishes may indulge as a pastime or a hobby or a vocation, without harm or injury to anybody, or to the general welfare, or the public health and morals, or the peace, safety and comfort of the people." Buehman v. Bechtel, 57 Ariz. 363, 367, 114 P. 2d 227, 229 (1941).

[47] Bramley v. State, 187 Ga. 826, 838-839, 2 S. E. 2d 647 (1939). And for similar views, leading courts to invalidate photographer licensing laws, see State v. Ballance, 229 N. C. 764, 51 S. E. 2d 73 (1949); Moore v. Sutton, 185 Va. 481, 39 S. E. 2d 348 (1946).

[48] People v. Brown, 407 Ill. 565, 95 N. E. 2d 888 (1951). In addition to the ground of decision discussed in the text, the Illinois court was also adversely impressed by the excessively long time required to advance through the lower plumbing grades to the highest.

[49] For another thrust at the master's control over access to a trade, see State ex rel. Whetsel v. Wood, 207 Okla. 193, 195, 248 P. 2d 612, 614 (1952), criticizing a requirement that a four-year apprenticeship must be served under and with the consent of a licensed watchmaker: " This provision has the effect of placing in the hands of those holding a license the power to limit the number of those allowed to engage in watchmaking in Oklahoma, and clearly tends toward creating a monopoly." And see State v. Walker, 48 Wash. 8, 92 Pac. 775 (1907), which upset a two-year apprenticeship requirement for barbers because the statute failed to recognize the possibility of a man's achieving proficiency by schooling without apprenticeship, or merely by his own unassisted efforts.

[50] For discussion of apprenticeship prerequisites, see Restriction of Freedom of Entry into the Building Trades, 38 Iowa L. Rev. 556 (1953); David Fellman, A Case Study in Administrative Law—The Regulation of Barbers, 26 Wash. U. L. Q. 213 (1941).

[51] The Georgia legislature's concern lest photographers be syphilitic was reflected in Ga. Laws 1937, p. 280, sec. 10(b).

[52] Templar v. State Board of Examiners of Barbers, 131 Mich. 254, 90 N. W. 1058 (1902) (held invalid). The Michigan court indicated approval, however, of citizenship requirements for liquor retailers and attorneys.

[53] Wormsen v. Moss, 177 Misc. 19, 29 N. Y. S. 2d 798 (Sup. Ct., N. Y. Co., 1941); Magnani v. Harnett, 257 App. Div. 487, 14 N. Y. S. 2d 107 (1939), aff'd 282 N. Y. 619, 25 N. E. 2d 395 (1940). And see, generally, David Fellman, The Alien's Right to Work, 22 Minn. L. Rev. 137 (1938).

[54] Clark v. Deckenbach, 274 U. S. 392, 397 (1927). Compare, however, Takahashi v. Fish and Game Commission of California,

334 U. S. 410 (1948), invalidating a statute that denied commercial fishing licenses to " persons ineligible to citizenship."

[55] As to irrelevant citizenship requirements see, e. g., New York Public Health Law, sec. 3421(2)(b) (embalmers must be citizens); Conn. Gen. Stat. (1953 Supp.), sec. 1763(c) (hypertrichologists must be citizens), and sec. 4556 (chiropodists must at least have declared their intention of becoming citizens).

[56] Yick Wo v. Hopkins, 118 U. S. 356 (1886), dealt with improper racial factors in licensing.

[57] As to the concealed use of improper limitations on license eligibility, Prof. Clyde W. Summers, in Admission Policies of Labor Unions, 61 Quarterly Journal of Economics 66, 83 (1946), says: " The Plumbers and Electricians (A. F. of L.) have openly advocated these [licensing] laws as devices for restricting the number of available workers and especially for excluding Negroes." Herbert Northrup, in *Organized Labor and the Negro* (Harper & Bros., 1944), 24, reports that in Baltimore the plumbers licensing board managed for years to keep Negroes out of the trade. At first this was achieved by requiring that each applicant be endorsed by two master plumbers, there being no Negro master plumbers in the city. The endorsement requirement was dropped when it was challenged by the Urban League. Then the licensing board rejected the Negro applicants by finding them deficient in theoretical physics.

[58] For judicial invalidation of residence requirements in licensing matters see, e. g., New Brunswick v. Zimmerman, 79 F. 2d 428 (C. A. 3, 1935); Lipkin v. Duffy, 119 N. J. L. 336, 196 A. 434 (1938); McGriff v. State, 212 Ark. 98, 204 S. W. 2d 885 (1947).

[59] Residence requirements may do more than cause inconvenience to an experienced man who desires to move. They also, in a very real sense, inhibit the movement of skills to places where they are most needed. National Manpower Council, A Policy for Skilled Manpower (1954), 243–45.

[60] For discussion of the differences between the creation of standards and, on the other hand, the imposition of disqualifications, see Francis D. Wormuth, Legislative Disqualifications as Bills of Attainder, 4 Vand. L. Rev. 603 (1951).

[61] Indiana Statutes Ann. (Burns, 1951), sec. 63–2315(1).

[62] For sweeping approval of the notion that past criminality denotes bad moral character, see Hawker v. New York, 170 U. S. 189 (1898), which endorsed a statutory exclusion from the practice of medicine of any person previously convicted of a felony, regard-

less of its nature. Good character is important in a medical practitioner, the Court said, and conviction of criminality bears on it.
To the same effect, see Barsky v. Board of Regents, 347 U. S. 442
(1954), upholding the disciplining of a doctor convicted by a
federal court of having committed contempt of Congress. Dr.
Barsky had refused to comply with an investigating committee's
command to produce the records of the Joint Anti-Fascist Refugee
Committee. There were no charges that bore in any way on his
professional conduct, abilities, or character; as Judge Fuld had
observed in the court below, 305 N. Y. at 102, 111 N. E. 2d at
228–29, the record was " barren of evidence reflecting upon appellant as a man or a citizen, much less on his professional capacity or
his past or anticipated conduct toward his patients." Justice Douglas,
in dissent, said (pp. 473–74): " The fact that a doctor needs a good
knowledge of biology is no excuse for suspending his license because
he has little or no knowledge of constitutional law." But the majority felt (p. 452) that the state, realizing " the importance of
high standards of character and law observance on the part of
practicing physicians," may permissibly " attain its justifiable end by
making the conviction of any crime a violation of its professional
medical standards. . ."

[63] Ernst Freund, *Administrative Powers over Persons and Property*
(University of Chicago Press, 1928), 128.

[64] As to procedure in " good character" cases, see, e. g., Perpente
v. Moss, 293 N. Y. 325, 56 N. E. 2d 726 (1944) (" license may
not be refused on the ground that the applicant ' is not a person
of good character ' unless the applicant has fair opportunity to meet
a challenge to his good character and unless the court of review is
apprised of the basis for the finding against the applicant. The
procedure . . . must conform to recognize standards of fairness ");
Smith v. Foster, 15 F. 2d 115 (S. D. N. Y., 1926) (a finding of
lack of confidence in an applicant's integrity cannot be made without
affording a full hearing); Gage v. Censors of the New Hampshire
Eclectic Medical Society, 63 N. H. 92 (1884) (medical license cannot be withheld on ground that applicant was " unworthy of public
confidence," without a hearing). And see Clark Byse, Opportunity
to Be Heard in License Issuance, 101 U. Pa. L. Rev. 57, at 100
(1952). Compare, however, Higgins v. Hartford County Bar Association, 111 Conn. 47, 149 Atl. 415 (1930): An applicant was
denied permission to take the bar examination upon a finding that
he lacked the requisite good moral character. He complained that

he had been given no notice, no charges, no knowledge of the sources of information adverse to him. The court refused to provide a suitable hearing, saying that he was not being deprived of a right or tried for a crime.

[65] The pharmacists' statute is Texas Civil Stat. Ann. (Vernon, Supp., 1952), art. 4542(a)(9).

[66] The Indiana regulation of pugilists is reported in *New York Times*, October 20, 1955; American Civil Liberties Union, Clearing the Main Channels, 35th Ann. Rep. (1955), 39.

[67] The piano tuner's difficulties are recounted in the ACLU report cited above, p. 38.

[68] The Washington veterinarian's oath requirement is reported in American Civil Liberties Union Weekly Bulletin No. 1744, April 2, 1956.

[69] The California legislature in 1955 defeated a proposal to revoke *any* of 450,000 outstanding state licenses if the licensee pleaded the Fifth Amendment in an official investigation of anything at all (later limited to Communism and advocacy of violent revolution). Discussed in the ACLU report cited in note 66 above, p. 36.

[70] See, as bearing on expurgatory oaths, American Communications Association v. Douds, 339 U. S. 282 (1950), which upheld the requirement of the Taft-Hartley Act that labor union officials file a non-Communist affidavit as a condition of the union's access to the National Labor Relations Board. The Court majority felt that Congress could reasonably view the affidavit as a necessary protection against politically inspired strikes. But the Court stressed that the required oath must be rationally related to purposes the legislature could seek to attain. And see also the concurring opinion of Jackson, J., in Thomas v. Collins, 323 U. S. at 545 (1945).

[71] The quoted phrase comes from Mr. Justice Frankfurter's dissent in Nugent v. United States, 346 U. S. 1, at 13 (1953).

[72] For discussion of port security measures, see Ralph S. Brown, Jr., and John D. Fassett, Security Tests for Maritime Workers: Due Process Under the Port Security Program, 62 Yale L. J. 1163 (1953). Parker v. Lester, 227 F. 2d 708 (C. A. 9, 1955), overturned an adverse determination because of procedural faults.

[73] For references to exclusion of communists from admission to the bar, see Rules for Admission to the Bar (West, 1953), 20, 39, 102. New York's Rules of Civil Practice, Rule 1(f)(1), harking back to the " red scare " days after World War I, have provided since 1921 that an applicant for admission to the bar must " furnish

satisfactory proof to the effect: (1) That he believes in the form of government of the United States and is loyal to such government." California's Business and Professions Code (Deering, Supp., 1951), secs. 6064.1 and 6106.1, provides that "no person who advocates overthrow of the government by force, violence, or other unconstitutional means" shall be licensed as a lawyer, and if he has already been licensed, such a person may be disbarred. There is no standard formulation. Maryland's law [Md. Code Ann. (Michie, 1955 Supp.), art. 10, sec. 3(c)] says that the admitting court must find that the applicant is "not a subversive person, as defined by the Subversive Activities Act of 1949."

[74] The quoted comment upon Communist lawyers comes from the Report and Recommendations of the Special Committee on the Matter of Communist Lawyers, submitted on November 29, 1955, and acted on at a meeting of the Association of the Bar of the City of New York on January 17, 1956.

[75] The statement about law teachers appears in Proceedings of the Association of American Law Schools (1951), 99.

[76] Ralph S. Brown, Jr., and John D. Fassett, Loyalty Tests for Admission to the Bar, 20 U. Chi. L. Rev. 480, 481 (1953).

[77] Criticism of Professor Brown's position comes from Vern Countryman, Loyalty Tests for Lawyers, 13 Law. Guild Rev. 149, 156 (1953).

[78] The Washington oath requirement is discussed in Washington Supreme Court Adopts Canons of Professional and Judicial Ethics and Non-Communist Admission Oath, 34 J. Am. Jud. Soc'y. 173 (1951).

[79] Ex parte Garland, 4 Wall. 333 (1886); and see also American Communications Association v. Douds, 339 U. S. 382, at 413–414 (1950).

[80] Schware v. Board of Bar Examiners, 291 P. 2d 607 (New Mex., 1955), involved an ex-Communist. Said the court: "We believe one who has knowingly given his loyalties to such a program and belief for six to seven years during a period of responsible adulthood is a person of questionable character. We do not think it an exaggeration to say that many have doubtless been denied entry into or expelled from membership in the legal profession for far less serious offense against ethic."

A petition for certiorari had been filed with the United States Supreme Court in Schware's behalf, but had not been acted upon by the Court when these pages were printed.

[81] Wieman v. Updegraff, 344 U. S. 183 (1952).

[82] Rejection of the guilt-by-infection concept is reflected in Application of Levy, 348 U. S. 978 (1955), reversing 214 F. 2d 331 (C. A. 5, 1954).

[83] The case of the Christian Fronter is Application of Cassidy, 268 App. Div. 282, 51 N. Y. S. 2d 202, affirmed 296 N. Y. 926, 73 N. E. 2d 41 (1947). And see In re Margolis, 269 Pa. 206, 112 Atl. 478 (1921); In re Smith, 133 Wash. 145, 233 Pac. 289 (1925), which also dealt with the affected individuals' own attitudes rather than their associations.

[84] The conscientious objector case is In re Summers, 325 U. S. 561 (1945). Mr. Justice Black, for the dissenters, was unable to " agree that a state can lawfully bar from a semi-public position a well qualified man of good character solely because he entertains a religious belief which might prompt him at some time in the future to violate a law which has not yet been and may never be enacted." (325 U. S. at 578.)

[85] The New York attitude toward conscientious objection is shown by Application of Steinbugler, 297 N. Y. 713, 77 N. E. 2d 16 (1947).

[86] In re George Anastaplo, 3 Ill. 2d 477, 121 N. E. 2d 826 (1954), cert. den. 348 U. S. 946 (1954).

A description of the Anastaplo case appears in The Illinois Bar and Individual Freedom, 50 Nw. U. L. Rev. 94 (1955).

[87] For further discussion of the problems of determining an applicant's fitness, see John R. Starrs, Considerations on Determination of Good Moral Character, 2 U. Det. L. J. 195 (1955). Ralph S. Brown, Jr., and John D. Fassett, Loyalty Tests for Admission to the Bar, 20 U. Chi. L. Rev. 480, at 508 (1953), quote Robert E. Seiler, Esq., secretary of the Missouri Board of Law Examiners as saying: ". . . I do not think that inquiry into political beliefs has any place in bar examination work. I think that the study of law is the best training anyone can have for becoming a good American and I do not think it should be cluttered up with investigations about political beliefs and whether or not the applicant happens to agree with what a majority of the people may or may not consider at the moment to be subversive."

[88] The lines of questioning described in the text are reported in the Brown-Fassett discussion cited in note 87 above, pp. 494, 500–501.

The perils of answering such an open-ended question as put in

Hawaii are richly suggested by the fantastic images of the Communist recently disclosed by Professor Stouffer's study of the general public from which investigative agencies obtain much of their "unevaluated" information. Only 3 per cent of the population cross-section knew a person who admitted he was a Communist. Another 10 per cent knew someone whom they *suspected* of being a Communist. Samples: "He was always talking about world peace." "Would not attend church and talked against God. He was always against local politics." "Her activities in distributing literature about the United Nations." "Just his slant on community life and church work. He was not like us." "During the war I used to say Russia was our enemy and he got mad at me." "He had a foreign camera and took so many pictures of the large New York bridges. A young man but never associated with people his own age." "My husband's brother drinks and acts common-like. Sometimes I kind of think he is a Communist." See Samuel A. Stouffer, *Communism, Conformity, and Civil Liberties* (Doubleday, 1955), 176–78.

[89] For the 1950 proposal of a "non-Communist oath" for lawyers, see 36 A. B. A. J. 948, 972. At about the same time, the Michigan State Bar Association proposed that every lawyer should swear that he does not adhere to "Marxism-Leninism," a condition of mind that was not defined. See 30 Mich. State B. J., no. 9, p. 70 (1951). For discussion of the problems suggested by these proposals, see Constitutional Issues Raised by the Proposed Loyalty Oath for Lawyers, 36 Iowa L. Rev. 529 (1951).

[90] For criticism of the ABA proposal, see The Proposed Anti-Communist Oath: Opposition Expressed to Association's Policy, 37 A. B. A. J. 123 and 125 (1951).

[91] The proposal for investigation of a lawyer who invokes the Fifth Amendment appears in 78 A. B. A. Rep. 388 (1953). This was followed in 79 A. B. A. Rep. 122 (1954), by a call for automatic disciplinary action against an attorney who claims the privilege against self-incrimination. The proposal now has the qualified support of the New York and Washington State Bar Associations, among others. See 27 N. Y. State Bar Bull. 247-265 (1955); 29 Wash. L. Rev. 345 (1954). On the other hand, it has been rejected by the California State Bar [30 Journal of State Bar of California 348 and 385 (1955)] and by the Association of the Bar of the City of New York, which on January 17, 1956, rejected two of the recommendations laid before it by a special committee, in the following

terms: (a) "That this Association should bring disciplinary proceedings against lawyers who are members of or who participate in Communist organizations with knowledge of their purpose"; (b) "This Committee recommends that in any case where a member of the bar invokes the Fifth Amendment in a proper inquiry as to Communist activities, and there is evidence of his connection with such activities, the Grievance Committee should make such investigation as it deems appropriate under the circumstances."

For views favorable to the A. B. A. proposal, see editorial, 39 A. B. A. J. 1084 (1953); Loyd Wright, The Lawyer's Responsibility and the Fifth Amendment, 34 Neb. L. Rev. 573 (1955). For critical comment, see Ralph S. Brown, Jr., Lawyers and the Fifth Amendment: A Dissent, 40 A. B. A. J. 404 (1954); Stanley A. Weigal, The Fifth Amendment and the Lawyer's Responsibility, 34 Neb. L. Rev. 586 (1955).

[92] Sheiner v. State, 82 So. 2d 657 (Fla., 1955).

The New York cases referred to in the text are Matter of Grae, 282 N. Y. 428, 26 N. E. 2d 963 (1940); Matter of Ellis, 282 N. Y. 435, 26 N. E. 2d 967 (1940). These cases did not in terms involve an invocation of the privilege against self-incrimination. They involved, rather, a refusal to sign a waiver of immunity when called upon to testify in an investigation. Thus, there was not a naked refusal to testify, but a refusal to testify unless the witness were first given absolution. The court declined to hold that guilt could be inferred from this refusal.

[93] Erwin N. Griswold, *The Fifth Amendment Today* (Harvard, 1955), 53.

[94] In connection with objections to constricting an appointing authority's choice, consider also Emmette S. Redford, The Protection of the Public Interest with Special Reference to Administrative Regulation, 48 Am. Pol. Sci. Rev. 1103 (1954). Stressing the need "to maintain remoteness from particularistic viewpoints and an attachment to general interests," Professor Redford recommends (p. 1110) avoiding "representation of the interests in the composition of public authority (as on regulatory boards) or occupational qualifications which are equivalent, except where necessary to obtain consent of parties to a mediatory process (as in some aspects of labor relations)."

[95] For comments on transferring administrative power into the hands of those regulated, see Avery Leiserson, *Administrative Regulation: A Study in Representation of Interests* (University of Chi-

cago Press, 1942) 130–33; Walter Gellhorn, *Federal Administrative Proceedings* (Johns Hopkins, 1941), Ch. 4.

[96] For further discussion of the internal realities of what appears to be a " group," see The State Courts and Delegation of Public Authority to Private Groups, 67 Harv. L. Rev. 1398, 1406 (1954) : ". . . in formulating general rules a public body will probably be more receptive to the special problems of a minority within a group; the general good, whether of the society or of a group within it, is not achieved simply by a majority vote of interested members, but by responsible deliberation upon the claims of all those affected." E. E. Schattschneider, in *Politics, Pressures and the Tariff* (Prentice-Hall, 1935), 217, cautions against " the oversimplification implicit in the assumption that individual industries and economic groups act as indivisible wholes actuated throughout their membership by identical motives of equal intensity." V. O. Key, Jr., *Politics, Parties, and Pressure Groups* (3d ed.; Crowell, 1952), 154 et seq. critically examines the " representative quality of group action." And see also Earl Latham, *The Group Basis of Politics* (Cornell, 1952), Ch. I.

[97] The quoted praise of "bureaucrats " as against " self-regulators " comes from Report of the Virginia Advisory Legislative Council, Administrative Agencies, Their Creation, Jurisdiction and Powers (1943), 5–6.

[98] The Governors' Conference is reported under the heading of " Examining and Licensing Boards," 24 State Government 280 (1951).

[99] As to centralizing of license agencies: In both Illinois and California, for illustration, more than twenty separate boards had been consolidated into a centralized organization for bookkeeping, enforcement, and investigation, though separate bodies remained for the purpose of giving examinations. By 1952 eighteen states had at least partially coordinated their licensing agencies; in every one of the eighteen states, from two to twelve occupational licensing agencies retained their separate identity outside the central administration. See Council of State Governments, Occupational Licensing Legislation in the States (1952), 29–31.

[100] The criticism of state enforcement of the guild system appears in State v. Harris, 216 N. C. 746, 6 S. E. 2d 854 (1940). Compare Robert L. Hale, *Freedom Through Law* (Columbia University Press, 1952), esp. pp. 335–66.

[101] For a statement of the contention that only the regulated occupation can provide qualified administrators, see Edwin W. Pat-

terson, Administrative Provisions for Licensing of Chiropractors, Chiropodists and Osteopaths, 7 Iowa L. Bull. 35, at 36 (1921): ". . . as a practical problem of means to an end, it is usually impossible to secure a board with the requisite technical equipment to pass upon the technical fitness of applicants for licenses, without appointing those already members of the profession; and the chiropractor and osteopath statutes simply follow in this respect the statutes creating the state board of medical examiners, the board of law examiners, and the state board of engineering examiners."

[102] Discussion of the need for expertise in test-construction appears in Council on State Governments, Occupational Licensing Legislation in the States (1952), 52.

[103] Description of the educational requirements for the barbering business may be found in Council of State Governments, Occupational Licensing Legislation in the States (1952), 26. The eighteen-state study in 1929 was made by Hugo Wall in satisfying the requirements for the Ph.D. degree at Stanford. His dissertation, " A Study of the License Laws in Eighteen Selected States," is available in mimeographed form in that university's library.

[104] The licensing provisions of the Emergency Price Control Act appeared in secs. 205(f), 56 Stat. 34, 35.

[105] Harvey Mansfield et al., A Short History of O. P. A. (U. S. Office of Temporary Controls, 1948), 264 remarks: " In operation, however, few license suspension suits were brought; injunction suits were found generally more flexible and efficacious."

[106] As to rationing suspension orders, see Mansfield, cited in note 105 above, pp. 264, 291–93; and see also Victor A. Thompson, The Regulatory Process in OPA Rationing (King's Crown, 1950), 7, 227, 356–58. The validity of a suspension order in rationing was sustained by the Supreme Court in L. P. Steuart & Bros., Inc. v. Bowles, 322 U. S. 398 (1944). Similar suspension powers were used elsewhere in order to prevent economic abuses that hindered the war effort. See John Lord O'Brian and Manly Fleischmann, The War Production Board Administrative Policies and Procedures, 13 Geo. Wash. L. Rev. 1, 46–54 (1944); Priorities—Enforcement by Suspension Order, 41 Colum. L. Rev. 1448 (1941).

Index

Acheson, Dean, on dangers of personnel security procedures, 43

Administrative Process, growth, 3; achievements, 5–7; criticism by the organized bar, 8–10; Senatorial views about "subversion of the administrative process," 10; reversals of positions concerning, 10 ff.; enlarged powers, 14–15; national security as influencing attitudes toward, 16–17; characteristics of decisions, 19 ff, 29 ff.; expertness and inexpertness, 20 ff., 72–73, 95–96; shift from service to suspicion, 38–46; powers to invade individual rights, 46–47

Adorno, T. W., studies of "authoritarian personality," 160

Advisory Committee on Prisoners of War, report to Secretary of Defense, 71

Aliens, procedures affecting, 15, 35 ff.; deportation of, 23–25; visas for, 25–27; plenary power of Congress over, 29–30; numbers expelled, 30–31; administrative bail, 33–35

Anastaplo, In re George, 136–37

Asheim, Lester E., on book selection, 66

Bagehot, Walter, on persecution, 18; on eradicating heresy, 178

Becker, Carl, on liberty, 40

Berle, Adolf A., Jr., evaluation of American Consuls, 25

Blanshard, Paul, on right to read, 159, 179, 183, 190

Bontecou, Eleanor, on unreliability of personnel security informants, 44; on federal loyalty-security program, 170, 194

Brown, Ralph S., Jr., on impact of personnel security programs, 41, 194; on qualifications of lawyers, 132; on inutility of character tests, 151

Butler, William J., on limits of expertise, 22–23

Cain, Harry, on impact of personnel security programs, 41

Cairns, Huntington, lawyers' role in censorship, 55–56; personal qualifications of, 181

Carr, Cecil T., description of Lord Brougham's venture in early popular education, 52; on British crisis legislation, 167

Carr-Saunders, Alexander Morris, on loss of professional leadership, 107–108; on characteristics of professions, 195; on achieving social recognition through licensure, 196

Censorship, absence of protests concerning, 14; philosophic foundations of, 50–52; of paperbound books, 53–55, 75–78; of violence and "horror," 59–60; of comics, 60; as cure for juvenile delinquency, 60 ff.; suppression of ideas, 67–72; methods of, 72 ff.; volunteer censors, 73–74; police censors, 74 ff.; in Detroit, 76–78; in Army post exchanges, 78, 79; public libraries, 79; of textbooks, 79–83; of foreign propaganda, 83–88; customs seizures, 88 ff.; by postal authorities, 90 ff.; in World War I, 95; governmental withholding of information, 159; Gathings Committee, 174

Chafee, Zechariah, Jr., on theatre censorship, 72–73; on jury trials of obscenity charges, 97; on cus-

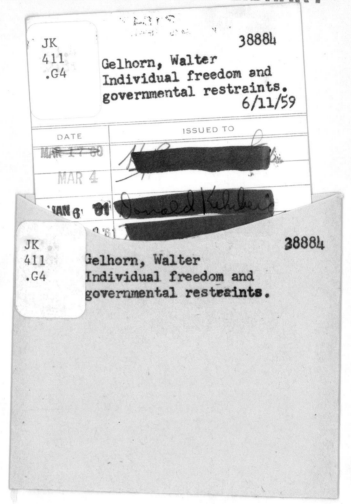